ADVANCED STUDY IN THE HISTORY OF MODERN INDIA

Volume III (1920-1947)

Published by
Lotus Press

ADVANCED STUDY IN THE HISTORY OF MODERN INDIA

Volume III (1920-1947)

G S CHHABRA

LOTUS PRESS
4263 / 3, Ansari Road,
Daryaganj, New Delhi-2

Lotus Press
4263/3, Ansari Road, Darya Ganj, New Delhi-110002
Ph.: 32903912, 23280047, E-mail: lotus_press@sify.com
www.lotuspress.co.in

ADVANCE STUDY IN THE HISTORY OF MODERN INDIA
Volume III (1920-1947)

ISBN: 81-89093-08-8

Reprint 2011

Published by: **Lotus Press**, New Delhi-110 002
Printed at: Anand Sons, Delhi

PREFACE TO THE FIRST EDITION

What originated as a middle-class movement, later on turned into a mighty mass upheaval against the British, determined to reach its goal of national independence. This happened from the twenties of the twentieth century when Mr. Gandhi entered the Indian political arena and gave it the magic touch of the non-violent, non-cooperation formula. Mr. Gandhi did not always achieve his objectives; he often failed and committed what were known as the 'Himalayan Blunders'. He was termed by some of his critics in India as 'vague mystic' out of touch with the ordinary human nature. He is said to have rather retarded than hastened the pace of India's march towards independence. Yet the period from 1920 to 1947 with which this volume deals, is known as era of Gandhi who dominated the Indian scene and guided the country's destiny. India's rising political demands, the constitutional reform of 1935 and the reports of the different commissions and committees appointed to thrash out the problems posed by India, till ultimately the British left in 1947 and India joined the community of independent sovereign nations of the world; all this and more, has been discussed in this volume.

G.S. Chhabra

PREFACE TO THE SECOND EDITION

The second edition of this volume, as it goes to the press, if not given entirely new shape, has been enriched with a lot of entirely new material that has come to light since the last edition was placed in the market. Besides enlargement and improvement of the existing chapters, some new ones have also been added; and the author is sure that the reader will not find the new findings about this period of Indian History missing in this work.

G.S. Chhabra

PREFACE TO THE THIRD EDITION

There is difference between intelligence and intellect. In the former lie objectivity, comprehension and spontaneity, while the latter is subjective and concerns itself with reasoning and a calculated action. An intelligence-based action is holistic, and is truly religious, while an intellect based action is fragmentary and not even remotely concerned with religion however much one may try to give it a religious color. Mr. Gandhi who dominated the period of History dealt with in this volume, was a confused person. He was well-meaning and often tried to hear the voice within, but when one preconditions oneself with concepts, good or bad, the voice from within and its interpretation will only be that of intellect and never of the formless wisdom. Which is why Mr. Gandhi's political actions often resulted into negation of the very objectives he wanted to achieve. Gandhi was a strict disciplinarian, determined only to do good and avoid evil, little knowing that concepts both good and bad are the product only of knowledge, and knowledge always blinds comprehension

The people of India are religious by nature and Mr. Gandhi's outward appearance and readiness always to personally go through suffering made them to look to him as to a *messiah* capable of accomplishing wonders. But every time they got disillusioned it was Mr. Ganghi's honest acknowledgement of his 'Himalayan Blunders' and self-inflicted punishments only that brought them back to a faithful allegiance. The wonder is that if Mr. Gandhi was confused, he was successfully able to confuse not only the people but also most of the other contemporary political leaders who worked with him. Even the British themselves got confused and often did not know how to deal with a situation that was the handiwork of this *messiah* of the people.

Be that as it may, the period dealt with here may truly be called the Gandhian era of the Modern Indian History, as the perusal of thoroughly revised and enlarged edition of this volume will reveal.

G.S. Chhabra

New Delhi

CONTENTS

1. **Viscount Chelmsford, 1916-1921** .. 1

   Non-cooperation, The Rowlatt Act, The Khilafat Movement

2. **Marquess of Reading, 1921-1926** .. 20

   The Swaraj Party

3. **Lord Irwin, 1926-1931** ... 34

   The Simon Commission 1927, Simon Commission Report, An Appraisal, The Nehru Report, The Broken Promises, Independence Declared, Non-Cooperation Again, The First Round Table Conference, The Gandhi-Irwin Pact, The North-West Frontier and the Red Shirts.

4. **Lord Willingdon, 1931-1936** ... 58

   Second Round Table Conference 1931-32, The Communal Award, The Poona Pact 1932, Third Round Table Conference and the White Paper.

5. **The Government of India Act, 1935** ... 67

   The Proposed Federation, The Federal Executive, The Instrument of Instructions, Federal Legislature, States and the Federal Government, Provincial Autonomy, Dual Policy of Repression.

6. **Marquess of Linlithgow, 1936-1943** ... 118

   Provincial Autonomy in Operation, The August Offer and the Cripps Mission, Proposals of the Cripps Mission.

7. **The Quit India Movement** ... 147

   The Congress Resolution, Gandhi's Fast and Release, Other Developments.

8. **Earl Wavell, 1943-1947** ... 166

   The C.R. Formula, The Wavell Plan, Cabinet Mission Plan, Failure of the Mission.

9. Lord Louis Mountbatten, 1947 ... 185

On to Independence, Attlee's Statement of February 1947, The 'Dickie Bird Plan,' The Mountbatten Plan, The Indian Independence Act.

10. The Great Divide ... 196

The Indian States, Radcliffe Award, The Indian Army, Independence, The Holocaust, The Assassination of Gandhi, Why did the British Leave India?

11. Some Indian Personalities of the time ... 213

Swami Dayanand Saraswati, Dadabhai Naoroji, Surendra Nath Banerjee, Lokmanya Bal Gangadhar Tilak, Bipin Chandra Pal, Lala Lajpat Rai, Allen Octavian Hume, Mahadev Gobind Ranade, Sir Pherozeshah Mehta, Swami Shradhanand, Mrs Annie Besant, Gopal Krishna Gokhle, Motilal Nehru, Sardar Vallabhbhai Patel, Maulana Abul Kalam Azad, Subhas Chandra Bose, M.K. Gandhi, Dr Rajendra Prasad.

Bibliography ... 244

Index ... 258

I

Viscount Chelmsford 1916-1921

NON-COOPERATION

With the year 1920, begins a new era in the history of the nationalist movement in India. For, in that year Mohandas Karamchand Gandhi popularly known as Mahatma Gandhi or Gandhiji entered the Indian Political scene bringing into the field his novel political experiments, which resulted in exceptional stress and strain culminating in the ultimate independence of this country in 1947. It would be instructive to have a short account of his early experience before discussing his experiment of non-cooperation in the country.

It was in South Africa that he introduced his weapon of passive resistance for the first time against the Anti-Asiatic legislation of Transvaal which won him a measure of success followed by great fame. Gopal Krishna Gokhale being impressed, extended his active sympathy and support and on his return to India in 1914, Gandhi offered to join Gokhale's Servants of India Society, which proves that he accepted his moderate views in Indian politics. At that stage of his career Mr. Gandhi professed himself to be a loyal citizen of the British Empire, and during the First World War offered his services to the Government of India in the ambulance corps, also rendering a considerable help in the recruitment campaigns. All this earned him the gratitude of the British authorities who bestowed on him the title of Kaisar-i-Hind.

Before offering satyagraha against the Rowlatt Bills of 1919, he used this weapon on several occasions in India itself, in his efforts to perfect its techniques. In this country he started with the establishment of a Satyagraha Ashram on the Sabarmati river near Ahmedabad; and his March into the Champaran district of Bihar to enquire into the conditions of the peasants suffering under ruthless exploitation of the European indigo planters, was perhaps the most important of his early experiments in passive resistance. His refusal to oblige the Commissioner, who served him with a notice to quit the district immediately, landed him into the court of a magistrate. And he stood firm facing the consequences of his action when the Lieutenant Governor of Bihar intervened, permitting him to carry on enquiries which ultimately resulted in the passing of the Agrarian Bill in the provincial legislature, whereby the major grievances of the peasants were removed. This success of Mr. Gandhi while developing his confidence in satyagraha on the one hand, won him the acclaim of several important Indians on the other, thus making it easier for his newly forged weapon to be accepted.

This early use of passive resistance, however, did not make Mr. Gandhi a non-cooperator with the British Empire. He was only fighting against certain evils of the system without any effort to destroy it. His being an active cooperator with the Government with a faith in its honesty of purpose is proved from the part he played in getting the Reform of 1919 accepted by the All India Congress. The Moderates having left it and formed in November 1918 their separate party, the National Liberal Federation, under the leadership of Surendra Nath Banerjee; the Amritsar session of the Congress in1919 was not in a mood to accept the reforms which had been characterized by Tilak as "unsatisfactory and disappointing–a sunless dawn", and by Mrs. Besant as something "unworthy of England to offer and India to accept". It was only as a result of Mr. Gandhi's efforts that the Congress not only agreed to try the new constitution, but also offered "its warmest thanks" to the Rt. Hon. E.S. Montagu for his labours in connection with the Reforms Act.

Soon, however, the situation changed, and he who was a loyal cooperator with the Government turned into an active non-cooperator wielding his sharp weapon of satyagraha in a manner which brought about a revolution in this country. Mr. Gandhi summed up the reasons, which brought this change in him in his statement before Mr. Broomsfield who tried him for having preached sedition in his *Young India;* He stated, "the first shock came to me in the shape of the Rowlatt Act, a law designed to rob the people of all freedom. Then followed the Punjab horrors beginning with the massacre at Jallianwala Bagh and culminating in crawling orders, public floggings and other indescribable humiliations. I discovered, too, that the plighted word of the Prime Minister to the Mussalmans of India regarding the integrity of Turkey and the holy places of Islam was not likely to be fulfilled." It would be instructive to have a short account of the events mentioned above, which turned Mr. Gandhi into a non-cooperator.

From Loyalty to Rebellion

"In the hour of England's peril," thus wrote Pearay Mohan: "India rushed to her help with unfailing faith and loyal enthusiasm. The voice of controversy was hushed and the grievances which the people had against the Government, were laid aside."[1] Or as Lord Hardinge said, India allowed herself to be "bled white," and contributed freely in men and money. And in this, the Punjab did more than any other province in India could do.

About one million men were sent overseas by India to fight battles of the British Empire, and upto 31 March 1919, £127.8m. had been incurred as her share towards the war expenses. Out of the former, the Punjab contributed as much as 60 per cent of the total, and in her contributions towards the war expenses, the Punjab competed successfully with the richer provinces of India. Everything was done to raise recruits in the Punjab. And when the Home Government asked for 21,000 combatant recruits in the last four months of the year 1914, 28,000 were raised, if whom 14,000 came from the Punjab 3,000 from Nepal, 3,000 from the Frontier and trans-Frontier and 8,000 from the rest of India.

In 1915, 93,000 combatants were enrolled, of whom 46,000 were from the Punjab, 14,000 from Nepal, 6,000 from the Pathan areas, and 28,000 from the rest of India. The first two and one-third years of the war had brought to the colours about one hundred and twenty thousand Punjabis, "The cream of the fighting races"[2] and their number increased as the war prolonged.

The "Legislative Council of the Punjab at its first meeting after war was declared, unanimously passed a resolution assuring the King Emperor of the devotion of the people of the Province and of their determination to serve His Majesty, in every form in which their help might be required, against the enemies of his Empire. The council was composed mainly of elected or nominated representatives of the Mohammedan, Hindu and Sikh communities and the resolution gave expression to the feeling of active loyalty that inspired the Province as a whole."[3]

The sacrifices made by Amritsar in the war were greater than those made by Lahore, so much so that in a speech at Karur, Sir M. O'Dwyer the Lieutenant-Governor of the Punjab solemnly declared that he would transfer the seat of Government from Lahore to Amritsar as a reward for the great war services of the latter and as a punishment to the former for its slackness in providing recruits.

But soon the picture changed. From loyalty the Punjab changed in 1919 to a scene of rebellion, and the city of Amritsar of which Sir Dwyer was so proud, was the first to come in the field. Different theories were assigned to these outbreaks in the Punjab, some of which were supported by Sir Dwyer himself.

In the beginning it was believed that there was a huge conspiracy to subvert the British Government in India and to seduce the Indian army. The conspiracy was supposed to be financed by Bolshevic money, the ramification of which had enveloped the whole country. The Punjab being the home of warriors, the conspiracy was more active here than in any other province of the country. As, however, no evidence could be forwarded for the Bolshevic origin of the outbreaks, the theory failed.

Later on, Afghan agency was substituted for the Bolshevic hand, but this theory too failed for want of any evidence. After this, Mr. Gandhi was blamed as being the chief conspirator who wanted to overawe the Government by criminal means, and secure the repeal of the Rowlatt Act. An order for his externment from the Punjab was passed by the Lieutenant Governor of the Punjab, who was informed by a Hindu friend that "Gandhi had been heard to say that the British were now full of pride in their victory and considered themselves the masters of the world; but that he was master of a weapon which would soon bring them to their knees. That, ofcourse, was his policy of passive Resistance." The Hindu friend told him "to be on the look out for Gandhi's next move."[4] But this theory too failed.

Then some local conspirators were blamed who agitated locally though not on provincial basis, but whose agitation developed a provincial character. The persons blamed were such as Lala Harkishan Lal, Lala Duni Chand, Dr Kitchlew, Dr Satyapal, Mr Labh Singh and Diwan Mangal Sen. But this view too failed as a result of the cross examination of Lord Hunter's Enquiry Committee. And as a result of all this, the theory of conspiracy was given up as a whole, in disgust.

The most widely accepted view, as also supported by the Government of India's resolution of 14 April 1919, was that the agitation against the Rowlatt Act was directly responsible for these disturbances. The real cause, however, seems to be that the very atmosphere which existed at the time was explosive, and it was an agitation against the Rowlatt Act which set it afire. There were other disruptive forces at work too.

Excessive recruitments had been made for the Indian Army in the Punjab. The Punjab, as we have seen, supplied as much as 60 per cent of the total number of recruits raised all over the country. And this means that of its twenty million population, recorded in the census of 1911, (1/15 of the total population of the country), the Punjab supplied during the war as many as 4,60,000 of her best men to fight the British wars. The Secretary of State himself admitted once that "many a family was left without its breadwinner or breadwinners". The Punjabis had fought for no national cause. The chains of slavery seem rather to have been strengthened. And Sir O'Dwyer admitted on 7 April 1919, that this had "led to some serious riots and lawless outbreaks in the Multan Division and in shahpur."[5]

The methods adopted for recruitments in the Punjab under the ruthless regime of Sir O'Dwyer, too were objectionable. To win a distinction in the supply of soldiers, Sir O'Dwyer assigned a quota to each district in the Punjab, and it was understood to be compulsory for the district authorities to supply the required number of recruits. Promotion of officers depended on the number of recruits furnished. Police got false cases against the villages that failed to furnish the assigned quotas. And the recruits in the Punjab became an economic commodity to be bought and sold by those who were aspirants to honours and rewards, and who thus made extensive transactions in the trade. These things were not loved by those who loved liberty and nationalism.

The Europeans in India were looked upon as superhumans. But when the Indian soldiers in Europe saw them lame, blind and beggars as well, the spell was broken. Many Indian soldiers had been acclaimed and received as saviours in ''France by men and women alike. But when they came back to their country, they had to face the same old *sahib* as proud and arrogant as ever he was.

In the collection of war-loans considerable severity had been used. The district revenue officials brought a good deal of pressure on the villagers to subscribe. Though the officers did not compel their subordinates to make their contributions, yet the very suggestions from them had to be complied with if the subordinates wanted to keep their favour. And then, the common man due to his illiteracy did not understand the Government's need for loans. To him it was a sure sign of bankruptcy of the so-called rich *sircar* which had to borrow from an ordinary man.

Then there were economic causes. The prices had been rising. Wheat sold in 1912 at 12 seers and 4 chattaks for a rupee, while by 1919, the price rose to 5 seers and 9 chattaks per rupee. Maize sold at 16 seers and 3 chattaks for a rupee in 1912, while by 1919 the price rose to 6 seers and 6 chattaks per rupee. As compared to this more than cent per cent rise in the price, the rise in wages was only 50 per cent.

And further, the excessive recruitment of soldiers drained the land of its working hands, and the produce per acre declined. The foreign imports were dearer. Influenza broken out. Monsoons failed. And in fact the Railway employees were just on the verge of a strike when the disorder broke out. "Rebellions of the belly are the worst", as Bacon wrote.

The Punjab had hoped that the British victory in the war would bring boons, which it did not. The common man had bled white, while honours and titles went only to the capitalists and high Government officials well known for the recruitments of soldiers. Instead of getting freedom after the war, they got only the Rowlatt Act.

Thus the atmosphere was already explosive when the Act was passed. Its provisions were so monstrous that no Indian with the slightest spirit of self-respect could bear to put up with it. It was a slur on India's loyalty, so definitely proved during the war, and about which the King Emperor himself had written in a message to the princes and the people of India, that India "had fulfilled my faith in her single-minded devotion to my person and Empire, and she has vindicated my confidence in her loyalty."

India had no desire to embarrass the British Government during the war, and therefore she had accepted the provisions of the Defence of India Act without demur. But it was more than a year before its expiry that the Rowlatt Act was hurled upon her. The Government of India had enjoyed some emergency powers during the war, which they wanted to perpetuate under the Rowlatt Act, under the pretext, that some mysterious anarchists existed in the country, who with foreign help were determined to subvert the Government. Even persons such as Sir O' Moore Creagh, formerly the Commander-in-Chief of India, had denied that there existed any need for such a measure.

THE ROWLATT ACT

A brief account may be given of the different provisions of the Act, to prove its monstrousness. The Act was divided into five parts.

Part I. It applied to the state of things when the Governor-General-in-Council was satisfied that in a part of the country anarchy prevailed and it was expedient for public safety to provide for speedy trial of such offences.

Such trials were to be conducted in tribunals specially instituted for the purpose. There was a safeguard that if judges in a tribunal differed, no death sentences could be awarded to a person being tried. But since such difference could arise only in cases of doubtful guilt, more illogical part of the Act was that the right to appeal above the tribunal was denied.

The trial was to be held in camera. And this means that no opportunity was given to the public or to the relatives of a person under trial, to understand his case and arrange for a defence.

The height of maliciousness was that the Local Governments were authorized to give a retrospective effect to the provisions of this part of the Act.

Part II. The provisions of this part were preventive. If the Governor-General -in-Council was satisfied that such conditions prevailed under which precautions for the maintenance of law and order were necessary, he declared the applications of this Part.

Under the provisions of this, if a Local Government was satisfied that a particular person was a potential criminal, it could place the papers relative to him before a judicial officer qualified to sit in a High Court. The person concerned, however, was not entitled to claim a hearing, nor was the Local Government bound to follow the officer's opinion.

After receiving the opinion of the officer, the Local Government could in writing direct the person to give a bond not to commit the scheduled offences. He was to notify a change in his address, was to reside in an area specified by the Government, and report himself to the nearest police station at stated periods, for the duration of a year. After issuing these orders the Local Government was to forward the case for opinion to an investigating authority consisting of three persons, two of them being above the rank of District or Sessions Judge, and a third who was not in the service of the Crown.

The enquiry, again, was to be held in camera, in which the person concerned was not entitled to claim presence, there being no provisions even for informing him.

The Local Government again, may not accept this report and it may pass the order upon the person for one year more. Thus the punishment could be given to a person even without a proper trial.

Part III. When the conditions referred to above were widespread to endanger public safety, this part was to be applied, under which any suspected person could be arrested directly and put into confinement. His house could be searched and then the enquiry under Part II was to follow.

Part IV. This part was more drastic in its provisions and Part V laid down that "no order under this Act shall be called in question in any court."

The assurance that the Act was to be used only for public safety proved to be false. And while the Government contended that the Act was limited in its application to anarchical and revolutionary crime, it refused to incorporate in the Act the definition of such crimes with the result that the application of the provisions extended to the extent of absurdity. It is a measure, thus wrote M.A. Jinnah, "admittedly obnoxious and decidedly coercive at a time of peace, thereby substituting the executive authority for the judicial"[6].

The natural result of the measure was protest meetings and resolutions, but while in other provinces this might have resulted in disturbances, not a single instance of violence occurred in the Punjab. The climax was reached on 6 April when at least a million persons took part in protest meetings all over the province, yet no violence was anywhere committed.

But the ruthless regime of O'Dwyer tried to suppress the agitation with an iron hand. Dwyer had a particular hatred towards the educated classes, and before the Act was passed he tried gagging the newspapers of the Province, discouraged the independent criticism and isolated the Punjab from the rest of India. The Mohammedans had already been agitated on the fate of Turkey and the Khilafat. There was a general atmosphere of discontent and lack of confidence in the Government. And when the people agitated against this Act, he took it as a direct challenge to his ideas of a good Government. As the agitation and demonstrations in peaceful manners grew, Dwyer grew violent. Freedom of speech in public and the freedom of writing of persons such as Dr. Kitchlew and Dr. Satyapal were suppressed. He issued orders prohibiting Mr. Gandhi from entering into the Punjab on 4 April, but the order was shown to him only when he reached Palwal, a small railway station on the border of the Punjab. Mr. Gandhi politely refused to obey the order, and he was arrested and taken to Bombay. This happened on 9 April, and when its news reached Lahore on the 10th, people were stunned. A complete *hartal* was organized throughout the town in half an hour, and a mob collected to protest against this action of the Government. But they were fired at and dispersed.

This was a signal for disturbances all over the Punjab. On the same date as a mob was fired at in Lahore, a mob rose in Amritsar and endeavoured to force its way into the Civil Station where the British officials and non-officials resided, but was held up by the small British pickets on the bridge over the railway which connected the city with the civil station. The havoc and destruction, which this mob brought about, is too well known to be repeated. There is no doubt that several people in a fit of fury lost their balance of mind.

Government property worth millions of rupees was destroyed. Some Europeans were butchered and their property put to fire. Similar disturbances occurred at Kasur and other places. But the retaliation of the alien Government was yet more brutal.

"If your house is on fire and you call in the fire-engines," said Mr. Joseph, an offical member of the Punjab Legislative Council in 1921, "and the fire-engines pump water into the house so fast and furiously that they ruin all your furniture, all your carpets, it is no use afterwards to discuss how many buckets full of water might have been sufficient to extinguish the conflagration". But this was no good an argument.

Jallianwala Bagh Incident

As the agitation continued, on 13 April 1919 the people from all parts of the Province collected in the Jallianwala Bagh at Amritsar. On the previous day, the inhabitants of the city had been warned not to hold meetings, but they, according to the notorious Brigadier-General Dyer, did not pay any heed. In his own words: On 13th April at 16 hours I received a report from the police that a gathering was begining in the place mentioned above. I immediately sent pickets to hold various gates of the city (to prevent a renewal of the attack of the 10th on the British quarters) and marched with 25 Rifles 9th Gurkhas, and 25 Rifles from detachments of 54 Sikhs F.F. and 59 Rifles F.F making a total of 50 Rifles, and also 40 Gurkhas armed with Kukris I entered the Jallianwala Bagh by a very narrow lane which necessitated leaving my armoured car behind. On entering I saw a dense crowd, estimated at about 5,000 (those present put it at 15,000 to 20,000): a man on a raised platform addressing the audience and making gesticulations with his hands.

"I realized that my force was small and to hesitate might induce attack. I immediately opened fire and dispersed the mob. I estimate that between 200 and 300 of the crowd were killed. My party fired 1,650 rounds."[8]

This is an underestimation of the number thus killed. And besides, the number of those who were injured is too high to make a mention. General Dyer, writes Rupert Furneaux. "when he marched his men away from the Bagh, left behind him a scene of horror. At least 1,500 Indian…lay either dead or writhing in agony from wounds great or small. Many of them were children. Over 20,000 people struggled frantically to escape from the death trap…Two half hour only remained until curfew, when, if caught in the streets, they could be shot down. Those Indians who returned to the Bagh that night to seek relations and friends or to succour the wounded risked death."[9]

Blood of hundreds of the Punjab's heroes who were fired at on the day, still runs in the fibres of the plants which grown in the Bagh, and tells us the story of woes and sacrifices of the illustrious sons of the Punjab who fought for India's independence and laid down their lives.

But this was not the end of the alien retaliation. On 14 April a mob was bombed from an aeroplane and fired at by machine-guns at Gujranwala. Outbreaks in Gujranwala, Gujrat, Lyallpur, Gurdaspur and other places in the province were ruthlessly crushed. Martial law was proclaimed in Amritsar and Lahore on the 15th regarding the atrocities of which much has been said and written. The view of the Hunter Committee on this may be quoted:

"As regards martial law and orders and cases arising out of the breach thereof, we think it unfortunate that in several important aspects, martial law assumed as intensive a form as it did...*Some of the orders issued were injudicious. They served no good purpose and were not, in our opinion, drawn with sufficient tact to prevent undue annoyance to the civil population*".

They then refer to:

1. General Dyer's *Crawling Order* (which no one attempted to defend).
2. General Campbell's *Salaming Order* prescribing that the people of Gujranwala should accord to British officers "wherever met, the salutation usually accorded to Indian gentlemen of high social position in accordance with the customs of India."
3. Colonel Frank Johnson's orders directing that the students of four out of the ten Colleges at Lahore which had been implicated in the disturbances, should attend roll calls four times a day to keep away from spreading sedition.
4. The order of the same officer arresting and interning in the Fort for twenty-four hours from fifty to one hundred students of a College where the martial law orders had been torn down.
5. Public floggings at Lahore and the excessive number of floggings generally.
6. "Fancy punishments by Captain Doveton at Kasur, e.g. making convicted men touch the ground with their forehead and skipping, in lieu of the ordinary but more severe punishments—such as whipping, fine, and imprisonment."[10]

But still more interesting was the fact that after having butchered those who were said to be taking a more active part and after having punished through courts those who were said to have been taking less active part in the movement, an Indemnity for the damage in the city of Amritsar was imposed on those who were taking no part at all. The estimated assessment was Rs. 2,056,000. The charge for police Rs. 1,43,000 and the remainder for the compensation of those who lost their property. The Amritsar municipality was to recover it by taking temporarily certain higher rates of terminal taxes and by imposing higher rates on the sale of immovable property. The compensation was assessed by the District Magistrate under Section 15-A (2) (c) of the Police Act and was subject to the revision of the Commissioner of the Division or the Local Government. Similarly, the cost of additional police was assessed by the District Magistrate under Section 15 (4) of the Police Act.

Sir Rabindranath Tagore gave up his knighthood in protest against these inhuman acts of the Government, and wrote to the Viceroy in a letter: "The time has come when badges of honour make our shame glaring in their incongruous context by humiliation." Sir Shankaran Nair resigned his membership of the Viceroy's Executive Council. And this created a stir against the Government trying to draw a veil on the gruesome bloodshed of the Jallianwala Bagh. The Government was compelled to appoint an enquiry Committee under Lord Hunter in October 1919, the report of which was published only in March 1920. A shameless effort was make in the report to let off the perpetrators of the crime without any seething condemnation. The Lords in the English Parliament rather eulogized General Dyer as champion of the British Empire, presenting him with a fat purse of £12,000 and a sword of honour. "The real face of imperialism was now unmasked for all Indians to see," thus observes Hirendranath Mukherjee, "and we could never efface from our mind its horror and its diabolism."[11] Mrs Annie Besant was "shocked to read the evidence given by the Military authority before the Hunter Committee", and of the shameless behaviour of the Lords.

In the meanwhile the Congress also had appointed a Committee of enquiry which included Mr Gandhi, Pandit Malaviya, Pandit Motilal Nehru and others. The report of this Committee condemned very severely the ruthless behaviour of the military authorities at Amritsar, and demanded adequate compensation for the families of the dead and the wounded and proper punishment for those guilty. This report went unheard and uncared for, the Government having in the meanwhile passed the Indemnity Act, which absolved of punishment all those connected with the firing. And this was thus one of the factors which shook Mr Gandhi's confidence in the Government's sense of fair play and converted him into a non-cooperator.

THE KHILAFAT MOVEMENT

The Muslims of India had been feeling uneasy at the prospects of ill-treatment towards Turkey at the end of war. But their fears had been brought to rest by a promise made by the British Prime Minister assuring that Turkey would not be deprived of the rich lands of Asia Minor and Thrace and that no vindictive policy would be followed towards her. The Muslims being satisfied, they gave their wholehearted cooperation in the British war campaigns. But as the war ended, it became manifest that the pledge given by the British Prime Minister would not be kept. Mr Gandhi deemed it essential to come to the help of the Muslims at this time in order to narrow down the gulf dividing them from the Hindus. A Khilafat Conference was held at Delhi on 24 November 1919 under the chairmanship of Mr Gandhi and a deputation under the leadership of Mr Ansari was sent to the Governor-General which proved of no avail. Maulana Mohammad Ali and his brother Shaukat Ali deputed to England in March 1920 also drew a blank. The terms of the Treaty of Sevres having become public in May 1920, the worst fears of the Indian Muslims proved correct. The treaty signed on 10 August 1920 dispossessed Turkey of the richest area of the Asia Minor and of the whole of Thrace. Her Arab Provinces were to go to England and France as mandated territories, and the Sultan of Turkey virtually imprisoned, seemed on his way to losing the office of Khalifa, the spiritual head of the Muslims. 'It was arranged to so destroy the Turkish Empire as to leave it only a despicable relic of its past glory." And this, thus became another cause for Mr Gandhi to become a non-cooperator.[12]

Under these circumstances in May 1920, under the advice of Mr Gandhi the All-India Khilafat Committee adopted his non-cooperation programme. This was followed after four months by the Congress session of Calcutta. The Liberals having already left the Congress in 1912, the extremists controlled it now. Yet, however, Mr Gandhi's proposal of non-cooperation did not find smooth sailing, and Pandit Malaviya, Mrs Annie Besant, C.R. Das, B.C. Pal and Mr Jinnah opposed it. The resolution for non-cooperation was eventually adopted by the Congress by a narrow majority of seven votes. This put Mr. Gandhi at the pinnacle of the Congress organisation, and when it met in its Nagpur session in December 1920, Mr. Gandhi's programme was reaffirmed by an overwhelming majority. The Nagpur session of the Congress, writes K.M. Munshi "looked like less a political body than a religious gathering celebrating the advent of a Messiah."[13]

The Nagpur session of 1920 was another turning point in the history of India's freedom movement for three reasons. First, the old constitutional means to secure political concessions were abandoned, and all the peaceful and legitimate means were now to be adopted by the Congress for the purpose. Secondly, the old aim of self-government within the British Empire was renounced, and "Swaraj within the British Empire, if possible, and outside, if necessary," was declared the necessary goal. And thirdly, Tilak having died on 31 July 1920 Mr Gandhi became an undisputed leader of the Congress and directed its destinies through his novel experiments till his death.

Non-cooperation Movement

The non-cooperation programme adopted by the Congress at Nagpur consisted of two parts. First, the country was to be asked to boycott (1) the coming elections under the Government of India Act, 1919, (2) the law courts set up by the Government, (3) the Government and aided schools and colleges, (4) and the foreign goods, (5) The nominated posts were to be resigned from and honorary offices and titles surrendered. (6) Nobody was to attend the Government Durbars and levies, and the official and non-official functions held either by or in the honour of the Government officials. And (7) the martial, labouring and the clerical classes were to be asked to refuse to join Government services in Mesopotamia. And secondly, (a) private arbitration courts were to be established to assume the role of the Government law courts, (b) national schools and colleges were to be set up for education, (c) hand spinning and weaving was to be revived and pure *swadeshi* to be adopted, and (d) the evil of untouchability was to be fought.

The non-cooperation movement started in its full fury in the beginning of 1921. The lawyers such as Moti Lal, C.R. Das, Vithalbhai, Rajendra Prasad, Vallabhbhai Patel gave up their lucrative practices. Government schools and colleges were deserted and the national institutions like the Bengal National University, and Jamia Milia of Delhi, the National Muslim University of Aligarh, the National College of Lahore, the Tilak Maharashtra Vidya-Peeth, the Gujarat Vidya-Peeth, etc. were set up. Consumption of the Swadeshi cloth increased, while that of the foreign cloth declined. About 20,000 Charkhas were manufactured and about forty lakhs joined as Congress volunteers. The *charkha* also found its place on the Congress flag. The enthusiasm of the people is manifest in the fact that the Congress expressing its need for a crore of rupees in March 1921, the whole amount was subscribed within a very short time. An annual sum of one lakh rupees was promised by Seth Jamuna Lal Bajaj for the maintenance of the non-practising lawyers. Titles were surrendered and law courts abandoned. The Congress did not contest elections and the opportunist and loyalists got the opportunity to fill the reformed Councils. Only 6 of the 774 seats went uncontested.

The Chlemsford Government retaliated and undertook certain very severe measures to suppress the movement. The Seditious Meetings Act was passed and many leaders were put behind the bars. But this made the movement more violent. In the meanwhile Chelmsford retired and was succeeded by Reading as Viceroy. Under him the violence reached a terrible height on 20 August 1921 at Malabar where the Moplahs wreaked their vengeance and paralised the whole administrative machinery. The unfortunate part of the Moplah uprising, however, was that many Hindus too fell victims to their violence. The Moplahs uprising was so successful that the Government machinery was replaced by Khilafat Republic. The Government struck back by arresting Ali brothers on 17th September 1921. The Working Committee of the Congress condemned this action of the Government and as a mark of protest decided to observe *hartal* on the day of the arrival of the Prince of Wales in India for the inauguration of the new Constitution. The Prince immediately on landing in Bombay on 17th November, was greeted by a very successful public *hartal* all over the city, but unfortunately this *hartal* had to witness certain violent clashes between the Cooperator and Non-Cooperator which in a way taught one of the greatest lessons to Mr. Gandhi who condemned these incidents in the strongest terms [14]. The Government too became more repressive and declared the Khilafat volunteer organization as unlawful. Firing and lathi charges began to be resorted to and public meetings were for forbidden, but the anti-government activities still continued.

The Prince was to visit Calcutta in December 1921. Lord Reading made certain efforts to reach a settlement with the Congress before that but the Congress refused to cooperate unless the Ali brothers were released. Viceroy Reading, according to K.M. Munshi offered that he "would call a round Table Conference at Calcutta a week prior to the Prince's visit there, he himself representing the British Government and India to be represented by her politicians including Gandhiji and other Congress leaders. Reading further offered that at this conference, he would, on behalf of the British Government, concede full provincial autonomy and discuss the possibility of dyarchy in the Central Government. All the political prisoners were to be released."[15] Several leaders asked Mr.Gandhi to accept the proposals, but the latter under influence of half-a-dozen Maulvis refused to agree unless Khilafat movement prisoners were also released. The negotiations came to an end. This was unfortunate. C.R. Das was beside himself with anger. According to him, "The chance of a lifetime has been lost." Be that as it may, the Ahmedabad session of the Congress was held towards the close of 1921 where it was decided to start civil disobedience movement and intensify the non-cooperation activities. All the executive authority of the Congress was handed over to one man, Mr. Gandhi. Thus the struggle continued with the increasingly repressive measures of the Government. Wherever the Prince went, empty streets greeted him and all the functions held in his honour were boycotted. About 30,000 nationalists were put behind the bars, and this included the popular leaders like Motilal Nehru, Lajpat Rai, Abul Kalam Azad, Ali brothers and others. Gandhi alone of the popular leaders remained outside.

Suspension of the Movement

The movement, however, despite its apparent success, was going fast to pieces. Gandhi's slogan was non-violent non-cooperation, but for the Congressmen the movement was hardly constituted on non-violence. The rising wave of indiscipline and disorganization reached its height when almost all the leaders were put in the jails. The principles and objectives of the struggle were not defined and a "vague Swaraj with no clear ideology behind it and a particular technique of non-violent struggle," writes Pt. Nehru,[16] could not sustain popular enthusiasm. The frightful repression and coercion of the Government demoralize the people yet further. And the effectiveness of the movement was considerably marred by the insurrection of the Moplahs.[17] Nor was the Moplahs uprising the only violent incident. Mr. R.W.D. Willoughby, the Deputy Commissioner of Kheri in U.P., was assassinated on 26August 1920 by a Muslim fanatic. The Hindu-Muslim front started cracking up and there was a possibility of communal and class violence breaking out all over the country. The things grew worse after the Ahmedabad session of the Congress reaching their climax in February 1922 when a mass violence broke out at Chauri Chaura, a village in the Gorakhpur district of the United Provinces. Here a large number of Congressmen supported by about a thousand ordinary peasants clashed with the authorities and when the police opened fire they retaliated by burning alive 21 policemen and a Sub-Inspector in the police station. This horrified Mr. Gandhi and declaring that the people were not yet trained to carry on a non-violent struggle. He announced the suspension of the movement.

For the rank and file of the Congress this declaration was a bolt from the blue. The most important of the Congress leaders like Motilal Nehru, C.R. Das, Lajpat Rai, Ali brothers and Jawaharlal Nehru criticized this action of Mr Gandhi. Romain Rolland, one of the great admirers of Mr. Gandhi, aptly summed up the feelings of these leaders thus: "It is dangerous to assemble all the forces of the nation, and to hold the nation panting before a prescribed movement to lift one's arm to give a final command; and then at last moment, let one's arms drop and thrice call a halt just as the formidable machinery has been set in motion." Mr. Gandhi, in fact, all of a sudden fell from the estimation of people, and it was here that the Government struck. Gandhi being arrested; his prosecution was sanctioned on 10 March 1922. The historic trial started at Ahmedabad in the court of Mr. Broomsfield, the Sessions Judge. Gandhi pleaded guilty and he was sentenced to six years' imprisonment, Thus did the Non-cooperation Movement come to an end at the time. Gandhi was released on 5 February 1924, much before the term of his imprisonment ended, on medical grounds and till then at least the Non-cooperation Movement seemed to have had its last cremation rites.

An Appraisal

The novel experiment of non-violent non-cooperation of Mr. Gandhi has been a subject of great criticism. Sir C.Y. Chintamani calls it "just one of those double negatives, if there be any, which do not make an affirmative."[18] Mrs Annie Besant, called non-cooperation as "only a clumsy method of expressing widespread resentment against the inferior positions to which India was relegated."[19] In a passage of Christian Scripture," continues Annie Besant, "the warning is given that Satan can appear as an Angel of Light, and the simile is apt for the N.C.O movement which has been distinguished from the beginning by speaking 'words smoother than butter' on non-violence while war has ever been in its heart and its practice"[20]

The *hartals* and non-cooperation, in fact, had been provocative of rioting and bloodshed since the very early days. The first all-India hartal had caused a riot in Delhi. Then the serious riots occurred at Bombay at the time of the visit of the Prince of Wales. It was this instrument of hartal that began the Punjab troubles.[21] In the elections that were held under the new Constitution the non-cooperators hurled disgrace in the most objectionable manner upon those who had the temerity to stand as candidates. Chintamani observes: "I speak from personal knowledge when I say that there was no end of non-violent violence or violent non-violence whichever phrase may be preferred, to embarrass the men who dared to think for themselves."[22] *Hartals* and non-violence being always accompanied by its intimidation, it was not a good weapon to be given to the Indians. But Mr. Gandhi, writes Besant, was a "vague, dreamy mystic, out of touch with ordinary human nature."

The movement brought a great misery to thousands of families. Great many left their employment, the youth leaving the schools and colleges became demoralized and developed the spirit of revolt against all authority, parental, tutorial and government. If the lawyers and the others left their professions and services, no proper arrangement was made to collect funds for their maintenance. And so much sacrifice and suffering led the people not to Swaraj but back to the Councils. The party to take the utmost advantage of the situation was the party against which the movement was directed. In fact he committed certain Himalayan blunders, which produced an immense mischief. If Mr. Gandhi had not come forward with his movement of the new reforms, the Indian Nationalists "would have remained a united body of men and would have in office, in legislatures and outside in public life, brought to bear upon the British Government a pressure the result of which" would have been much better. Mr. Gandhi, in fact, threw away "a splendid opportunity of stating his policy in the calm and quiet discussion among men of different opinions."[23]

Mr. Gandhi's assertion that he would secure Swaraj in a year was, perhaps, childish. For, a whole nation could not be raised to the great heights of perfect non-violence in just one year, nor could the bureaucracy be overawed to bow before his magic wand in that time.[24] But even if we supposed that he succeeded. "What then? We know what has been done already. The Khilafat Raj in Malabar, the horrors of which his followers ignored but which has killed the Hindu-Muslim entente and N.C.O.... If he snatches it (Swaraj) away, he cannot just keep order. We shall anarchy, murder, arson, rape, robbery, the uprising of have-nots and slaughter of the haves."

Nor could the consequences of the defiance of law for the mere sake of defiance be overlooked. This, according to Annie Besant, "encourages the spirit of lawlessness among the ignorant and the criminal classes, which strikes at the very foundations of the society. If the present Government permitted this to continue unchecked, they would bequeath to their Indian successors the painful task of reducing to order the chaos they had permitted instead of handling over to them well-ordered and law-abiding people."[25]

Mr. Gandhi believed in practising the precepts of the "Sermon on the Mount." (If a man strikes thee on one cheek turn to him the other also, etc.) Commenting on this Bishop Magee said that if the sermon were practised by a nation it would be destroyed in a week. The observation of the Bishop does not seem to be wrong if considered in the context of the later position of independent India in the Indo-Chinese conflict. It would not be an exaggeration to say that Mr. Gandhi's policy had been one of the major causes of India's unpreparedness and humiliation.

Mr. Gandhi's alliance with the Khilafat Committee again was nothing but a 'Himalayan blunder." Even if the British Prime Minister violated his promises and the demands of Khilafat were entirely correct, "the introduction of a purely religious question, affecting Musalmans only, as an integral part of

Indian politics marked a new and fatal departure and has had a far greater part in the creation of" the deplorable conditions which then existed.

Mr Gokhale was not perhaps incorrect when he told Mrs Annie Besant that "Gandhi will cause a great set-back to our political movement."[26] Even Dr. Tagore when called upon by a European friend to give Gandhi's three strongest and three weakest points, summed up all his qualities in one word: "Inconsistency."[27]

Yet, when all this is said, let us not forget that the novel movement started by Mr Gandhi brought about a general awakening in the masses. The masses became brave, fearless and self-reliant; the Law of Sedition began to be freely criticized, jail was looked upon as a place of pilgrimage and the Congress leaders had a successful experience of an open clash with the British authority. On its constructive side, prohibition got a great deal of encouragement, hand-spinning and hand weaving became popular and khadi became an honourable uniform of the popular leaders.

Chelmsford retired from India in 1921, and returning to England he was made Viscount. In 1924 the Labour Government made him First Lord of the Admiralty. He worked in several other important offices before he suddenly died in 1931. Reading, the successor of Chelmsford as Viceroy, wrote of him, "For my own part, although I found him singularly lacking in charm and geniality, which may perhaps account for some of the difficulties in his path, he was actuated by high purpose and strove his utmost for India."[28]

NOTES

1. Mohan, Pearay, *An Account of the Punjab Disorders and the Working of Martial Law*, p. 121.
2. O' Dywer, Sir M., *India as I knew it*, pp. 216-222.
3. *Ibid*., p.213.
4. O' Dywer, *op. cit.*, p. 363.
5. O' Dywer, *op. cit.*, p. 365.
6. See Gwyer, Maurice and Appadorai A., *Speeches and documents on the Indian Constitution* (2 vols), Vol I; Banerjee A.C., *Indian Constitutional Documents*, 3 vols; III 1949, pp. 158-67.
7. *Legislative Council Report*, Punjab, 1921.
8. Dyer's testimony to the Hunter Committee—see Furneaux, Report, *Massacre at Amritsar*, London, 1963, pp. 17-24, 108-11; also see Datta, V.N., *Jallianwala Bagh*, Ludhiana, 1969, pp. 111-118.

9. Furneaux Rupert, *op. cit.*, p.25.
10. See O'Dywer, *op. cit.*, pp. 302-3; Wally, S.D., Edwin Montagu, pp. 206-9; Mukerjee, Hirendranath, *India's Struggle for Freedom,* p. 110.
11. Mukerjee, Hirendranath, *India's Struggle for Freedom*, p. 110.
12. Caveeshar, Sardul Singh, *India's Fight for Freedom*, 1936, p. 17.
13. Munshi, K.M., *op. cit.,* 1, p. 23. Mr Jinnah followed by some others left the Congress after this session. For they were sure that such an unconstitutional movement would lead to large-scale violence.
14. Sitaramayya, P.B., *History of the Indian National Congress*, I, p. 221.
15. Munshi, *op. cit.*, I. p. 23.
16. Nehru, Jawaharlal, *Autobiography*, p. 269.
17. *Indian Constitutional Documents, 1757-93* (3 vols.) Vol.III, 1917-1939, edited by A.C. Bannerjee, 1949, p. 164.
18. Chintamani, Sir C.Y., *Indian Politics Since the Mutiny*, p. 187.
19. Besant, Annie, *The India That Shall Be*, p. 25.
20. *Ibid.*, p. 114.
21. *Ibid.*, pp. 150, 174.
22. Chintamani *op. cit.*, p. 84.
23. See Chintamani, *op. cit.*, p. 137.
24. Caveeshar, *op. cit.*, p. 112.
25. See Besant, Annie, *op. cit.*, pp. 139-144.
26. *Ibid.*, p. 103.
27. Caveeshar, Sardul Singh, *India's Fight for Freedom,* 1936, p. 109.
28. Hyde, H. Montgomery, *Lord Reading,* p. 340.

2

Marquess of Reading
1921-26

Son of a fruit merchant named Finsbury Square by Sarah, the daughter of one Daniel Davis, Rufus Daniel Issacs, who later became Marquess of Reading, was born on 10 October 1860. Isaac's family came of a Jewish stock. He got his education at the University College School and in Brussels and Hanover, but without getting any higher degrees he entered into service as ship's boy when he was only sixteen. He visited South America and India. After coming back to England he tried his hand at the family business but could not succeed. He decided to turn to the Bar and in 1887 was called at the Middle Temple. In the same year he married Elice Edith, who was daughter of a Hamburg merchant. At the bar he secured a phenomenal success so much so that in 1904 when he became M.P. his annual income was £ 28,000. Having proved a great success in the Commons as well, in 1910 he was appointed by Asquith as Solicitor-General and after a short time was raised to the post of Attorney-General. In 1912 he was made Privy Councillor and given a seat in the Cabinet. Next year saw him appointed Lord Chief Justice of England. A few months thereafter he was created a baron as Lord Reading. He was made G.C.B. in 1915, was later on sent as High Commissioner to Washington and Ottawa, then as Ambassador in the USA and finally in 1921 he was appointed Viceroy of India in succession to Lord Chelmsford.

His appointment as Viceroy was criticized by some journals such as *Morning Post* on the grounds of his being a Jew. In India, however, the Press opinion was generally favourable, and it was hoped that his Jewish wisdom would enable him to understand the minds of the Eastern people more intimately. At a farewell function before he embarked for India he remarked: "To be the representative of the King-Emperor in India is to be the representative of Justice.

I leave this seat, the Judicial Bench, not forsaking or abandoning the pursuit of justice but rather pursuing it in larger fields, and where I feel the road is not so certain or well-laid..."

Such were the circumstances under which Reading arrived. We have already seen in our previous chapters how the Congress having boycotted the Reforms Act of 1919, in 1920 Mr Gandhi had started his experiment of non-violent non-cooperation. The movement started by Gandhi was still going on when Reading succeeded Chelmsford. Besides the non-cooperation movement of Mr Gandhi there had been large-scale disturbances in the Punjab, leading to the Jalianwala Bagh tragedy of 1919. In 1920 the Sikhs had started Gurdwara Sudhar Movement and it had not yet ended when the new Viceroy came in. As a result of the harsh terms imposed by the Allies on Turkey by the Treaty of Sevres in 1920 the Muslim community in India had been extremely excited. Reading was quite sympathetic towards the Muslim feelings, not only because he was convinced of the weight of the Muslim objections to the Treaty but also because he thought that only encouraging the Muslim community against the non-Muslims could control the political situation in India. Even before he arrived in India he had written to the Prime Minister in England as to "How important it is, in my judgement, to make concessions to Mohammadan opinion, if you think they can safely be made. After all that has happened in India in relation to the Treaty, there will be the greatest disappointment if no revision is made..."

Almost the first thing that Reading did in India was to calm the feelings of the Sikhs in the Punjab. He personally went to Lahore and heard full accounts of the Sikh agitation from the Punjab Governor, Sir Eric Maclagan. From Lahore the Viceroy insisted on going to Amritsar where he went round the Jalianwalla Bagh and the Golden Temple. Returning to Lahore he received a deputation of the Punjab leaders and pleaded before them for racial cooperation, and promised that a monetary compensation would be given to the Indians who had suffered by the events of Jalianwalla Bagh and elsewhere. He said: "Can we not now do our utmost to banish suspicion, to cease imputing evil motives, to breathe again in the sympathetic justice of the Government, to concentrate in the united effort to reach by peaceful and constitutional means the end which is promised under your new Reforms and which indeed is already in course of fulfillment?"[2]

In order to ease the political atmosphere in India he also made use of the services of Pandit Madan Mohan Malaviya who brought about an interview between Mr Gandhi and the Viceroy. In May 1921 the Mahatma had as many as six interviews with the Viceroy at Shimla. The Viceroy was not much impressed by Gandhi's appearance but he considered his religious and moral views as admirable. Mr Gandhi was supremely courteous "with manner of distinction." When the Viceroy asked Gandhi as to what made him pursue the policy of non-cooperation with the Government, the latter replied that every action of the Government, which appeared good, was actuated by the sinister motive of trying to fasten British dominion in India. This was the root cause of his present attitude. The meetings took place in a very cordial atmosphere but they could not stop the Non-cooperation Movement that had been going on.

On 17 November 1921, the Prince of Wales arrived on a visit to India accompanied by his naval A.D.C. Sub-Lieutenant Lord Louis Mountbatten, who later became the last Viceroy of India. Gandhi urged his followers to boycott all celebrations planned to welcome the Prince. The "King-Emperor's heir made his way across the subcontinent to the accompaniment of galloping hoofs on the polo-fields and half empty and deserted streets, mute testimony of the success of the *hartals* proclaimed by Gandhiji. By the time he reached Calcutta six weeks after leaving Bombay, the Prince was thoroughly disillusioned and felt ashamed that so much should have been spent – '£ 25,000 of English money and goodness knows how many lacs of rupees'– on a tour which so far could not be described as successful." In fact later on the Prince bluntly told Montagu, that "India is no longer a place for a white man to live in." Northcliffe, a great Press Lord and friend of Reading who visited him in India expressed similar views. He told the Viceroy that he did not care for India 'a wearisome country.' He asked: "What do we want India for? Prestige? Perhaps. Cash? We certainly don't get any from it. The thousands of able men from home could do far better almost anywhere else."

The Prince of Wales' visit to India was a failure, but as we have already seen Mr Gandhi's Non-cooperation Movement started in 1921 was also not a success. As the Movement slowly became violent, the Mahatma suddenly suspended it, and openly recognized its failure. On 10 March 1922 he was arrested on a charge of sedition. The Mahatma, Reading wrote to the Prime Minister in England, had become "more the politician than the holy man." He, according to the Viceroy had seized hold of the Mohammedan discontent and the Punjab disturbances for the purpose of "making a combined movement in favor of Swaraj. Thus his power grew, but equally he had to meet all the difficulties of a political combination of this character." His promises to get Swaraj within three months remained unfulfilled and the more sensible people had begun to wonder "whether he would achieve anything beyond agitation and disturbance." In 1924 Gandhi underwent an operation for appendicitis. Reading took the opportunity and released him, but he was happy that he no more enjoyed the popularity that he previously used to. "It is pathetic," the

Viceroy remarked, "to observe the rapid decline of the power of Gandhi and the frantic attempts he is now making to cling to his position as leader at the expense of practically every principle he has hitherto advocated."

While doing everything to weaken the Indian National Congress and its leader, Mr Gandhi, the Viceroy, true to his policy of divide and rule, did not forget to placate the Muslims and to wean them away from the popular political movement. Reading believed that if peace was to be restored among the Muslims of India, Turkey must somehow be placated. On 28 February 1921 he sent a telegram to Montagu, the Secretary of State: "The Government of India are fully alive to the complexity of the problem, but India's services in the War, in which Indian Moslem troops so largely participated, and the support which the Indian Moslem cause is receiving throughout India, entitle her to claim the extreme fulfilment of her just and equitable aspirations." He insisted that the Treaty of Sevres should be revised in conformity with the wishes of the Indian Muslims and after proposing how it could done, he concluded: "so important is it for the Government of India to range itself openly on the side of the Muslim India that we press for permission to publish the foregoing…forthwith."[3] Montagu published this telegram in haste without even securing the permission of the Prime Minister Lloyd George, and this cost him his office. The constant hammering of Reading on this subject, however, ultimately secured his end. The Treaty of Sevres was ultimately revised and its harsh provisions modified or knocked off by the new peace that was concluded in Lausanne in 1923.

Reading like Minto, believed that while the Muslims should be set up as a counterpoise to Hindus, a third force of the princes should be reorganized and strengthened as a counterpoise to both. Reading made special efforts to woo the princes and to bring them together as a strong reactionary force against the growing nationalist movement. He made State visits to several of the states starting with Kashmir.[4] During his whole period of viceroyalty he received the hospitality of more than 20 princes having a wild elephant hunt in Mysore, getting his first tiger with the Maharaja of Gwalior and making friends with Bikaner, Patiala and Nawanagar. It was as a result of the encouragement of Reading and his predecessor that Sir Ganga Singh, the Maharaja of Bikaner, succeeded in developing the Chamber of Princes from the annual conference of the Indian Princes. The Chamber of Princes was inaugurated in 1921. It consisted of 120 members of whom 12 represented 127 states, while the rest of the states were members in their own right, except the 327 states which got no representation. The chamber originally met once a year presided over by the Viceroy. It elected its own Chancellor who presided in the absence of the Viceroy, and acted as the permanent President of the Standing Committee of the Chamber which met at least twice a year at Delhi and submitted yearly reports to the Chamber. Besides the princes also held formal conference when visiting Delhi for a session.

Though the Chamber could not do much beyond acting only as a deliberative body, yet the important purpose served was that the Princes could come together and discuss their relations with the Paramount Power and other matters of common interest. And moreover, as the Simon Commission commented: "The establishment of the Chamber of Princes marks an important stage in the development of relations between the Crown and the States, for it involves a definite breach in the earlier policy, according to which it was rather the aim of the Crown to discourage joint action and joint consultation between the Indian States and to treat each State as an isolated unit apart from its neighbours."

The Conservatives having won in the General Elections in October 1924, Mr Baldwin came to power in England. Lord Birkenhead was appointed the Secretary of State for India. Although the latter had never been to India, his study of Indian history was said to be extensive. It may be interesting to quote his views with regard to the Indian problem, which naturally affected the Viceroy's thinking in India. Writing about the Montagu reforms thus, he informed the Viceroy that, "too much has been given away, I will not say through weakness, but through general malaise which succeeded the War in India, Ireland and Egypt. On any point, therefore, on which you hold a strong view that the line must be firmly drawn, you are unlikely to lack support...from me." Again, "to me it is frankly inconceivable that India will ever be fit for Dominion Self-Government." In ultimate analysis, the strength of the British position is that we are in India for the good of India. The most striking illustration of the truth of the position is of course supplied by the infinite variation of nationality and religion in the subcontinent....I, as you know, never liked or believed in, the Montagu-Chelmsford reforms. I distrusted dyarchy, though I realized that dyarchy was an indispensable experiment in attempting to begin grafting Western parliamentary institutions upon an Oriental population, wholly uneducated for their receipt."[5]

"An oft-told incident deserves to be repeated here. One evening at a dance at Viceregal Lodge (Shimla), Lady Reading turned to the A.D.C. in waiting, whose first night on duty it happened to be, and asked what was the name of the tune the band was playing. Just at that precise moment the music stopped, and in the minute's silence, which followed the voice of the A.D.C., could be clearly heard across the ballroom replying, "I shall remember your Kisses', your Excellency, "When you have forgotten my Name." The effect of this announcement on the assembled company, it need hardly be added, was sensational."[6]

THE SWARAJ PARTY

The circumstances, which led to the formation of the Swaraj Party, are interesting. After the Moderates had left the Congress, the National Liberal Federation had been formed in 1918. The Congress having boycotted the first elections under the Reforms Act of 1919, the Liberals who fought them were returned to the legislatures in large numbers towards the end of the 1920. The policy of the National Liberal Federation in the legislatures was what has been known as "responsive cooperation", or in other words cooperation with the Government where possible and opposition where necessary. Immediately after their election to the Central Legislature, the Liberals tried to move for a revision of the constitution. Thus, on 23 September 1921 a resolution was brought in which they demanded a full provincial autonomy and introduction of responsibility in the Centre. The intervention of the Home Member Sir William Vincent, however, brought about a compromise and his formula being adopted, the Assembly passed the resolution: "That this Assembly recommends to the Governor-General-in-Council that he should convey to the Secretary of State for India, the view of this Assembly that the progress made by India on the path of responsive government warrants a reexamination and revision of the constitution at an earlier date." The report of the resolution was duly submitted by the government to the Secretary of State, but the latter rejected it saying that the existing constitutional machinery had not yet been fully worked out as a whole and progress was still possible under it. In reply to this Diwan Bahadur T. Rangachariar moved in the Assembly in February 1923, yet another resolution expressing dissatisfaction with the reply of the Secretary of State. But nothing came out of it and the Liberal Party seemed to have bitterly failed in its programme. Although it was successful in getting some undesirable Acts repealed and in getting some useful Acts–like the Special Law Repeal Act 1922, the Indian Criminal Law Amendment Repeal Act 1922, and the Criminal Law Amendment Act, 1923 placed on the Statute Book, yet its achievements were unsatisfactory, and this in a sense paved the way for the formation and the success of the Swaraj Party.

The increasingly stiff policy of the Government towards 'responsive cooperation of the liberals was yet another factor which alienated the masses against the Government and prepared the way for the Swaraj Party. The declaration of the Government on 2 November 1922, that no early revision of the constitution was possible; the Governor-General Reading's certifying the Princes Protection Act into law, when it had been rejected by the Assembly;

and his use of extraordinary powers in doubling the Salt Tax although the Budget containing the measure had been rejected by the assembly; these were thus only a few of the steps of the Government which exhibited their unreasonable stiffness.

Nor was the well-known 'steel frame' speech delivered by the British Prime Minister, Lloyd George on 22 August 1922 less helpful to the organization of the new party. His eulogising of the Indian Civil Services and emphasis that they were going to play a major role in the Indian administration for a long time to come, convinced some Indian leaders that with such a policy of the Government cooperation was just impossible and the policy of obstruction was the only way which could profitably be followed.[7] The injustice meted out to Indians in the Crown Colony of Kenya in Africa, and the Government's failure to do anything in this connection. The efforts of the Government inflamed the Swarajists. To save the princes, as a power of reaction against the progressive movement in India also prepared the ground.

Yet another factor was the difficulty of the Muslims as a community to comprehend the ethics of the principle underlying non-violence. Non-violence seemed to be foreign to their elements. If they accepted it in the initial stages that was only for the Hindu support for the Khilafat Movement. But when this support was no more needed the value of non-violence began to diminish in their minds till it became a thing of ridicule. And finally, came the abrupt decision of Mr Gandhi, whereby the non-cooperation launched with such high hopes was suspended. A desperate situation was created and the leaders like Motilal Nehru and Lala Lajpat Rai wrote letters to Mr Gandhi from jails assailing his decision. In the All India Congress Committee on 24 February 1922 Mr Gandhi had to face bitter criticism. His arguments to defend his policy failed to win the ground and the gulf between the cooperators and non-cooperators widened.

These thus were the circumstances, which paved the way for the organization of the Swaraj Party.

The Gaya Session of the Congress was held towards the close of 1922. C.R. Das who presided over it placed his scheme of entering the legislatures for the purpose of fighting the Government from within and bringing its administrative machinery to a standstill before the members. But the supporters of Mr Gandhi yet being strong enough, his scheme was outvoted. C.R. Das resigned his office and announced his programme to organize the Swaraj Party which would contest the ensuing elections. He was given every support by Pt. Motilal Nehru and thus were the foundations of the Swaraj Party laid which according to the desire of its organizers was to work from within the Congress and fight the government on the parliamentary plane.

A special session of the Congress was held at Delhi in September 1923 under the presidentship of Maulana Azad. And by this time the atmosphere had yet further changed in the favour of the Swaraj Party. It was between these two sessions that the Salt Tax had been doubled despite the opposition of the Assembly. Those who desired to have some sort of clash with the Government, thus developed their strength and the programme of the 'council entry' was adopted by the Congress officially. Gandhi being released on medical grounds in February 1924, expressed his dissatisfaction with the new Congress programme. But the circumstances as they were, it was impossible for anybody to bring back the masses to an active non-cooperation and therefore a sort of compromise being reached in 1925, the Congressmen were given freedom to decide for themselves, i.e. to work for the Council entry or to carry on the constructive work outside the Council. Mr Gandhi gave his blessings to the Swarajists at Belgaum in 1924, and thus the last obstacle in the way was removed.

The Programme of the Swarajists

So far as the programme of the Swaraj Party was concerned, it was declared in its manifesto in 1923, that the demand of the right for the Indians to control their own government would be the first duty of the Swarajists after their entry into the Council. The capture of seats by the Swarajists was declared to be necessary in order to prevent undesirable persons from entering the Councils and thus giving a false show of popular support to the British by cooperating with them. The Swarajists also hoped that they would generate new enthusiasm in the masses by fighting the elections. After their entry into the Council, their programme was to make the Montford Reforms unworkable and to bring the administrative machinery to a standstill. They were to reject the offers of participating in the government bodies and in the functions held by and in honour of the Government officials.

The more constructive side of their programme, however, was that they would move resolutions for the advance of the constitution and bring proposals for new legislation to facilitate the growth of the arts of civilization. Outside the Council they were to whole-heartedly assist the constructive activities of Mr Gandhi. And they also promised that if their scheme failed in bringing down the Government to the Indian way of thinking, they would come back and ungrudgingly follow Mr Gandhi in his civil disobedience programmes.

At the Polls

The Swarajists fought in 1923 the second elections under the new constitution of 1919. In these elections they secured 45 out of 145 seats in the Central Legislative Assembly, thus emerging as the largest and most disciplined group in the Assembly. Although a working majority had not been secured, yet their success in winning the support of National Party and of the Independents, made it possible to make the smooth running of the British Government difficult. In the provinces the Swarajists in the Central Provinces won a clear majority; while in Bengal they emerged as the largest party in the provincial assembly. Elsewhere their achievements were not very enviable.

Their Work

So far as the work of the Swarajists in the Central Provinces was concerned, they being in clear majority, the working of the Dyarchy was actually made impossible and the Governor had to assume control of the transferred subjects in his own hands. In Bengal too, some Muslim members having come to the support of C.R. Das, the working of Dyarchy was made difficult. C.R. Das declared on 21 February 1924, that he would not cooperate with the Government and help in forming the ministry in Bengal unless the existing constitutional set-up had been changed. In the remaining provinces, however, the Swarajists having gained no worthwhile strength, a few of their members who were able to enter the Legislatures, continued only putting forward demands for an improvement in the constitution.

In the Centrral Legislature the Swarajists moved in 1924, that the Government should take early steps to revise the existing constitution and that a Round Table Conference should be called to make recommendations for the purpose. In the Conference the British should sit together with the Indian representatives and the recommendations made by them, after approval by the Central Assembly, should be taken to the British Parliament for the new enactment.

The Labour Party having won the elections, Ramsay Macdonald known for his sympathetic attitude towards India, became the new British Prime Minister in January 1924. It was hoped that the resolution passed by the Central Legislature would receive a favourable consideration at his hands, but the Swarajists had nothing but discouragement in store. Their proposal was rejected and they swore to stiffen their attitude against the Government. Thus, as a result of their efforts the Finance Bill was rejected in the Assembly in 1924-25 and Governor-General Reading had to carry it with the help of his extraordinary powers of certification. A similar certification had to be made by the Governor-

General in the case of the rejected budgets of 1925-26 and 1926-27. The Swarajists were able to secure passage of a resolution in the teeth of Government opposition, demanding the repeal of the Regulation III of 1818 and release of certain political prisoners. Walkouts were common, offers of membership to the government bodies were rejected and the functions held by and in honour of the Governor-General were boycotted. Nor did all this go without an effect on the Government. The die-hards in the Government were moved and in February 1924, was appointed the well known Muddiman Reform Enquiry Committee under the chairmanship of the Home Member, Sir Alexander Muddiman, to report on the working of the Dyarchy.

The Muddiman Committee Report

In the Muddiman Committee thus appointed, some Indian members were invited to join. Although Pt. Motilal Nehru declined the offer, persons like Sir Tej Bahadur Sapru and M.A. Jinnah joined the Committee. But the official majority in the Committee was retained. The investigations were duly made in the working of the Reform Act of 1919, but the official majority found it difficult to agree in its findings with the non-official minority. Two reports were thus prepared; the majority report appreciating the system of Dyarchy and recommending its continuation with some insignificant changes here and there, while the minority report condemning the system of Dyarchy as an unworkable system and stressing the need of its early abolition. According to the minority report, the Dyarchy was working 'creekily', and to "our mind the proper question to ask is not whether any alternative transitional system can be devised but whether the constitution should not be put on a permanent basis with provisions for automatic progress in the future so as to secure stability in the Government and willing cooperation of the people."[8] The Government accepted the majority view and proceeded with the consideration of its recommendations. In September 1925, thus, the report of the committee was brought in the Central Legislature for discussion. Pt. Motilal Nehru delivered a brilliant speech condemning the dyarchical system. He moved a resolution, which was carried by an overwhelming majority in the teeth of Government opposition. The resolution demanded among other things that (a) certain immediate changes should be made in the existing constitution in order to make the Government fully responsible and (b) a Round Table Conference or Convention should be held to prepare a detailed scheme for the purpose, which should be placed before the Assembly for its approval and then be taken to the British Parliament to be embodied in the statute. The Government, however, remained adamant in its opposition to the Indian aspiration and on 24 January 1924 Lord Reading expressly declared that the British Parliament would not be coerced by such resolutions. But the Swarajists' activities did not go entirely in vain. Hardly had nine months passed after Lord Reading's declaration when the Home Government announced the appointment of Royal Commission as promised in the Reform Act of 1919. This Commission was appointed two years earlier than the date of stipulated in the Act.

An Appraisal

Commenting on the work of the party thus wrote Mrs Annie Besant: "A most astounding position has arisen in the country in consequence of the success of the Swarajist Party in the Assembly. Before they were elected they roared like lion; now they are gentler than cooing doves." Swaraj was the main aim of the Party, but the moment they entered the Assembly, this aim was entirely forgotten. Their fall from the high ideals is revealed from their proposal of a conference for the purpose of making a constitution for India and in the conference they were prepared to offer the Government one-third of the seats. "If I were a Swarajist," thus wrote Annie Besant, "I should cry aloud and say that they had been bought by the Government."[9]

In fact all those who joined the body and through the party entered the Assemblies were not persons very selflessly devoted to the national cause. There is no doubt that the Swarajists courted imprisonment during 1924-26, but not all of them were capable of receiving *lathi* blows. There were many among them who were undesirable for becoming members of the Assemblies. These persons, in fact, aimed at social and political positions more than at the national independence. The Swarajists on the whole were incapable of following extremist methods and it was only due to this reason that they decided to follow the easy parliamentarianism. There was little wonder; therefore, when they entered the Assemblies all the old promises were forgotten. An important wing among them began openly to advocate the merits of the policy of responsive cooperation. Those in favour of wholesale obstruction could not like this and hence, the split between them was bound to appear.

In fact the whole policy that the Swarajists were to follow seemed ill-desired and ill-aimed at. They were determined to bring administrative machinery to a standstill. But in the administrative machinery that existed, there was much that could keep it working and foil the Swarajist ambition. The Government was not brought to a standstill and even in C.P. and Bengal where they had considerable hold in the Assemblies, the King's Government went on as it ever did.

The death of C.R. Das in 1925 also weakened the Party to a considerable extent. And even he, it is said, during the closing years of his life had developed doubts in the utility of obstructionism. Moreover, such an obstructionism could be followed advantageously only in the Assemblies where the Swarajists had a majority. But in the majority of the provinces where such majority did not exist, the wholesale obstruction was nothing but futile.

Then there was the continuous opposition of the orthodox followers of Mr Gandhi to face. The moral courage the Swarajists in the beginning had, began slowly to wane. The seductive policies of the Government also had their way and slowly the Swarajists began to feel that the indiscriminate opposition to the Government was after all not in the best interests of the country.

Yet another factor soon appeared. The Hindus and Muslims had been fighting together in India so long as the Khilafat problem remained unsolved. But with the abolition of Khilafat in Turkey in 1922, no inducement was left for majority of the Indian Muslims to cooperate with the Hindus. The Muslim League eclipsed during the Khilafat agitation, thus found a breathing space once again. The divide and rule policy of the Government and the vigorous work of its secret agents created dissensions. The Non-cooperation Movement, which had also been a factor in bringing about Hindu-Muslim unity, had ebbed. Thus with the passage of time the discord between the Hindu and the Muslim began slowly to appear. The Hindus suffered in 1922 in the Moplah uprising and in 1923 there were as many as 11 Hindu-Muslim riots. The political unity between the two communities was becoming a thing of the past and the Swarajist Party began to experience too great a risk in constantly trying to alienate the Government with its obstructionism. For in that case the Government would woo the Muslim League and the gulf between the Hindus and the Muslims would become too wide to bridge. And then, Mr Gandhi too had never seen eye to eye with the Swarajists, He being released from the jail on 5 February 1924 on grounds of ill health, began to regain his popularity with the masses at a very fast pace.His constructive activities and his efforts at a Hindu-Muslim accord began to win him a general sympathy and his 21 days' fast in September 1925 undertaken as a self-imposed penance for the sins of all the Hindus and the Muslims who had participated in the communal riots, made him a popular national leader once again.

On the other hand the Swarajists slowly lost ground. Their policy of obstruction began to change fast. In 1924 they thus accepted seats on the Steel Protection Committee. In 1925 the Skeen Committee, appointed to recommend measures to rapidly Indianise the Army, secured Pt. Motilal Nehru as its member. Mr V.J. Patel saw no harm in being elected Speaker of the Central Assembly. S.B. Tambe became an Executive Councillor in C.P. And all this slowly but surely stole away the thunder of the Swarajists' programme. The selfless workers began to be looked upon as self-seeking adventurers. In the elections of 1926 the Swarajits fared but badly. All their glamour was thus lost and Mr Gandhi who was slowly regaining his ground found himself about 1926 to have been brought once again at the helm of affairs as an undisputed master of the Congress.

Thus did the Swarajist Party fail. But in our criticism of the activities and achievements of the Swarajist Party, let us not forget that considering the circumstances under which it was organized, it did render some services to the national cause. The Party was organized just at the time when the non-cooperation movement of Mr Gandhi had failed. The great enthusiasm aroused among the people was finding no channel through which to express itself. It was only the Swarajist Party, which gave the Indian masses an alternative programme. Their enthusiasm was thus kept up and resistance against the Government continued which killed the existing cooperation of the Liberals with the Government in the Assemblies. Nor could the importance of Swarajists be minimized in the fact that they exposed the irresponsible and autocratic nature of the Government in the Legislative Assemblies. The rejection of the Government budgets and the refusal of supplies were, in fact, some of the achievements of the Swarajists which while discrediting the Government on the one hand, enlightened the masses on the other. Let us also not forget that the proposal of a Round Table Conference accepted by the Government in 1930, had originally been brought forward only by the Swarajists. The appointment of the Muddiman Committee was another of its achievements. The minority report of the Committee was a very valuable contribution, which paved the way for an ultimate burial of the dyarchical system. The appointment of the Simon Commission two years earlier than the stipulated date was also a feather in the Swarajists' cap. Thus, although the Swarajists did not do as much as it was expected of them, yet they did fill up the gap in India's war of independece but for which the ultimate attainment of independence may have been delayed.

Before closing, it may be interesting to quote the official view with regard to the Swaraj Party, revealed from the Secretary of Stare Birkenhead's letter to Lord Reading: "Your conclusions agree with those of this Office and, for what my own opinion is worth, with my own. I see many signs that the Swarajists are slipping. In my opinion they neither know where they are, nor where they are going. The split between them and the Independents is a new promising and unexpected development. I hope that it will grow. But I have always placed my highest and most permanent hopes upon the eternity of the Communal situation. The greater the political progress made by the Hindus, the greater, in my judgement, will the Moslem distrust and antagonism become. All the conferences in all the world cannot bridge over the unbridgeable, and between these two communities lies a chasm which cannot be crossed by the resources of modern political engineering."[10]

Reading retired from India in 1926 and was immediately raised to marquessate. He continued taking interest in the Indian affairs, and was firmly opposed to granting Dominion status to the country. In 1930 he participated in the India Round Table Conference as leader of the Liberal delegation. The next year he was made Foreign Secretary and Leader of the House of Lords under the National Government. But he remained in this office only for a few months. In 1930 he had lost his wife, the next year he married Stella, who had been his wife's private secretary. He died at 75 in December 1935.

NOTES

1. Reading to Lloyd George—Hyde, H, Montgomery. *Lord Reading,* London, 1967, pp. 331-332.
2. *Ibid.*, p. 234.
3. *Ibid.*, pp. 327-372.
4. See Butler, Iris, *The Viceroy's Wife*, pp. 146-149.
5. Hyde, H. Montgomery, *Lord Reading*, pp. 381-383.
6. *Ibid.*, p. 348.
7. See Bose, S.C., *The Indian Struggle*, p. 143.
8. *Reform Enq. Committee Report,* pp. 201-03.
9. Besant A., *India That Shall Be,* p. 59.
10. Hyde, H. Montgomery, *Lord Reading*, p.38.

3

Lord Irwin, 1926-1931

Fourth son of Charles the 2nd Viscount Halifax, Edward Frederick Lindley Wood who later became Lord Irwin and the Earl of Halifax, was born on 16 April 1881. His mother, Lady Agnes Elizabeth Courtenay belonged to a distinguished family, being the only daughter of William, 11th Earl of Devon. Edward Wood was educated at Eton and Christ Church, where he was elected a Fellow of All Souls. He was yet a boy when all his elder brothers died and he became heir to his father's titles. At the age of 28 he married Lady Dorothy Onslow, who was the daughter of William, the 4th Earl of Onslow. In 1910 he became a Member of Parliament and soon distinguished himself for his courage and qualities. In 1917 he became Assistant Secretary in the Ministry of National Service. In 1921 he was promoted Under Secretary in the Colonial Office, becoming Privy Councillor and President of the Board of Education in 1922. In the next year he was made Minister of Agriculture and Fisheries and two years thereafter, was selected to succeed the Viceroy, Lord Reading, in India. He left England in April 1926 to take charge of this office.

In India as we have already seen, the Montagu Declaration of 1917 had promised that a responsible government would be established by stages, and that a substantial step towards the direction would be taken immediately. The promised step was taken in the Reforms Act of 1919 under which dyarchy had been established in the provinces. The fact that the British proved honest to their promises made in 1917, pleased even the extremist leaders in India, and Bal Gangadhar Tilak offered himself as a candidate at the first elections. Although the parliamentary government introduced in 1919 was only in a truncated form, yet even the Congress decided to accept it, and prepared to put up candidates at the elections. Soon however, as a result of the Rowlatt Act and Jalianwalla Bagh killing the situation changed and Mr Gandhi started his novel movement of non-violent non-cooperation. This new method of political agitation was based on the belief, as Gandhi said, that: "an Englishman never respects you till you stand up to him. Then he begins to like you. He is afraid of nothing physical; but he is very mortally afraid of his own conscience if you ever appeal to it, and show him to be in the wrong. He does not like to be rebuked for wrong-doing at first: but he will think it over, and it will get hold of him and hurt him till he does something to put it right."[1]

Mr Gandhi had probably understood the English character correctly, but he was not able to comprehend whether the common man in India would be able to stand up to the new and novel method of political agitation that he started. His Non-violent Movement soon turned violent. Gandhi was disillusioned and recognizing that India was not mature to grasp its spirit, called a halt to it. Soon he himself was arrested and put behind the bars. Sudden calling off of the movement left some of his staunch followers in the lurch and the Swaraj Party was organized to follow an alternative programme of political agitation from within the Legislative Councils. This party too, however, could not deliver the goods.

It is in these circumstances that Irwin came to India. The politics that the Congress at that time was following was said to be the politics of 'suspense'. *The Times of India* probably correctly summed up the situation when it wrote of "the completeness of the Congress collapse, that utter futility of the so-called Congress creed and the total absence among Congress supporters of a single responsible political idea."[2] When Irwin arrived in India, there was almost a political calm. Not only the Congress lay low, there was no other party or group which could cause concern. Although the Communist Party had been organized in 1925, it had not yet made a headway. There was tranquillity in the North-West Frontier as well.

The one problem that Irwin had immediately to face was that of communal riots. How serious this problem was may be judged from the fact that during the first year of his office there were as many as forty communal riots, Hindus killing the Muslims and the Muslims butchering the Hindus. There was a large-scale destruction of property and in several parts of the country the atmosphere was tense. The first thing that Irwin therefore did was to appeal to the people to develop a sense of toleration and live together in the name of true religion. Some leaders like Maulana Abul Kalam Azad and Pandit Motilal Nehru responded to the call, and a non-political body named Indian National Union was organized with its branches proposed to be established in all localities to combat communalism. This body however, could not achieve much success and in 1926 a respected Hindu, Swami Shradhanand was murdered by a fanatic Muslim. Intense emotions were aroused which resulted in counter-attacks and loss of much life and property. The communal agitation spread also to the North-West Frontier where a large number of Hindus were expelled by the

Afridis and other fanatic tribes, although later on good sense prevailed and if not all, at least some of these expelled Hindus were able to go back to their homes. Generally, however, the communal situation continued deteriorating and in August 1927 Irwin gave a warning in the Legislature that unless the people corrected their behaviour, the slogans of self-government would prove only empty. Soon, however, the situation took yet another turn, and what the Indian National Union or the Viceroy could not do, the announcement on 8 November 1927 of the personnel of the Statutory Commission appointed to consider the Indian Constitutional Reforms, accomplished.

THE SIMON COMMISSION, 1927

According to Section 84 of the Reform Act of 1919 statutory commission had to be appointed "at the expiration of the ten years after the passing of the Act for the purpose of enquiring into the working of the system of Government and the development of representative institutions in India, with a view to extend, modify or restrict the degree of responsible Government then existing in India." But as already referred to, the Commission was appointed two years earlier. There were several reasons why this was done. Firstly, there was the pressure of public opinion outside as well as within the Central Legislature, which forced the Government to take this step. Secondly, it was supposed that the Labour Party would certainly come to power in the next general elections, and the Conservative Government would not like the Commission to be appointed by them. Lord Birkenhead, the Secretary of State for India, frankly wrote to Lord Reading the Governor-General of India: "I am sure that having regard to political contingencies in this country, we must keep the nomination of the personnel of the Commission in our own hands. In this matter, we cannot run the slightest risk." These were, thus, the reasons for the earlier appointment of the Commission.

Indian opposition. The Commission thus appointed, landed in Bombay in February 1928. Its term of reference was, *inter alia*, to report on the extent to which it would be desirable to introduce a responsible government in India. But the Indians who had been anxious for the appointment of such a Commission, instead of welcoming it, showed a very serious opposition right from the beginning. The most important reason for this was the constitution of the Commission in which not a signle Indian has been taken as a member. The Commission consisted of representative of the different parties of England i.e. two Labourites, one Liberal and four Conservatives. It was to work under the Chairmanship of Sir John Simon of the Liberal Party. The British excuse for not appointing any Indian to its membership was that according to the terms of the Reform Act of 1919 only members of the British Parliament could be appointed to it. But this excuse was nowhere appreciated in India, for there were two Indians in the British Parliament, Lord Sinha in the Lords and Mr. Saklatwala in the Commons, who could have very well been included in the Commission. It was indeed insulting to the Indian aspirations and self-respect that the outsiders should sit in judgement on them and decide on their capabilities for a measure of responsible Government, which they could handle. Yet more so, when adding insult to injury, the Viceroy declared: "It would be generally agreed that what is required is a Commission which would be unbiased and competent to represent an accurate picture of the facts to Parliament, but it must also be a body on whose recommendations. Parliament should be willing to take action which a study of these facts may indicate to be appropriate.[3]" Sir Stanley Reed writes thus: "Indian politicians who had grown grey in the public life of their country were summoned to headquarters and told that they might be heard as witnesses: but they were to have no major part in fashioning the instrument of the Government. No greater insult was ever offered to a proud and sensitive people."[4]

Secondly, it was felt that Lord Birkenhead was posing as a conqueror and imposing his will on a subject people. The Indian leaders had not forgotten his speech to Oxford student in 1927 in which he had said: "India is our prize possession. We in England have to live on it; the Indian may live in it..... It is the task for you, the younger generation, to hold India to the last drop of your blood."

Nor was the cooperation of Labour and Liberal Parties with the Conservatives on the Commission less shocking to the Indian nationalists. This shook "their confidence in the professions of the British Liberalism and Socialism."[5]

Just in 1927 Miss Katherine Mayo's book entitled *Mother India*, had been published, in which the evils of the social and religious structure of the Indian society had been picked up with a special effort and given to the Western World to understand as if they were the general features of the Indian life. India was painted as the most backward and barbaric country and all this caused a great excitement among the Indian leaders. They saw in it the hand of the British Imperialists who by applying such subtle means wanted to perpetuate their hold on this country. Moreover, the Commission was to implement no definite policy towards India and this omission was resesnted by the loading brains of the communities.

The All-White Commission thus appointed was doomed to utter failure. All the Indian Parties, including the Congress, the Muslim League and the Liberals, protested vehemently against the composition of the Commission. And the All-India Leaders Manifesto signed by Sir Tej Bhadur Sapru, Annie

Besant, Mr M.A. Jinnah, Mr Yakub Hasan and others issued on 16 November 1927 declared its intention to give the Commission no cooperation whatsoever, Mr. S.Srinivasa Iyengar, the Congress President summed up the reasons for the Indian opposition thus: (i) "Indian people…are entitled to determine their constitution … That claim has been definitely negatived." (2) "…we cannot be parties to an enquiry into our fitness for Swaraj." (3) "The third reasons is undoubtedly the affront to Indian self-respect involved in the deliberate exclusion of Indians from the Commission." (4) "Commission is imposed which is not wanted and when it is not wanted." (5) "The last reason for the boycott is the spirit which lies behind these proposals. There is no change of heart except in the direction of greater hardening."[6]

The Commission however started its work by commencing its tours all over the country and collecting the facts with the assistance of the bureaucrats and their sycophants in the country. But it was greeted by the popular opinion with black flags, hartals and boycotts wherever it went. 'Simon Go Back' was the slogan which it had to face everywhere. The police had to open fire in Bombay and Madras and make lathi charges in places like Lahore in an effort to clam the public protests. But all this went in vain. Lala Lajpat Rai received lathi blows at Lahore[7] and Pt. Jawaharlal Nehru and G.B. Pant were badly molested in the United Provinces for their leading protest procession. The Commission, however, continued its work and ultimately did submit its report which was published in two volumes; the first on 11th June and the second on 24th June 1930.

SIMON COMMISSION REPORT

In its report, after studying the existing situation, and after emphasizing that the new constitution "should as far as possible contain within itself provision for its own development" and while "contemplating and conforming to an intimate objective" it "should not attempt to lay down the length or the number of stages of the journey," the Commission made several recommendations.

Regarding Provinces

Regarding the Provinces, the Commission recommended that (1) the Dyarchy now having lived its purpose should abolished and Ministers nominated by the Governors from among those commanding majorities in the legislatures should be entrusted with the full control of the Provincial administration. These Ministers among whom the Governor would distribute portfolios, and on whose meetings the Governor would preside, should be jointly responsible to the legislature. But the constitution of the Cabinet should be elastic so as to enable a Governor to introduce an official element into it if he considers it necessary. (2) The Central Government should not unnecessarily interfere in the administrative and legislative functions of the Provinces, but the Governors should be granted some special powers there-with to override the advice of the Ministers where thought necessary. The powers of the Governors for some essential purposes, such as protection of minorities, should be clearly defined and they be empowered subject to the direction of Governor-General, to retain full powers in case of constitutional breakdown. (3) The franchise in the Provincial Legislature should be widened so as to treble the electorate and include in it the largest number of women voters. (4) Unless some better method was agreed upon, certain important minorities should be adequately protected by continuing the system of communal electorates. The depressed classes should be given representation by special reservations of seats. (5) The Legislatures should be enlarged, while the constituencies should be reduced to a manageable size. And the Provincial Councils instead of being purely legislative bodies should be given certain powers of recasting their own representative system. (6) The Provinces should be given enlarged financial resources. (7) The question of re-distribution of provincial areas should be taken up at once and the cases such as of Sind and Oriya speaking people should be considered first. (8) Burna should be separated from India and provision for a separate constitution for it must immediately be made. (9) North-West Frontier Province should acquire a separate legislature and both it and Baluchistan should be given the right to representation at the Centre. (10) In future, the Commission said, each province should be, as far as possible, a mistress in her house.

The Centre

Dealing with the Central Legislature, the Commission recommended that (1) The Central Legislative Assembly to be called "Federal Assembly", should be constituted on the basis of the representation of the provinces and other areas in British India, in proportion to their population. (2) Members representing Governor's provinces should be elected by Provincial Councils by method of proportionate representation so as to ensure adequate representation of minorities. Members from N.W.F.P. and other areas outside the provinces, should be returned by methods appropriate to each. (3) The official members of the Federal Assembly should consist of such members of Governor-General's Council as sit in the Lower House together with the other nominated officials. (4) Numbers of and proportion between non-elected and elected members should remain unchanged, and (5) Life of Assembly should be five years.

The Council of States

(1) The Council of States with its elected and nominated Members should continue with its existing functions. (2) Its members having high qualifications;

so far as they are elected, they should be chosen by indirect election carried out by Provincial Second Chambers, if such bodies are constituted, or failing this, by the Provincial Councils. (3) Life of the Council should be seven years. (4) The existing financial and legislative powers of the two Central Chambers should continue, but the Federal Assembly should be given special functions of voting certain indirect taxes collected by the Centre, the net proceeds of which go to the Provincial Fund for distribution amongst different units represented in the Federal Assembly.

The Executive

(1) Governor-General-in-Council should continue as the Central Executive, that henceforward the Governor-General himself should appoint Executive Councillors. (2) The existing qualifications of the Councillors would remain. (3) Among the members of this Council, there should be one who leads the Federal Assembly. (4) The Commandein-Chief should no longer be a member either of the Executive Councils or of the Central Legislature. (5) Dyarchy could not be introduced in the Centre, because unity "in the Central Executive must be preserved at all costs."

The Army

The need for the Indianization of the army was admitted, but the Commission recommended that the defence of India should be treated as a matter which falls within the responsibilities of the Governor-General advised by the Commander-in-Chief as representing the Imperial authorities, instead of being a part of the responsibilities of the Government of India in relation to the Central Legislature.

Civil Services

The Commission said: (1) The Security Services as Indian Civil Service and Indian Police Service should continue to be recruited as All-India Services by the Secretary of State. Similar recruitment of Irrigation Service and Forest Service should also be considered. (2) The rates of Indianisation as laid down by the Lee Commission should be maintained. (3) In addition to the existing Public Service Commission, similar bodies covering the Provincial and Subordinate Services in the Provinces should also be constituted.

For the India Office

It was recommended that (1) The Governor-General-in-Council should remain in constitutional theory, under the superintendence and control of the Secretary of State. The extent to which this control is relaxed, should depend on the future practices and it cannot be laid down in the Statute. (2) The

Secretary of State will exercise no control over the Provincial Governments save so far as he does so in connection with the special powers vested in the Governors. (3) Functions and composition of the Council of India should be modified, its size should be reduced and majority of its members should have the qualification of a more recent India experience. The Council should be an Advisory Body, but its independent powers should continue for the control of service conditions and for the control of non-violence Indian expenditure.

The Indian States

The Commission recommended for the institutions of a 'Council for Greater India' containing both the representatives of the Princely States and the members representing the British India, to deal with a scheduled list of matters of common interest. This, the Commission said, will be a beginning of the process which may lead to the Federation of Greater India. The establishment of a Federation in the immediate future should, however, be impossible.

AN APPRAISAL

Such thus were the recommendations of the Commission. The Commission, as is obvious, made no mention of the future goal of India and this was naturally strongly resented by the public. The Central Government remained as irresponsible as ever and the indirect elections to the Central Legislature, as recommended by the Commission were obviously a reactionary step. In the provinces also the Governor remained strong with his powers to nominate ministers, distribute work among them and preside over their meetings. Still, however, though outrightly denounced and condemned by the Indians, the recommendations were of a great significance. Keith thus observes, that it was probably wrong on the part of the Indians "to repudiate the report out and out. If it had been accepted...responsible government in the provinces would have been achieved much earlier than it could be under any later scheme." It must, however, be remembered that the report although shelved, its recommendations were not altogether disregarded. Some of them found their way into Act of 1935. And another significance of the report was that it made certain observations regarding the Federation and the part the Princes of India could possibly play in it. This suggestion was later on taken up and the Federal scheme was put forward. The failure of the Reforms of 1919 was virtually recognized by the Government, and for this too the credit went to this Report.

THE NEHRU REPORT

The Conservative Secretary of State Lord Birkenhead challenged the Indians in 1925 and again in 1927 to produce a constitution, which should be acceptable to all the political parties of the country. The Congress took up the challenge and called an All-Parties Conference which met in Delhi on 28th

February 1928 and to which as many as 29 organizations sent their representatives. The Conference discussed certain preliminaries at Delhi and meeting again in Bombay on 19th May 1928 it set up a small Committee of nine members with Pt. Motilal Nehru as its Chairman to go into the matter and draft a Constitution for India by July 1928. This Committee known as the Nehru Committee held as many as 25 sittings and ultimately prepared a unanimous report which was placed before the All-Parties Conference meeting again, at Lucknow, under the Chairmanship of Dr Ansari. The Report, which was "masterly and statesmanlike." As Dr. Zacharias observed, presented a Constitution which was a proof of the deep and masterful understanding of the subject by the Indian leaders. The more important recommendations of the Report were as follows:

Recommendations

Regarding the general principles of the Constitution, (1) the Report accepted Dominion Status as "the next immediate step," not as an ultimate goal. This was, in fact, a compromise between the two groups in the Committee one of which held a majority and favoured a Dominion Status, while the other would like the words replaced by complete national independence. On the rest of the recommendations the members were unanimous. (2) The Constitution was to be secular giving no State recognition to any one of the religions of the country, (3) The principle of the communal electorates was dispensed with. The system of joint electorates was recommended; the safeguard for the minorities being that they would have reserved seats in proportion to their population, with a right to contest the additional seats if they so desired. No seats, however, were to be reserved for any community in Punjab and Bengal. (4) The Constitution enumerated as many as 19 fundamental rights for the people to be embodied in the Statute, and expressly declared that the Government derived all its authority from the people.

Regarding the Central Executive, the Constitution said. (1) That the Governor-General of India would be appointed by the British Crown but he would be paid from the Indian revenues. No adverse alteration was to be made in his salary during the term of his office. (2) The Governor-General would act on the advise of the Executive Government. He would appoint the Prime Minister. The Executive Government thus constituted was to be collectively responsible to the Parliament. (3) The Central Cabinet once thus appointed could not be removed during the first three years of the Constitution except for certain special reasons such as corruption. After the passage of first three years. However, the cabinet could be removed by vote of censure by two-thirds majority in the Lower House. A similar provision was made for the provincial cabinets as well. (4) The Governor-General in the Centre was to appoint a

Committee of Defence which would consist of the Minister of Defence and that of Foreign Affairs, Commander-in-Chief, Commander of Air Forces and that of Naval Forces, Chief of General Staff and two other persons who should be expert on the subject. The Committee would work under the Chairmanship of the Prime Minister and would advise the Government on problems of Defence. The rules and regulations regarding the organization, discipline and maintenance of forces were to be made only on the recommendations of this Committee. For the Defence Budget a due approval of the House of Representative (the Lower House in the Centre) was necessary, though in case of an emergency created by foreign aggression or by a responsible apprehension of it, the Government could undertake the defence expenditure even without such authorization.

The Report also recommended that (1) A Parliament of two Houses should be established in the Centre. These Houses should be, Senate or the Upper House with its total membership of two hundred and the House of Representatives or the Lower House with its total membership of five hundred. The life of the Upper House was to be seven years while that of the Lower would be only five. (2) The members of the House of Representatives were to be elected by direct votes on the basis of adult suffrage while those of the Upper House would be elected indirectly by the members of the Provincial Councils.

Regarding the Provinces, the Report said (1) that the Provinces would be created on linguistic basis with a view to "planning of Muslim-majority Provinces against Hindu-majority Provinces." (2) The need for a complete Provincial autonomy was admitted and the Report said. (3) Powers should be divided between the Centre and Provinces on the basis of federal structure: the residuary powers going to the Centre in order to make it strong. In this recommendation the lines of the Canadian Constitution were adopted. (4) The Governors of the Provinces would be appointed by the Crown while they would be paid from the revenues of their respective Provinces. (5) A Provincial Governor was to act on the advice of the Provincial Executive Council which would consist of not more than five members; the Chief Minister being selected by the Governor while the other ministers being appointed by him on the advice of the Chief Minister. (6) Every Province was to have a Legislature, known as Legislative Council, the members of which would be elected by a direct vote on the basis of adult franchise. Life of a Provincial Legislature was to be five years unless it was dissolved earlier by the Governor who could also extend its life under certain special circumstances.

Regarding the Princes, the Report said (1) that their rights would be duly respected and protected by Government of India, but that they were expected to go according to the dictates of the time and not deny the democratic rights to their people. (2) The paramountcy was, in a way to lapse to the Government of India thus succeeding the British, for it was laid down that the new Government would duly exercise the rights and authority of the Crown on the Princes.

The Report also provided for a Supreme Court, the constitution of which was duly laid down. This Court was to be the Court of Final Appeal in India, no appeals going henceforward to the Privy Council in England.

The Civil and Army employees in India were to continue enjoying their rights and continuity of service as before. And it was provided that the Governor-General would appoint a Public Service Commission for selection to the Civil Services.

This, thus, was the Nehru Report which after its adoption by the All-Parties Conference at Lucknow, came up for further discussion in the All-Parties Convention held in Calcutta in December 1928. Here, however, the progressive trends outwardly visible in the Lucknow Conference were entirely reversed and the earlier hopes that the challenge of the Secretary of State would successfully be met, were dashed to the ground. At this Convention, as Bose writes, all "Those who did not have a hand in drafting the Nehru Report now made a dead set against it. Mr. M.A Jinnah, who a year earlier had advocated a progressive nationalist point of view at the Muslim League Conference in Calcutta, now came forward with his 'fourteen points' in order to amend the communal settlement embodied in the Nehru report.[9]"

Jinnah's Fourteen Points

It may be advisable to give here more important of these fourteen points of Mr. Jinnah, which spelled the ruin of all hopes of communal accord which was a glory of India a short while before when the challenge of Secretary of State was sought to be accepted. (1) Mr. Jinnah wanted a Federal Constitution for India in which the residuary powers were to be vested in the provinces. (2) All the Legislatures and the other elected bodies were to be constituted on definite principles of adequate and effective representation of minorities without reducing a majority to a minority or even to an equality. (3) The number of Muslim members in the Central Legislature was not to be less than one-third of the total. (4) The system of communal representation was to continue. (5) No bill or resolution or a part thereof would be passed in any Legislature or any other elected body of the country, where three-fourth members of any community in that body opposed it. (6) A provision was to be made in the Constitution, giving the Muslim an adequate share in all the services of the State and those of the local self-governing bodies having a due regard to the requirements of merit and efficiency. (7) Proper safeguards should be made in the Constitution for the protection of the Muslim culture, for the promotion of Muslim education, etc. (8) No Cabinet, Central or Provincial, was to have less than one-third Muslim Ministers. (9) No change in the Constitution could be introduced by the Central Legislature except with the concurrence of the States constituting the Federation.

This attitude of Mr. Jinnah, although developing his popularity in the reactionary section of his community, gave a severe blow to the value and importance of the Report. Mr. Jinnah moved several amendments to the Report to the above effect, all of which, however, were rejected with the exception of one concerning the amendment of the Constitution. This attitude of Mr. Jinnah elicited an interesting remark of Sir Tej Bahadur Sapru, who said: "If he is a spoilt child, a naughty child, I am prepared to say, give him what he wants and be finished with it." The attitude of Mr. Jinnah was soon copied by the other communities like Sikhs, who did not want to be left behind. A confusion and pandemonium were natural in such circumstances when the Hindu Mahasabha pitted itself against the Muslims and the die-hards and reactionaries had the best of the day.

Separately, however, the Muslim League was divided in its attitude towards the Report. One group led by Sir Muhammad Shafi, advocated the rejection of the entire report and cooperation with the Simon Commission. The Nationalist bloc desired a complete boycott of the Simon Commission and a whole-hearted acceptance of the Nehru Report, while the third group led by Mr. Jinnah was reactionary in its attitude on the communal question but advocated a complete boycott of the Simon Commission. When a meeting of League was summoned at Delhi in March 1929 to consider the Nehru Report the warring sections clashed between themselves and it ended in a complete pandemonium.

Nor was even the Indian National Congress unanimous in the matter. The Working Committee of the Congress had endorsed the Report in September 1928. Mr. Jawaharlal Nehru was against the Congress having diluted its goal to Dominion Status by accepting the Report and resigned his Secretaryship of the party. In the Calcutta Congress of December 1928 when the question of ratification of the Report was brought up, Mr. Subhas Chandra Bose and Jawaharlal Nehru tried to strike against the Moderates, advocating complete independence as the immediate goal. It was only a masterful intervention of Mahatma Gandhi, which saved the situation. A compromise was struck and thus the inevitable rift was avoided. In the resolution that was passed, an ultimatum was given to the Government that if the Nehru Report which demanded only a Dominion Status, was not accepted in its entirety on or before

31 December 1929, the Congress would be compelled to "organize non-violent non-cooperation by advising the country to refuse taxation and in such other manner as may be decided upon." An amendment favouring a complete independence was moved by Mr. Subhas Chandra Bose and seconded among others by Jawaharlal Nehru, but when put to vote, it was lost by 1,350 against 273 Mr. Gandhi thus won the day once again and his compromise resolution had its way.

An Estimate

Speaking generally on the Nehru Report we may say it was a mischief on the part of the Secretary of State to have challenged the Indian leaders to draft a constitution to which all the political parties should agree. And it was an utterly hasty action on the part of the Congress to have accepted this challenge. In fact such a unanimity on the political question has never been possible any where in a democratic State. Even in England the most important political problems have always been decided only by a majority vote. In India too the responsibility for producing a constitution was an exclusive right only of the party, which fought for the country's independence. The support of all the parties to a constitution was simply impossible, more particularly when the country was yet under a foreign yoke and one or another party was bound to be under the thumb of the ruling authorities.

However, it cannot be denied, as Zacharias observes: "The Nehru Report deserves to be read and studied in all its details, as it sheds light on every subject it touches and displays a practical commonsense which never loses itself in doctrinaire utopian, but which equally spurns to shelter itself behind the enunciation of some platitudes."[10] It was the first attempt of the Indian leaders to devise a constitution for their country, and although the British Government looked at it with a studied indifference, it was a blueprint from which the essentials even of the present Constitution of India were drawn. If nothing else, this in itself is a great compliment which one can pay to the genius of the leaders who produced this report.

THE BROKEN PROMISES

May 1929 saw a lucky change in Great Britain for the Indians. The Labour Party having won the elections, its leader Ramsay Macdonald become the new Prime Minister of England, with Wedgwood Beun as the Secretary of State for India. Mr Macdonald had expressed a keen hope shortly before the elections that it would not be more than a few months before India would become yet another Dominion in Commonwealth. It was a new ray of hope for the Indians and they looked forward with keen delight for something promising to happen. Lord Irwin paid a hurried visit to England and on his return he declared on

31st October 1929 "on behalf of his Majesty's Government" that "it is implicit in the Declaration of 1917, that the natural issue of India's constitutional progress, as there contemplated, is Dominion Status". And further, before the Simon Commission Report had yet been published, he said it had been suggested in the Report and Government had agreed to it, that a Round Table Conference of the different Indian as well as the British interests would be held to seek the greatest measure of agreement.[11]

The statement of the Viceroy was good, but every Indian leader was not happy. The Dominion Status as a contemplated goal was agreed to but nobody could say after how much time it would come. The statement had perhaps been issued in reply to the Congress ultimatum of the Nehru Report to be accepted before 31 December 1929. But it was vague. Nor was the statement considered happy even in certain sections of the English opinion. Mr Simon, leader of the Liberal Party, thus found all of a sudden the thunder having been stolen out of his Report, and in a way his Report having been side-tracked before the public knew even its terms.

The Indian reaction to the Report was prompt. The most important leaders of India met with the Congress Working Committee at Delhi, and issued a manifesto over the signatures of Mr Gandhi, Motilal Nehru, Jawaharlal Nehru, Dr Ansari, Pt. Madan Mohan Malaviya, Sir Tej Bahadur Sapru, Mrs Annie Besant and others. The manifesto placing a confidence in the British sincerity, expressed its belief that the proposed Round Table Conference would be held to thrash out a scheme for the Dominion Constitution, and not merely for discussing a date when the Dominion Status should be given. A predominant representation for the Congress was expected on the Conference, and the manifesto suggested that a general amnesty should be granted to those having taken part in the political agitation, so as to convince the people that a new era had commenced.

The ray of light on the dark Indian horizon, however, soon proved false, and the subdued fear in the manifesto proved correct. The extremists in the Congress had shown their disgust that the manifesto had agreed to something less than the *Purna Swaraj* or complete independence, and Mr Subhsh Chandra Bose had even resigned from the Congress Working Committee as a protest. But even the veiled and limited promise in the Viceroy's statement began to melt away as it was placed on the anvil of practicability. The Liberals showed an open resentment against the cold treatment given to the Simon Report, and Mr Churchill declared in his characteristic die-hard way that the promise of Dominion Status to India was "a crime". The Labour Government having no absolute majority of their own in the Commons, refused to risk their career for the sake of India. As the clouds of mischief and political pilferage arose from

England, Mr Gandhi sought an interview with the Viceroy on 21 December 1929. Pt. Motilal Nehru, Sir Tej Bahadur Sapru and Mr. M.A. Jinnah also accompanied Gandhi. But replies of the Viceroy were indefinite and vague. Clearly thus, the last date of the ultimatum having expired, the Nehru Report stood rejected and uncared for by the Government.[12]

INDEPENDENCE DECLARED

The Lahore Session of the Indian National Congress met towards the end of December 1929. Mr. Nehru who had all through stood for an immediate declaration of complete independence as the Congress goal, and who presided over this session, came out with his plutonic heat and lightning, and at the fateful hour of the midnight of 31 December 1929, was adopted that historic Independence Resolution which threw upon the gates of determined clashes of interest, and a heroic march of India through the mire of its blood and sweat on to victory. The Resolution declared in measured words:

"The Congress is of the opinion that nothing is to be gained in the existing circumstances by the Congress being represented at the proposed Round Table Conference. This Congress ... declares that the word Swaraj in Article I of the Congress Constitution shall mean complete Independence, and further declares the entire scheme of the Nehru Committee's Report to have lapsed. This Congress calls upon the Congressmen and others taking part in the national movement to abstain from participating directly or indirectly in future elections and directs the present Congress members of the Legislatures and Committees to resign their seats. The Congress authorizes the All India Congress Committee, whenever it deems fit, to launch upon a programme of Civil Disobedience, including non-payment of taxes, whether in selected areas or otherwise and under such safeguards, as it may consider necessary."

Nor was this the end. 26 January was decided to be observed every year as the day of Independence, when the people would meet and solemnly take the pledge:

"It is the invaluable right of the Indian people to have freedom and to enjoy the fruits of their toil, and have the necessities of life, so that they may have full opportunities of growth. We believe also that if any Government deprives the people of their rights and opposes them, the people have a further right to alter it or to abolish it. The British Government in India has not only deprived the Indian people of their freedom, but also based itself on the exploitation of the masses and has ruined India economically, politically, culturally and spiritually... we hold it to be a crime against man and God to submit any longer to a rule that has caused this fourfold disaster to our country.

We will therefore...prepare ourselves for Civil Disobedience including non-payment of taxes...we therefore hereby solemnly resolve to carry out the Congress instructions issued from time to time for the purpose of establishing *Purna Swaraj*."[13]

NON-COOPERATION AGAIN

The Nehru Report rejected, there were other factors which intensifying the atmosphere, hastened the clash. The closing twenties of the twentieth century had brought a general economic depression all over the world under the strain of which the peasantry as well as the labour groaned; the business community cursing its fate no less than the others. India could be no exception. The peasants formed their associations, the labouring classes prepared for agitation, and the Communists preparing to make the best use of all this, invited the heavy hand of the Government to fall on them. March 1929 had witnessed the brute force of the administrative machinery in play, when the Communist leaders of India found themselves imprisoned at Meerut awaiting a regular trial, which coming scandalously after four years, transported some for life, putting the rest under varying terms of rigorous imprisonment. The minds all around were agitated, when Pt. Jawaharlal Nehru presiding over Indian Trade Union Congress in November 1929, got a resolution passed which demanded India to be established a Socialist Republic. By this time, in the Surat District of Gujarat the Lion of Bardoli, Sardar Vallabhbhai Patel, under whose leadership the peasants of Bardoli had refused to pay their Land Revenue unless their grievances were redressed, too had demonstrated the possibility of Satyagraha winning the game.

In short, the atmosphere was explosive when the Congress declared for a *Purna Swaraj* and authorized the Civil Disobedience. If someone did not rise to canalize the energy into a disciplined non-violent movement, the people were expected to break out everywhere and create a chaos. "Here go the people," Mr Gandhi had to declare, "I must follow them, for I am their leader." He put himself at the top of the rising wave and the movement started.

Mr Gandhi wrote to Irwin once again as a last minute effort to see if the situation still could be saved. But discouragement was in store. The Congress Working Committee replied by authorizing Gandhi on 11 February to start the Satyagraha. On 11 March 1930 Gandhi again addressed a communication to the Viceroy through an English friend, Reginald Reynolds, to help and avoid the desperate action. But in vein. On 12 March he gave a notice to Viceroy declaring the programme of the historic Dandi March. And this opened yet another chapter in India's fight for independence.

The Dandi March

Dandi was a place situated on the seacoast, about 200 miles from Ahmedabad from where his journey commenced. The Mahatma took with him 79 of his selected followers, and the programme was that after covering this distance on foot and reaching the seacoast, he would break the Salt Law, which made it a legal offence to prepare salt even from the salt water. The salt tax had been doubled in 1923, and since this tax fell most heavily on the common man, the Salt Law was taken up to be broken first.

The March commenced on 12 March. At every place the villagers thronged around the Satyagrahis and accorded them a cheerful and enthusiastic reception. Press resounded with the stories for full 24 days during which the March was continued, and by 5 April when the Mahatma reached Dandi, the whole nation reverberated with a rare wave of enthusiasm and patriotism. After a day of prayers and fasting, on 6 April the civil disobedience started when the Mahatma appropriated a piece of salt which lay on the beach.

An English Journalist, Mr Brailsford, had scoffed the queer notion "that the King Emperor can be unseated by boiling sea-water in a kettle." But he had failed to understand the symbolic value of the Mahatma's action, which was a signal for almost simultaneous breaking of the Salt Law all over the country and picketing of the liquor shops—a work which the Mahatma had entrusted especially to women. In Calcutta the people publicly read seditious literature to break the Sedition Law; while in the C.P. Forest Laws were likewise violated. Bonfires were created to burn foreign cloth, the boycott of which cut down its import by about three-fourths, helping the Indian textile mills to raise their production by double shift to fill up the gap.

Brutal Retaliation

Retaliation of the Government was equally forceful, but brutal. The hands of the administrative machinery clamped down, and Delhi alone saw 1600 of its women put behind the bars. The most fearful reprisal was witnessed in Peshawar, where the story of the Jallianwala Bag seemed to repeat. Firing and the lathi charges killed hundreds. A gruesome story appeared in the *Young India* of 12 June 1930, wherein Miss Medeleine Slade gave an eye witness account of the injuries perpetrated on the non-violent volunteers at Bulsar in Gujarat. She said she had an evidence that (1) the lathi blows were carefully administered on stomach, chest, head and joint, (2) pointed thrusts were given in the abdominal regions and private parts. (3) Loin cloths were torn off and stick thrust into arms. (4) Testicles were squeezed till one became unconscious. (5) Pins and thorns were thrust in their bodies. (6) Wounded men were dragged and beaten mercilessly even when they became unconscious. (7) The most objectionable abuses were hurled upon them; and (8) making them sit or lie down, horses were ridden over their naked bodies.

Mr. Jawarharlal Nehru found his way to the prison house on 16 April 1930, followed by Gandhi who was sent to the Yervada Jail on 5 May. But all this, instead of cowing down, intensified the spirit of civil disobedience. While a major part of the Muslim population followed Mr Jinnah who declared the movement an attempt to throw the Muslims at the Hindu mercy, Khan Abdul Gaffar Khan, the Sarhadi Gandhi, led his Red Shirts into the campaign, and they gave their due share of sacrifices. The Government declared All India Congress Committee and the Local Congress Committees unlawful. The number of emergency ordinances exceeded a dozen. And over six million people filled the Government jails, creating an acute problem of jail accommodation. Yet the movement showed no sign of a abatement. The attempt of George Solocombe, a journalist, and of Sir Tej Bahadur Sapru and Mr. Jayakar, in August 1930, to bring peace by acting as mediators between the Congress leaders and Lord Irwin bore no fruit till 25 January 1931 when suddenly the Congress leaders were released. On 6 February 1931, the nation was plunged into utter grief, when Motilal Nehru, a stalwart of India's fight for freedom, passed away. On 17 February 1931, was signed the famous Gandhi-Irwin Pact. And on 5 March the Mahatma called the movement to a halt.

It would now be desirable to turn to the events of the first Round Table Conference, and the situation that led to the signing of the above referred to Pact.

THE FIRST ROUND TABLE CONFERENCE

First session of Indian Round Table Conference, boycotted by the Congress, was held at James Palace, London, on 12 November 1930. It was attended by 89 delegates, 57 of whom represented the British India, while 16 were the Princes nominated by the Viceroy to represent the states, and the rest represented the three parties in the British Parliament. Those from the British India too were nominated only by the Viceroy, and professed themselves to be representatives of the Hindus, the Muslims, the Sikhs, Christians, Scheduled Castes, Trade Unions, land-lords and the commercial interests. Meticulous care was taken to exclude the nationalist Muslims, and the Indian Legislatures were not even consulted on the matter. The British Prime Minister counted in the opening session the problems to be discussed, as (1) Federal Government for India, (2) Partial Responsibility at the Centre and (3) full Provincial Autonomy with certain safeguards.

The question of the federal type of Government for India came up for discussion, not one voice expressed disagreement, and surprisingly enough even the Princes nodded their heads in favour and expressed willingness to join it. It was said, and it could not be denied, that the Princes did so under the scandalous British whip which desired the perpetual presence of a reactionary element in Federal Government lest it should become too progressive to be controlled. The essential principles of the problems No. 2 and 3, as above, too found a general measure of agreement. But the endless and vituperative wrangling came when the Conference took up the matter of the distribution of exploits. Mr Jinnah insisted on his declared fourteen points to be accommodated, Dr Ambedkar would be satisfied with nothing less than communal electorates for the Scheduled Castes, while the Hindu delègates would put up with none of these demands. The Prime Minister summed up the three points on which the agreement had been reached, and victoriously concluded the conference in January 1931.

THE GANDHI-IRWIN PACT

The delegates came back home. And the Government slowly felt the need of making a compromise with the Congress. The urgency of the matter became acute as a result of certain international factors, i.e. Russia's advance in China, the problems of Italy and the general economic crisis all over the world. It was under these circumstances that the leading Congress leaders were unconditionally released on 25 January. Mr Gandhi lost no time in seeking an interview with Lord Irwin, which was willingly granted, and on 17 February 1931 was announced the famous Gandhi-Irwin Pact, which once again brightened the Indian hopes that their goal had after all come within reach.

The more essential terms of the Pact, were that the Viceroy agreed (1) that all the political prisoners in the country would immediately be released; (2) that a Federal Government would be established in the country and all safeguards in the transfer of powers to the Indians would be in the interests of India; and (3) that the Government would have no objection to peaceful picketing of the shops selling liquor, opium and foreign cloth. Mr. Gandhi on his part agreed (1) that he would ask Congress to suspend the Civil Disobedience immediately; (2) that the Congress would participate in the Second Round Table Conference; and (3) that the Congress would not press for an investigation of police excesses.

While majority of the Indian leaders appreciated Gandhi's step, the leftists in the Congress like Jawaharlal Nehru and Subhas Chandra Bose felt shocked over the terms of the Pact. The promise not to press for investigation into the police excesses was unfortunate, and the Mahatma's failure to get the death sentences of Sardar Bhagat Singh and his Comrades commuted to transportation for life was extremely disturbing. His acquiescence to the principle of safeguards was supposed to be detrimental to India's goal of full Independence, and as Mr Subhas Chandra Bose said, the Pact while going "into many petty and unnecessary details...had avoided the main issue of Sawarj." In the Round Table Conference the decision taken are always final and binding on the parties participating, but Mahatma had agreed to a Round Table Conference the decisions of which would have no binding force. Nor were the delegates to the conference to be elected by the Indians. The Government was to nominate. By not pressing the Government to confine the representation in the conference to the two belligerent parties only, the Mahatma permitted the possibility of all kinds of non-descripts who had no concern with the fight for Independence, getting into it. And finally the type of the Federal Government agreed upon, in which the autocratic Indian Princes would joint to act as a dead-weight against national aspirations, was supposed to be a step backward.[14]

The next session of the Congress was held at Karachi in March 1931, in which Subhas Bose and others raised the above points of criticism. The Session, in fact, was held in an atmosphere of utter gloom. Government had mocked at Mr Gandhi's spirit of accommodation by hanging Bhagat Singh and his comrades just on the eve of this session. The people said "Gandhi truce has sent Bhagat Singh to gallows." The Mahatma was greeted with black flags and the cry of "Down with Gandhi." The All-India Youth Congress held its session under the presidentship of Mr Bose simultaneously with the Congress, and there was an open move among the youths of Sind and Punjab to break away from the Congress and run a separate body. Mr. Gandhi, however, in his characteristic humble way, won over much of the opposition, and the Pact was eventually ratified. Thus ended one scene in the drama and Congress prepared to participate in the Round Table Conference.

THE NORTH-WEST FRONTIER AND THE RED SHIRTS

After the Third Afghan war a new policy termed the 'Modified Forward Policy' towards the frontiers had been adopted. Basis at Razmak and Wana were soon completed and the motor traffic developed right into the bare mountains to keep them fully supplied. Although this new policy was quite expensive and clumsy, yet for a considerable time it proved successful and peace was kept. Soon, however, certain new forces emerged, and once again destroyed the frontier calm.

The dyarchy under the Act of 1919 had not been extended to the frontier Provicne on the plea that the people here did not have the sufficient political education. The Government's partisan attitude in favour of a Shia Muslim as against the Sunni also affected the situation. The development of communication had brought about a greater intercourse between the people of the administered and non-administered areas of the province on the one hand and the settled and advanced provinces of the British India on the other. There was also a grumbling among the tribal people that their allowances had not been increased for the last 30 years. The news of the political agitation in India spread like wildfire and there were general rumours that the British would not remain in India for long. The Government legislation such as the Sarda Act also raised an alarm and it was alleged that in future no one would be able to marry without the consent of the Government.

It is in these circumstances that among the frontier people rose a six feet four inches tall Pathan, Abdul Gaffar Khan, who came into contact with Gandhi and Nehru and losing his Pathan ferocity adopted Truth and Non-violence advocated by Gandhi. In 1929 he organized his famous 'Khudai-Khidmatgars' or 'Servants of God' into which young Pathans were recruited and they were trained and drilled regularly to fight against the British rule. Since most of these people could not afford to have an elborate uniform, they wore simple shirts dyed in brick-dust after which they began to be known as 'Red Shirts'. This organization had a regular military hierarchy and badges of rank. Gaffar Khan's agents worked not only in the settled districts of the frontier province but penetrated into the non-administered areas also. He established his own underground government in the Peshawar district, and his prestige rose high, till on 20 April 1929, the Khan was suddenly arrested and sent away to jail. The arrest of the Khan and some of his followers proved to be a signal for general disturbances all over the Peshawar town. The civil government could not handle the situation and troops were called in. Fire was opened which killed at least 30 persons and wounded 33 as it was given out by the government, though the actual number of casualties was supposed to be much higher. From Peshawar the disturbances spread to Kohat and other towns, and even the tribal areas of Mohmands, Orakazais Afridis, etc., could not remain unaffected. It took the troops supported by aircraft quite some time before peace was restored.

Fazl-i-Hussain, a Muslim leader of the Punjab, who joined Irwin's Council in April 1930, advised that the growing political consciousness of the Frontier Province should be brought into constitutional channels. The general grievances of the people should be looked into and redressed. The Viceroy responded and it was announced that a committee would soon be set up to look into the demands of the frontier people. Pears, the Chief Commissioner of the province, also promised to introduced elections for local bodies and to set up an advisory committee to help in administration. At the same time an intense propaganda was started that the Congress was a Hindu organization in which the Muslims could have no place.

Force coupled with cajolery and promises served the purpose and frontier became peaceful. But the promises given were not fulfilled, with the result that towards the close of 1930 the Mahsuds, Afridis and others once again rose in arms, so much so that the whole province had to be placed under Martial Law. To restore the Government's waning prestige an expedition was sent inside the tribal areas to spread fire and destruction. Main approaches to Peshawar were occupied. But it took quite some time before peace could be restored. In March 1931 Abdul Gaffar Khan had been released under a Pact between the Viceroy and Gandhi, but on 24 December the same year the Government had to take emergency powers in hand to safeguard public services, property and public order. The Red Shirts were declared an illegal organization and Gaffar Khan was deported together with four of his followers to be gaoled in various parts of India. By the spring of 1932 the Red Shirt Movement ceased to be a force in the Frontier Province.

Gaffar Khan's agitation however, did not go in vain. For right in 1932 itself the North-West Frontier Province was raised from Chief Commissioner-ate to a Governor's province, with political rights and institutions equal to the rest of India. In 1935 the Province shared provincial autonomy equally with other provinces and Gaffar Khan's brother, Dr Khan Sahib rose to eminence as Chief Minister. Khan Sahib "was a devoted follower of Gandhi and National Congress, and was to play an important part in the struggles ahead."[15]

The Princes

Although a new policy had been initiated in the time of Lord Minto to woo the princes and set them up as a force counterpoise to the Nationalist Movement, the British throughout remained jealous of their paramount power. The Chamber of Princes had been established in 1921 which enabled the princes to come together for joint consultations, and even Irwin allowed them to set up a special Standing Committee of the Chamber which could hold talks with the Viceroy and his advisers whenever necessary. Yet the Princes were never allowed any undue familiarity. Irwin's predecessor Reading had declared in a letter to the Nizam of Hyderabad: "The sovereignty of the British Crown is supreme in India and therefore, no Ruler of an Indian State can justifiably claim to negotiate with the British Government on an equal footing. Its supremacy is not based only upon treaties and engagements, but exists independently of them." Irwin stuck to this policy and was never tired of telling the princes that the Viceroy personally, as representative of the Crown, without reference to his Council, had a responsibility towards the people they ruled. He repeatedly insisted on them to establish a reign of law and set up a machinery through which they would be aware of the desires of their subjects.

In fact the paramountcy of the Crown exercised by the Viceroy personally through his Political Department was increasingly becoming a source of irritation. In 1927 the Princes insisted through their leader the Maharaja of Bikaner that a committee should be appointed to examine the Crown's relations with the States. The Princes engaged an eminent counsel from England to argue their case. They said that when they entered into treaties and engagements with the British, they were fully sovereign and independent states. The relationship between them and the Crown was therefore contractual and no one party had the right to modify it without the full consent of the other. Their obligations with regard to the conduct of administration were reciprocal with the British, and therefore there was a limit beyond which the British powers to interfere in their internal affairs could not go.

Responding to the demands of the Princes, Irwin set up a committee headed by Sir Harcourt Butler in December 1927 to report on the matter. The Butler Committee report appeared in February 1929, declaring that the theory of paramountcy could not be considered static "the Crown's relations with the States were not circumscribed by contract but were a living Process moulded by circumstances and policies. Neither a tidy formulation of the principle of paramountcy nor a comprehensive codification of its practice was possible."[16] Obviously the Princes' theory of contract stood summarily dismissed. The Butler Committee also, however, had a few words in favour of the Princes. According to the report no direct relationship could exist between the Princes and the Government of India which was responsible to the Indian people, except with the agreement of the Princes themselves. The report recommended that instead of appointing a separate political Member of Viceroy's Council to deal with the Princes, the States portfolio should be handled by the Viceroy in person as a representative of the Crown. A special Committee should be appointed to consider disputes between the Government of India and the States, and yet another committee be appointed to enquire into the financial relations between the two. It also recommended that the political officers appointed to deal with the States should be recruited and trained separately.

Obviously, the recommendations of the Committee were aimed at raising a permanent wall between the Indian States and the people of British India. It secured the Indian Princes from the nationalistic and democratic movements in British India, and naturally invited the indignation of the popular Indian leaders. Chintamani thus remarked: "The Butler Committee was bad in its origin, bad in the time chosen for its appointment, bad in its terms of reference, bad in its personnel and bad in its conclusions."[17]

The people of the British India could not be happy with the Butler Committee Report. But the Princes were not pleased either. For paramountcy was not only strongly reasserted, it was pushed beyond the limits, which had so far been accepted. It is because of this reason that the Princes later on flirted at the Round Table Conferences, with the idea of federation with the British Indian provinces. They thought that by this they would escape the increasing burdens of the British paramountcy as well as the aggressive interference of the progressive and nationalistic forces in the British India. But they were wrong.

Irwin retired from India in 1931. In 1932 he was appointed President of the Board of Education. In 1934 his father died and he became 3rd Viscount Halifax. In 1935 he became Secretary of State for War and Lord Privy Seal. In 1938 he became Foreign Secretary. He was raised to an Earldom in 1944 and continued enjoying high respect in the House of Lords.

NOTES

1. Quoted. Gopal, S. *Viceroyalty of Lord Irwin*, p. 5.
2. *Ibid*., p. 50.
3. Gwyer & Appadorai, *Speeches & Documents...*, I, pp. 206-07.
4. Reed, Sir, Stanley, *The India I Knew* (1897-1947), pp. 191-92.
5. Banerjee, A.C., *Indian Constitutional Documents*, III, p. 196.
6. *The Indian Annual Register, 1927*, Vol. II, pp. 98-99.
7. Nehru, Jawaharlal, *Autobiography,* p. 174.
8. Keith, *Constitutional History of India*, pp. 293-94.
9. Bose S.C., *The Indian Struggle for Freedom*, pp. 218-219.
10. Zacharias, *Renascent India,* p. 240.
11. C.Y. Chintamani described Lord Irwin as an "honest and Godfearing" man, "the most righteous Viceroy after Lord Ripon". *op. cit.*, p. 173.
12. Sitaramayya, *op.cit*., I, p. 351.
13. Sitaramayya, *op. cit.*, I, pp. 351-53; Munshi, *op. cit.*, I, p. 26.
14. For further details see Gopal S., *The Viceroyalty of Lord Irwin,* pp. 89-122.
15. Swinson, Arthur, *North-West Frontier,* p. 319: Also see Gopal S., *op. cit:*, pp. 67-68.
16. Gopal, S., p. 127.
17. Chintamani, C.Y., *Indian Politics Since Mutiny*, p. 97.

4

Lord Willingdon 1931-1936

"Lord Willingdon entered India at the most formidable period of its national movement, and he devoted the best part of his ripe experience to the service of Britain's greatest charge. He saw the growth of constitutionally ambition and harnessed it for beneficial advance, he saw its militants and assertive youthfulness in the Home Rule Movement, and by the devolution of power to local bodies and elastic interpretation of provincial rights already conferred, gave it a constructive turn. He witnessed the surging wave of the non-cooperation movement and counteracted it by the most liberal translation of the Montagu Reforms. He experienced, as the Governor-General and Viceroy of India, the more devastating chaos of economic depression and Civil Disobedience, its political expression, and applied effective cement of comprehensive programme of politico-economic action," thus writes Victor Trench, a contemporary of the Viceroy, under the assumed present name.[1]

Freeman Thomas, who later became Earl and Marquess of Willingdon, was born on 12 September 1866. He was the son of Frederick Freeman-Thomas by Mabel Brand, daughter of the first Viscount of Hampden. He got his education at Eton and Cambridge, married in 1892, Hon'ble Mari Adelaide, the daughter of the first Earl of Brassey. In 1895 when Lord Brassey was appointed Governor of Victoria, Willingdon accompanied him as his A.D.C. After returning to England he became M.P. and as such distinguished himself as good-tempered, "shrewd and a good mixer." Between 1905 and 1912 he worked as Junior Lord of the Treasury. In 1913 he was appointed Governor of Bombay and in 1918 was transferred to Madras. In both presidencies he was much helped by his active and attractive wife, whom he called his "constant inspiration and encouragement," and he was generally considered, both in India and at home, as an ideal Governor."[2] As Governor of Madras he did much to make the Montagu Reforms a success. We have already seen how in 1920 Mr.

Gandhi started his Non-cooperation Movement which was wrecked by an outbreak of violence at places like Malabar. The Moplah rebellion in Malabar took place when Willingdon was the Governor of Madras. This rebellion was attended by an unfortunate event which may very well have turned into a second edition of the Jallianwala Bagh, but for the diplomacy and foresightedness of the Governor. On 19 November, 1921there took place a 'train tragedy' that sent a shudder of horror through the country. About 100 Moplahs convicted for rebellion were put in a goods train at Tirur destined for Coimbatore, but when the train arrived at Padanur, all the convicts were found to be unconscious and in a state of collapse. Forty six of them lay dead through asphyxiation, while six died when being taken out of the train. The rest were taken to the hospital but two more died before any medical aid could be rendered. Even the best treatment in the hospital, however, could not save all and out of the total of a hundred prisoners, as many as seventy succumbed to the hand of negligence. There was a wild clamour for enquiry and punishment of the guilty all over the country. Lord Willingdon realized the need of re-assuring the public of the Government's keen concern, and immediately announced a Committee of Inquiry. The Committee submitted its report on 30 August 1922, and by taking the proper action against the guilty as recommended by the Report, Willingdon saved the situation. It is such acts that earned him the appreciation of the people and developed his popularity.

After retiring from Madras, Willingdon was sent away to Canada as Governor-General. He receives several honours and titles and on the retirement of Lord Irwin he was appointed in 1931 as the next Viceroy and Governor-General of India.

When Willingdon took charge in Delhi, the country was in the grip of a deepening economic depression and political crisis. The Gandhi-Irwin Pact had created a semblance of lull but behind it still there were the seething forces of intransigence. There was still the big question mark. Whether Mr Gandhi would go and attend the Second Round Table Conference in London. The pact was said to have brought about no change of heart. There was the Hindu-Muslim problem, and there were the allegations that the officials were violating the pact. There was a lengthy correspondence between the new Viceroy and India's Prophet of Peace. A lengthy charge-sheet was received by the Viceroy against the local officials who were alleged to have breached the pact. If the Viceroy wanted Congress cooperation it was necessary that the guilty should be punished. Willingdon knew that if Gandhi did not go to London, the Second Round Table Conference would be as much a failure as the First Conference had been. But the situation was enigmatic and the Viceroy did not want to sacrifices his officers who stood by the government with ability and courage.

Mr. Gandhi was delayed at Simla. "The first batch of delegates had already left Bombay, the second one was about to start. Mr Gandhi created a classic denouement. The last train for the mail-boat had left; the conversations grew more and more frantic, and after the tension had reached the peak point, and the situation made dramatic, Mr Gandhi announced his agreement with Lord Willingdon's offer and the special waiting train rushed him down the plains to the hospitable shores of Bombay. This was considered the first diplomatic triumph of Lord Willingdon, for he sacrified no vital position nor surrendered the interests of Government officers; and succeeded in evolving an agreement that satisfied the conscience of one who looks above everything else for a true heart."[3]

SECOND ROUND TABLE CONFERENCE, 1931-32

Much water, however, had flown down the Thames before the Second Round Table Conference took place. In India Lord Irwin had been replaced by Lord Willingdon and the latter was sure that his predecessor had been too liberal with Mr Gandhi. In England, though Mr MacDonald still headed the Government, he had been expelled from the Labour Party, which now sat in Opposition, while their former leader led the Conservative National Government. Conservative member, Sir Samuel Hoare, replaced Mr Wedgwood Benn as the Secretary of State for India. The Round Table Conference now started, and while it was still in session, general elections were held in England and a purely Conservative Government headed by Mr MacDonald assumed office in November 1931. The whole atmosphere in the Conference was changed, and it looked as if a back-gear had been put into operation.

MacDonald presided over the Conference to which the Congress sent Mr Gandhi as its sole representative. Mrs. Sarojini Naidu and Pt. Madan Mohan Malaviya attended it as Government nominees in their individual capacity. And the representative of other communities and interests were invited as usual. The most important work of the Conference was assigned to two sub-Committees, on one "Federal Structure" and the other on "Minorities". The problems of the previous Conference were re-examined, and in the "Federal Structures" Committee, Mr Gandhi was dazed when safeguards were suggested with the real intention of perpetuating the British rule and spirit of the Irwin Pact was gagged to death.

The worse, however, was yet to come. In the Minorities Sub-Committee, all those who thrived on communalism filled every space on the stage. The nationalists like Dr Ansari has studiously been excluded. The venom soon began to be emitted. The Muslim delegates declared their determination not to be satisfied with anything less than an absolute majority in the Punjab and

Bengal, an excessive weight-age where they were in minority and at least one-third of the seats in the Centre. They would eat the cake and have it too. The Sikhs claimed a weightage in the Punjab exactly on the lines of that claimed by the Muslims in Madras, Bombay, U.P. and Assam. Depressed Classes wanted separate representation. Europeans claimed special weightage in Bengal, which was incompatible with Muslim absolute majority claim. They wrangled and disputed peevishly. "It was all jobbery." Mr Nehru writes, "big jobs, little, jobs ,and seats for the Hindus, for the Muslims, for the Sikhs, for the Anglo-Indians, for the Europeans, but all jobs for the upper classes, the masses had no look-in. Opportunism was rampant, and different groups seemed to prowl about like hungry wolves waiting for their prey—the spoils under the new Constitution. The very conception of freedom has taken the form of largesacle Jobbery."[4] A shameless secret agreement was reached between the European and the Muslim representatives, in which they promised mutual support and determination to fight the Congress tooth and nail.[5] It was in vain that Gandhi claimed that the Congress represented 85 per cent of India and therefore should not be treated as only one of the parties;[6] and that it was wrong to assume that the communal problem of India could not be solved except in the presence of the British.

And when everything failed, the self-seeking moralist, MacDonald, summed up that the formidable task had been the communal deadlock. "This conference," he said, "has twice essayed this task: twice it has failed...This would mean that His Majesty's Government would have to settle for you not only your problems of representation, but also to decide as wisely and justly as possible what checks and balances the Constitution is to contain to protect minorities, from the tyrannical use of power by majority." The net result of this declaration was the Communal award. Mr Gandhi moving a vote of thanks to the Prime Minister regretted, that he and the Prime Minister had "come to the parting of ways."

Lone Representative

Mr Gandhi came back home dejected. He had done his best to make gains for the Congress, but there were some who criticized the advisability of the Congress in having sent him as its sole representative. After rejecting the Government offer of 15 seats for the Congress Delegation, the Mahatma sat at the Conference "a single front individual in group of 107" thus observed Subhas Bose.[7] He took no advisers with him, and his frankness and confessing his ignorance of the intricate legal and financial questions could win him little fame in the midst of a society where leaders were looked on as wiser than actually they could be.

In fact the whole visit of Mr Gandhi to England was ill-planned, naturally perhaps because of his indecision regarding the advisability of attending the Conference till the last moment. He arrived in London late, and did so ill-equipped with facts as against the elaborate preparation of his adversaries. Then he went there in two capacities, as a world-teacher and as a Congress leader, and these two missions of his were sadly mixed up. Outside the Conference he discussed matters of spirit and morality in the company of missionaries, journalists, politicians and society ladies, when he should have been busy with the Conference problems and easily available to the Indian members who needed his advice. In fact, he had a stronger influence in the previous Conference when he was in jail, than in this Conference in which he participated.

If the Mahatma's time in London was not entirely well spent, it was no better spent when he visited the European countries. In Paris he missed all those whom he must have met, and in Geneva it failed to occur to him to try to win the sympathies for India, of those who mattered in the League of Nations. In Switzerland his meeting with Romain Rolland, and in Italy with the dictator, Signor Mussolini, was productive of much that could benefit India, but elsewhere he acted more as a missionary than as a watchful politician.

To continue the story, however when Mr Gandhi returned home on 28 December 1931, he discovered to his exasperation that Lord Willingdon has already struck hard and struck in time. Bengal was almost under a martial law. Ordinances ruled this Province, as they did U.P. and the N.W.F. Province. Jawaharlal Nehru was under detention, while Khan Abdul Gaffar Khan of the N.W.F.P. and his brothers were under arrest. The Mahatma sought an interview with the Viceroy, but met with a rebuff.[8] The Congress Working Committee authorized him to resume Satyagraha, but this found all its members, together with Mr. Gandhi, promptly landed in jail. The Government's reprisal did not end here. Several new ordinances made the executive autocratic: every office-bearer of Congress, big or small and even its sympathizers found themselves behind bars. The organization was declared unlawful. Press was placed under strict surveillance, shooting and beating became a commonplace, and over a lakh were forced into jails. Now came the Communal Award.

The Communal Award

The Prime Minister of England has said in the Second Round Table Conference that the British would decide for the Indians the system of communal representation they should have. And in this connection a Communal Award was issued. The Award decided for separate electorates for every conceivable community or an interest that existed in India. The Hindus, Muslims, Sikhs and Christians, then the land holders, mining and planting, commerce and industry, all got separate electorates, as did the women of India. British axiom of divide and rule, indeed reached the very home and hearth of the people. The most unfortunate fact, however, was the provision of such electorates for the so called "depressed classes" among the Hindus, who were simultaneously to enjoy a right to vote in the general constituencies too which were meant for those not specified as above. The depressed classes constituencies were to continue for twenty years, unless abolished earlier with their consent. The whole system could be revised after ten years if the communities affected agreed. The League accepted it.

The attempt to divide the "Caste Hindus" from the Scheduled Caste Hindus however was the bitterest blow which Mr. Gandhi could not stand and declared his decision to fast unto death unless the British revised their decision. The fast commenced on 20 September 1932, but the Government remained unmoved. The Indian leaders like Madan Mohan Malaviya, C. Rajagopalachari, Dr Rajendra Prasad and Dr. Ambedkar met at Poona in their bid to save the Mahatma's life. After six days of deliberations, the well known Poona Pact was ultimately evolved, which the Government agreed to incorporate in the Award, and thus the fast ended.

THE POONA PACT, 1932

The Pact reserved for the "Depressed Classes" a total number of 148 seats out of the general electorates. This was against the 71 seats provided in the Award. In Bengal, thus, 30 seats were so reserved; Madras too has 30, while U.P. has 20, Bihar and Orissa 18, and Assam 7. The election to these seats was to be by joint electorates but as follows. The members of the depressed classes registered in a general constituency, were first to form as Electoral College to elect by method of single vote a panel of four candidates for each one of the seats reserved for them. These four were then to contest in the general electorate, which will elect one of them. This practice was also to be followed for the Central Legislature in connection with which 18 per cent of the seats allotted to the general electorate for the British India were reserved for them. Subject to their educational qualifications, a fair representation was promised to the depressed classes in the public services as well as in the local bodies. A due financial provision was to be made for the development of education among them. And it was provided that the system of primary election to a panel of candidates for election to the Central and Provincial Legislatures would come to an end after ten years, unless abolished earlier by mutual agreement.

The satyagraha, however, in the meanwhile continued, though it has much slackened. The Independence Day celebrations on 26 January 1933, and the Congress Session at Calcutta in April were arranged to reinforce the warning inspiration. But the Government foiled the attempt.

On 8 May 1933 Mr. Gandhi commenced his 21-day fast in the Yervada jail, "for purification of myself and my associates, and for greater vigilance and watchfulness in connection with the Harijan work." On the same day the Government released him. Immediately after his release he advised the Congress to suspend the satyagraha for six weeks, and appealed to the Viceroy to release political prisoners and withdraw his ordinances. Nobody in the Government was, however, moved by this feeble voice of the tottering Movement, and Mr. Gandhi extended the suspension for another six weeks. Still there was no response from the Government. And ultimately convinced of the uselessness of beating the almost dead horse that the Movement now was, the Acting President was advised on 24 July to suspend it unconditionally. He however, advised the people to continue individiual satyagraha, and himself prepared to move for the same purpose to the village Ras in the Kaira district after disbanding his Sabarmati Ashram. But the heavy hand of the Government fell and he was removed once again to the Yervada jail for one year. Here his demand for facilities to continue the Harijan work having been refused, he resorted again to fast, with the result that he was released again from the jail. On coming out this time, he decided not to continue satyagraha till the expiry of one year, and advising the Congress at Patna to give up the individual disobedience as well, began to devote time to the Harijan welfare work.

Dr. B.C. Roy and Dr. M.A. Ansari called a meeting of some important Congress leaders at Delhi in March, 1934 and moved for the revival of the Swaraj Party. Mr. Gandhi was not against the idea, and the Patna Session of the Congress in May decided for going back to the Councils. The elections to the Central Legislative Assembly were fast approaching in November, the Congress set up a Parliamentary Board to select its candidates. Elections were fought and in all Provinces but the Punjab, the Congress swept the polls, such thus was the inglorious end which the Civil Disobedience Movement once again met, though the success of the Congress in the elections was glorious, and it effectively demonstrated to Lord Willingdon that the popularity and power of the Congress had not yet been ruined as he hadz so vaingloriously hoped to do.

An Appraisal

A few words of evaluation of the Satyagraha Movement will not be out of place. Although the Congress secured a grand success in the elections, its dismay and disillusionment could not go unobserved. The disappointment of Mr. Nehru and Mr Bose was usual. There was no doubt that the Mahatma had lost his game once again because a vague mystic as Mrs Besant called him, he was out of touch with the ordinary human nature. The violence at the hands of the untrained satyagrahis appeared again, and when the police beat up the people black and blue, a general demoralization crept in and the movement began to seek a way to go unworthily underground.

Nor was the Mahatma's changing of boats in mid-stream very helpful to the cause he was fighting for. His fast unto death was good at it aroused public opinion against untouchability. But it was not an unmixed blessing. The world at large came to know that Hindus themselves were divided between the 'Caste Hindus' and the Depressed Classes; and that the problem was so great that the national leader had desperately to resort to the 'epic fast'. To be more accommodating however, while on the advisability of this fast one may express a simple doubt, his sudden change of emphasis from politics to Harijan uplift was nothing but one of those blunders which he himself admitted he was not incapable of committing. The anti-untouchability work could very well have been postponed, or assigned to some other workers outside the Movement. Why should the political movement have been side-tracked?

Muslim League and the other communal organizations also did not make a mean contribution to see the Movement fail. But due credit must also be given to Lord Willingdon whose Government struck in time, smoothened in time and then hit again in time, and all this in balanced measures. If the Government had failed but once, say for instance that if they had not released Gandhi from the jail whenever he resorted to fast, the satyagraha spirit should have been rejuvenated and become too formidable to control. The Government had become wiser by this time by their experience in the first two Movements of 1920-21 and 1930. And while in these two Movements the initiative remained with Mr. Gandhi, in the Movement of 1932, it was stolen by the Government which was now on the offensive and the Mahatma on the defensive.

One firm contribution of this Movement, however, was that the roots of revolt went deeper into the soil, becoming more difficult to pull out.

THIRD ROUND TABLE CONFERENCE AND THE WHITE PAPER.

When the situation improved a little after the Government's acceptance of the Poona Pact, the authorities took up the question of Round Table Conference again, which was held for the third time in November 1932. In this Conference, however, both the Congress of India and the Labour Party of

England were conspicuous by absence. The Conference carried on its deliberations, the idea of a Federation of British India and the Indian States matured and it was on the basis of this that the White Paper was drafted and submitted for examination and report to the Joint Select Committee of the Parliament.

The more important terms of this paper were as follows: (1) A Federal Government consisting of the Indian Provinces and the Indian States was to be set up at the Centre with a bicameral Federal Legislature. (2) The Provinces would be given a complete autonomy with certain safeguards. (3) A demarcation between the Central and the Provincial spheres of legislation was provided. (4) Certain Federal institutions like a Federal Court, Reserve Bank and Railway Federal authority were also to be set up.

The White Paper was examined by a Joint Select Committee consisting of 16 members each from the Commons and the Lords under the Chairmanship of Lord Linlithgo, before which the Indian Association etc., submitted memoranda and appeared as witnesses. The Committee recommended certain changes as: (1) introduction of bicameral legislature in six Provinces and not only in three as proposed; (2) upper chambers in Centre as well as the Provinces to be indissoluble; (3) indirect elections in place of direct elections for the Federal Assembly; and (4) future restrictions on the power of the Federal Court.

A Bill was drawn up on the basis of these recommendations and passed as the Government of India Act, 1935.

NOTES

1. Trench, Victor, *Lord Willingdon in India*, Bombay, 1934, p. 21.
2. Mersey, Viscount, *The Viceroy*, p. 142.
3. Trench, Victor, *op. cit.*, pp. 187-188.
4. Nehru, Jawaharlal, *Autobiography*, p. 294.
5. Revealed in the confidential circular issued by Benthal, a European representative.
6. Gandhi, Mahatma, *India's Case for Swaraj* (Select Documents), p. 155.
7. See Bose, S., *op. cit.*, pp. 226-31.
8. See Gandhi, Mahatma, *India's Case for Swaraj* (Select Documents), pp. 23-33.

5

The Government of India Act, 1935

The Government of India Act, 1935, which was a very lengthy statute consisting of 321Sections and 10 Schedules, was in its material, drawn from the following sources: (1) The Simon Commission Report; (2) the Nehru Committee Report; (3) the discussion held at the Round Table Conference; (4) the White Paper; (5) the Joint Select Committee Report and (6) The Lothian Report. Besides others there were two special reasons why the Act was so lengthy: First it had to deal with a very complex type of Government, and second, it tried to provide legal safeguards against the wrong use of power by Legislators and Ministers.

A brief sketch of the main features of the Act, some of which are discussed in detail in the following pages, may be given here.

An interesting feature of the Act was that it had no preamble of its own. It borrowed the preamble from the Act of 1919. The preamble had envisaged Dominion Status for India by stages, and since the basic principle of this policy was not changed, the authors of the Act while repealing the Act of 1919, retained its preamble which they attached to the Act of 1935.

Supremacy to the British Parliament

The supremacy of the British Parliament was kept intact. According to the Act the Dominion status, which was the ultimate goal for India, was to be attained by stages and it was the British Parliament that was to decide the time and nature of each advance towards it. Although the Federal and the Provincial legislatures could recommend changes in certain specified matters under certain prescribed circumstances, the ultimate authority to amend or repeal the constitution of India was jealously kept with the Parliament.

Secretary of State and his Council

The people of India had been agitating against the India Council of the Secretary of State since long. The Council established in 1858 was abolished by this Act, which empowered the Secretary of State to appoint not less than three and not more than six advisers instead, to advise him on the matters referred to them. At least half of these must have served in India at least for 14 years and must not have been away from that country for more than 2 years at the time of their appointment. They were to be mere advisers, not authorized to sit in the Parliament, nor was the acceptance of their advice obligatory on the Secretary of State, though in the formulation of rules and regulations for Civil Services the concurrence of at least half of them was necessary.

The powers of the Secretary of State himself were curtailed with regard to the Provincial matters, handed over to the control of the popular Ministers. Still, however, the control of the special powers of the Governor-General and the Governor remaining in his hands, the Secretary of State remained supreme in the real sense.

Federation and the Federal Government

The Act envisaged the establishment of a federation of India, which was to consist of the eleven existing Provinces, the Six Chief Commissioner's Provinces and those of the States, which offered to join it. For the Provinces it was obligatory to join, but for the States it was voluntary. If a State desired to join the Federation, it was to sign an Instrument of Accession where in it would clearly lay down the matters with regard to which the control was being handed over to the Federation. The powers once handed over to the Centre could not be withdrawn, though they would be added to by signing a supplementary Instrument of Accession.

In order to demarcate the respective sphere of activities of the Federal Government and of the Provinces, the Act drew out three lists i.e., (1) the Federal List which consisted of 59 subjects such as Armed Forces, Railways, Currency, etc. with regard to which the Federal Legislature alone enact laws; (2) the Provincial List consisting of 54 subjects with regards to which the Provincial Legislatures alone could legislate; and (3) the Concurrent List with regard to which both the Federal and the Provincial legislature, could legislate, the Federal law prevailing in case of a conflict. The powers with regards to the residual matters not mentioned in any one of the lists were vested in the Governor-General who could authorize the Federal or any of the Provincial legislatures to legislate on any of these matters.

The Federal Executive was to consist of the Governor-General, the Councillors and the Ministers. The authority of the Governor-General was, on behalf of the Crown, to extend to all those matters with regard to which the Federal Legislature had the powers to legislate, to the raising of forces and to the treaties and engagements as entered into by his Majesty. Over and above, he was given certain special powers, which extended to almost all the matters, the Federal as well as the Provincial.

The Federal Legislature was to be bicameral, the Upper House named as the Council of States and the Lower House as the Federal Assembly. The Federal Legislature could legislate on all the matters included in the Federal and the Concurrent Lists and also on the residual as permitted by the Governor-General.

The All India Federation was to be inaugurated only after an address to the effect was presented by both the Houses of the Central Legislature to the King. The address could be presented only when at least half of the population of all the States acceded to the Federation, filling at least half of the total number of the seats allotted in the Upper Chamber to the States. And since this condition was not fulfilled, the Federal part of the constitution never came into force.

Dyarchy at Centre

The dyarchy established in the Provinces by the Act of 1919, was abolished. But the present Act established dyarchy at the Centre by which a part of the Federal Executive was declared reserved while another part was transferred. The reserved part consisted of the important subjects of Defence, External Affairs, the Tribal Areas and the Ecclesiastical Affairs. These subjects were to remain under the control of the Governor-General acting in his discretion and for their administration he could appoint Councillors, not exceeding three, who would assist him and would be responsible to him. The transferred part was to be administered by the Governor-General with the help of the popular Ministers, appointed from among the members of the legislature to which they were to be responsible. The Governor-General was instructed in a separate instrument of instructions, to appoint the Ministers in consultation with a person who was most likely to command a stable majority in the legislature, and to encourage joint consultations between the Ministers and the Councillors.

Bicameral Enlarged Legislatures

The Act established a bicameral legislature in the Centre as well as in each of the six of the total number of eleven Provinces. The membership of the Legislatures was increased. Thus in the Centre, the Legislative Assembly was to have 375 members while the Council of States would have 260. The Legislative Council of Bengal was to be the largest, with not less than 63 and not more than 65 members, while that of Assam the smallest with not less than

21 and not more than 22 members. Bengal, again, was to have the largest Legislative Assembly with the total membership of 250, while that of the North West Frontier Province was to be smallest with a total membership only of 50.

The Electorate

The Franchise qualification being lowered, the electorate was enlarged. As much as 10 per cent of the population got the right to vote for the Provincial Legislatures. The cures of communal electorate was, however, extended side by side. The electorate in 1919 was broken up into 10 parts, but now it was divided into 17 unequal bits. Separate electorates were now thrust on women and Indian-Christians.

Federal Court

The Act established a Federal Court with original and appellate, jurisdiction, to decide disputes between the Federating units, between the Federal Government and a unit or units and with regard to the interpretation of constitution. The final court, however, remained the Privy Council.

Reserve Bank

A Reserve Bank was established with a Governor and fifteen Directors to control currency and keep financial stability in the country.

Provincial Autonomy

The most important feature of the Act, however, was the establishment of autonomy in the Provinces. The old dyarchical system in the Provinces was dropped and the distinction between the transferred and the reserved subjects abolished. The entire Provincial administration was placed under the charge of the popular Ministers who were to be appointed by the Governor from among the members of the Provincial legislature on the advice of a person who commanded majority. They were responsible to the legislature and collective responsibility among them was to be encouraged.

An unfortunate feature of the Act, however, was certain wide special responsibilities given to the Governors who, from behind the smoke-screen of these responsibilities, could sweep away the whole business of the popular Ministers at any time and establish their dictatorship. That is why some people said the Provincial Autonomy was in fact the autonomy of these Governors.

Territorial Changes

The Act introduced certain far-reaching territorial changes. Burma being separated from India, was transferred to the control of the Colonial office.

The transfer was affected on 1 April 1937. Aden also taken away from the administrative control of India was instituted into a Crown Colony, Berar, though continuing under the Nizam's symbolic authority became a part of a Governor's Provinces called the Central Provinces and Berar.

Safeguards

The safeguards were a very special feature of the Act, which coming last but not least requires a more detailed reference. Safeguards are included in a constitution in order to check certain tendencies which it is desired not to develop. Such safeguards are included in all the constitutions, as for instance in that of the USA where they are included in order to check revolutionary activities. In India where the entire constitution of 1935 was based on suspicion and distrust, the provision of safeguards was bound to be in an ample measure.

It may be interesting to sketch briefly the origin and development of the idea of safeguards in India where different interests, i.e., the British, the Princely, communal and class interests existed, which all suffered from a bitter fear-complex and therefore had to be safeguarded in their respective spheres by the Constitution. The idea seems to have originated with the Simon Commission, but was discussed in detail in the First Round Table Conference in January 1931, where Sir Tej Bahadur Sapru agreed to their necessity so long as they did not counter the vital interests of democracy and secularism. The Gandhi-Irwin Pact agreed in March 1931 that such safeguards would be in the interest of India alone. In the Second Round Table Conference held in September 1931 Mr. Gandhi agreed to them on condition that they were "demonstrated to be in the interest of India," though in no case should they be prejudicial to the real interests of Great Britain. The Joint Parliamentary Report discussed the matter at length and agreed for the safeguards as an absolute necessity. Therefore, the safeguards were included in the Act of 1935.

These safeguards were many and varied dealing with different subjects as follows: (1) First, thus, the Defence, External Affairs, Tribal Areas and Ecclesiastical Affairs were placed in the hands of the Governor-General to be administered by him to his discretion, with the help of his Councillors responsible to him and not to the Legislature. These subjects were declared 'reserved' for their national importance and placed outside the control of the popular Ministers who could be consulted, but whose advice in these matters, was not necessarily to be followed. Then (2) there were the special responsibilities of the Governor-General and the Governors with regard to (a) the prevention of a grave menace to peace and tranquility of the country; (b) safeguarding the interests of the Princely States and their rulers; (c) protection of the legitimate interests of the minorities; (d) of the interests of the public services and (e) prevention of discrimination against the British commercial interests. Besides, (3) although finance was transferred to the control of a responsible Minister, yet the Governor-General had the special responsibility of maintaining the financial stability of the Federation, for which he was to appoint a Financial Adviser whose advice he could accept or reject and for which he cold veto any measure proposed by the Finance Minister. The monetary policy and currency was to be controlled by the Reserve Bank, the Governor, of which was to be responsible to the Governor-General. (4) A Governor, with the sanction of Governor-General, could at any time declare the constitution of his Province having broken down and after this assume the control of the entire administration himself. Then (5) the power for the amendment of the Constitution was kept in the hands of the Parliament alone; (6) Police and higher services were kept outside the control of the popular Ministers; (7) Second Chambers in some Provinces; (8) recognition of new communal and class interests by the extension of special electorates to them; (9) nomination by the Princes of their representatives to the Federal Legislature and (10) granting in this legislature the seats to the States much beyond the proportion of their population. Such thus were the safeguards.

The safeguards thus clearly prove that what was given with one hand was sought immediately to be taken away with the other. In the presence of these safeguards, in fact, the whole Act smacked only of distrust and mischief. Mr. Gandhi's view that these safeguards should be in the interest of India alone was hardly accommodated, and the only interest safeguarded was that of John Bull's imperialism. Firstly, the most vital affairs such as Defence and External were kept firmly in the British grip. Secondly, the special responsibilities of Governor-General and the Governors seemed to aim only at circumscribing the free movements of the popular representatives; thirdly, the safeguards with regard to finance made a mockery of the transfer of its control to the popular Ministers. Fourthly, the Governor's power to declare the constitution of a Province having broken down was like a Damocles, sword hanging on the Ministers' head. Fifthly, the incapability of Indians to amend their own Constitution was an insult to the popular aspiration for independence. The uncontrolled activities of the Services and Police were bound to invite a stigma of inefficiency on the Ministers. And then the Second Chamber was primarily intended to act as a retarder on the progressive movement of the Lower House: the recognition of the new class and communal interests indicated clearly the policy of divide and rule; the members of the Federal legislature nominated by the Princes were to sit with those elected on popular basis from the Provinces, and the grant to the States of seats much beyond what they deserved, all this was a naked and most shameless attempt at tying a heavy deadweight to the development of democratic trends. Attempt of some writers thus to divide the safeguards into two classes, those for the protection of the British interests and those for the protection of the Indian interests, seems to be misdirected.[1] In fact they all were intended and worked only to protect the British imperialism. For the Indians, as Mr. Jawaharlal Nehru aptly summed up, it was "all brakes and no engine."[2]

THE PROPOSED FEDERATION

The Government of India Act, 1935 proposed to establish and All India Federation, which was to consist of eleven Governor's Provinces, six Chief Commissioner's Provinçes and such of the Indian States as would like to join it by signing as Instrument of Accession. The Governor's Provinces were: Madras, Bombay, the Central Provinces, Bihar, Orissa, Bengal, Assam, the United Provinces, Sind, Punjab and the N.W.F Province. And the Chief Commissioner's Provinces were: Coorg, Ajmer–Marwara. British Baluchistan, Delhi, Panth-Piploda and the Andaman and Nicobar Islands.

While the membership of the proposed Federation was compulsory for the Provinces, it was voluntary for the Indian States. Such of the States as signified their desire to join, were required to sign a document, known as the Instrument of Accession. In this document, a State was to specify the particular subjects with respect to which it would permit the Federal authorities to interfere. The scope of such interference could be extended by a ruler's signing of a supplementary Instrument of Accession, subject to the approval of the Crown, but it could not be curtailed. Nor could a State withdraw from the Federation once it signed the document.

The most interesting aspect of the system, however, was that there was to be no uniformity in the states accession to the Federation. Each was to decide for itself with regard to the subjects it would ceded to the Centre, and thus the subjects ceded by one were not necessarily the same as ceded by another. There was a reason why so much freedom was given to the States. Before the passage of the Act of 1935, the Governor-General of India while being the chief executive authority for the British India, was also an authority in which the Paramountcy over the States vested. This Act, however, separated the two authorities. The Paramountcy over the States was now to vest in the Crown, and it was to be exercised by the Governor-General not as head of the state, but as Viceroy in the name of the Crown. The States being thus separated from the British India, it was now left to their option whether to join it in a Federation or not, and in case of joining what subjects to cede.

Another significant feature of Act was that whereas prior to it the British India presented a unitary system of Government under which both the Central and the Provincial Governments were run under the superintendence and direction of the Secretary of State, the Provincial Governments exercising only such of the powers as derived from the Centre; under the new system all the previous Acts of the Parliament relating to the Government of India were replaced, and the entire authority over the Centre as well as Provinces was resumed by the Crown. After this, the Provinces were separated from the Centre, created into autonomous units which would derive their power from the same source as that of the Centre, and then re-grouped into a Federation whether they liked it or not.

In the Federation thus instituted, the executive authority of the Crown was to be vested in the Governor-General as the representative of the Crown, and the legislative was to be vested in both the Governor-General as the Crown representative and the two Chambers which would be known as the House of Assembly and the Council of States. A Federal Court was provided for, to adjudicate the disputes between the Federation and the units and between the units themselves, and to protect and interpret the Federal Constitution. A Reserve Bank was provided for, for the issue of bank-notes and for the maintenance of the financial stability of the Federation. And the Federal Railway Authority, a statutory body, was provided for, to control the Federal Railways.

The Federation was to be proclaimed by His Majesty on an address to the effect having been presented to him by the two houses of the Central Legislature. And the Central Legislature was to present such an address only if (1) the states having at least half of the total population of the Princely India agreed to accede and (2) if the rulers of the States willing to join were entitled to choose at least 52 members of the Council of State. No direct time limit was prescribed for the establishment of the Federation, but the Princes being permitted a time of twenty years in which to make up their minds, evidently if not enforced the scheme was to lapse after this.

No Prince of India, however, thought it advisable to join the Federation. The enthusiasm shown by them in the Round Table Conference has in fact been an effect of the British whip. When the actual moment for joining the Federation came, they apprehended a danger to their very existence, if they in this manner associated their States with the progressive elements in the British India. Nor was the question of paramountcy solved entirely to their satisfaction. Hence they desisted from joining, and the All India Federation never came into existence, although the Reserve Bank was instituted in 1935, and the Federal Court started its operations on 1 October 1937.

THE FEDERAL EXECUTIVE

If the All India Federation had come into existence, it would have established in the Centre an Executive consisting of (1) the Governor-General, (2) the councillors and (3) the Council of Ministers.

The Governor-General

The most important office in the Federal Executive was that of the Governor-General who was a representative of the British Crown, and to whom the executive authority of the Crown was delegated. His appointment was to be made by His Majesty on the advice of the Prime Minister of England. His tenure of office was to be at least five years. Besides the other allowances, he was to get an annual salary of Rs 250,800, which was to be charged on the revenues of the Federation. And a palatial building at Delhi, another at Simla and a country house at Mashobra near Simla were given to him for his residence.

In his powers, the Governor-General was perhaps the greatest dictator of the world. These powers were to consist of three categories those, which he would exercise in his discretion, those to be used in his individual judgement and those, which he would exercise on the advice of the ministers.

The powers to be exercised by the Governor-General in his discretion, were vast and covered almost all the most important subjects to be handled by the Federal Government. In the exercise of these powers, if he liked, he could consult the Ministers, but was in no way bound by their advice.

They consisted of (1) the control of Defence, the Tribal areas and the Foreign and the Ecclesiastical affairs. These were reserved subjects, and with regard to these he was responsible to the Secretary of the State for India. (2) The appointment of the Councillors, Financial Adviser, Chief Commissioners, Chairman and members of the Federal Public Service Commission, Governor and Deputy Governor of Reserve Bank and the President of the Railway Tribunal, etc. (3) Choice, appointment and dismissal of Ministers; and presiding over the meetings of the Council of Ministers.

Then, the Governor-General was to make rules for (1) the convenient transaction of Government business and for the allocation among the Ministers of the said business. This he was to do in his discretion, but after consulting the Ministers. While making these rules he was to provide that every Minister would consult the Finance Minister upon every proposal that affected the Federal finances, that no Minister would make any re-appropriation within a grant except with the concurrence of the Finance Minister, and that if there was a difference of opinion in this connection, the matter would be placed for decision before the Council of Ministers. The Governer-General was also to make rules for (2) keeping him informed of the business and for (3) authentication of the orders and instruments of the Government. To the same category belonged his powers of (4) suspending the Constitution; (5) issuing ordinances and emergency proclamations; (6) refusing assent to bills, disallowing their introduction and sending messages regarding them; (7) summoning, dissolving or proroguing the lower house; (8) enacting Governor-General's Acts and (9) controlling the Governors when they exercised powers in discretion or in individual judgement.

The powers which the Governor-General was to exercise in his individual judgement, were enumerated in Section 32 of the Act. These powers were: (1) the prevention of any menace of the peace or tranquility of India or any part thereof; (2) the safeguarding of the rights and legitimate interests of the public services; (3) the safeguarding of the legitimate interests of the minorities; (4) the safeguarding of the financial stability and credit to the Federal Government; (5) prevention of commercial discrimination; (6) the prevention of action which might subject goods of the United Kingdom or of Burmese origin imported into India to discriminatory of penal treatment; (7) protection of the rights of the Indian States and of the rights and dignity of rulers thereof and (8) securing discharge of an action taken by the Governor-General himself in his discretion or individual judgement. Besides, there were certain other matters, which came under the same category, such as the (9) appointment, determination of the salary and the dismissal of the Advocate-General of the Federation. In such matters, however, he had to work under certain limitation, as for instance that a person appointed as Advocate-General must be qualified to hold the office of a judge in the Federal Court.

In the exercise of these powers, however, the Governor-General was bound to consult the Ministers, though he enjoyed the option between accepting or rejecting their advice. Obviously, therefore, the position of the Ministers was slightly better here. But on the whole it was hardly enviable.

The residuary executive powers to be exercised by the Governor-General on the advice of the Ministers. But these were of no great significance. All the important powers were placed in the first two categories, and those of the powers given to the Ministers to enjoy were reduced almost to a nullity, for here too the Governor-General enjoyed the final and the overriding authority. Moreover, the Ministers at best were only his henchmen, to be selected, appointed, maintained and dismissed by him. They were not expected to go much against his authority.

He was, however, instructed in the Instrument of Instructions that for a close and harmonious cooperation both in his discretionary powers for which he was responsible to the Secretary of State, and in others which were to be exercised by him on the advice of the Ministers responsible to the Federal Legislature, he should develop the practice of joint consultation between himself, his councillors and his Ministers. Particularly so in matters of Defence which should admittedly be the concern of the Indians to an increasing extent.

Financial Powers. A special reference may here be made to the Governor-General's financial powers. It was by his orders that an annual statement of the estimated receipts and expenditures was to be laid before the Federal Legislature. No demand for grant could be made except on his recommendation, and it was with in his power to restore a cut imposed on it by the Legislature. He was to decide the votable and non-votable items in the expenditure, and in an emergency he was empowered to incur any amount of expenditure he liked. For the maintenance of the credit and the financial stability of the Federations he was to appoint a Financial Adviser and fix his salary and conditions of service in his discretion. And this Adviser, in a way, was as strong as the Finance Minister, it being contended by the public criticism that the functions and authority of these two offices may actually overlap.

The extraordinary legislative powers. Nor may the Governor-General's extraordinary powers of legislation be passed unnoticed. (1) Section 45 of the Act empowered the Governor-General to issue a proclamation whereby the entire constitution of the Federation could be suspended. This power could be exercised when he was satisfied that the existing circumstances made it impossible for the Federal Government to be carried on. And when the proclamation was issued, he could assume to himself all or a part of the powers exercised by any federal authority with the exception of the Federal Court. The proclamation to this effect was, however, to be immediately communicated to the Secretary of State for India, through whom it was to be laid before the two houses of the Parliament. The proclamation was to remain in force for a period of six months, unless another proclamation revoked it earlier.

(2) And another extraordinary power is related to the promulgation of ordinances, which were of two types. The first were those, which he could promulgate at any time, being satisfied that his discretionary powers and the powers to be exercised in individual judgement necessitated them. Such ordinances could remain in operation for six months with the full force of law, and could be renewed for another six months if he desired. The second were those which he could promulgate at the time the Federal Legislature was not in session. These ordinances could concern his powers to be exercised on the advice of the Ministers; and they had to be sanctioned by the Legislature within six weeks of the commencement of its next session, failing which they would lapse.

A Dyarchy

A passing reference may be to a sort of dyarchic government that the Act established at the Centre. The whole executive business was to consist of two wings, the one dealing with the reserved subjects consisting of the Defence, the External Affairs, the Tribal Areas and the Ecclesiastic Affairs, and the other dealing with the Transferred subjects consisting of the residuary matters.

The reserved subjects were to be administered by the Governor-General in his discretion but with the help of his Councillors whose number would not exceed three. These Councillors were to be appointed by the Crown, but they were not to act as Ministers. They were simply advisers to the Governor-General to whom they were responsible for their functions; the Governor-General himself being responsible to the British Parliament. The Act fixed no qualifications and no tenure for this Councillors, who could sit in either of the two Federal Chambers as ex-officio members, but without a right to vote.

On the other hand, the residuary or the transferred subjects were to be administered by the Governor-General with the help of the Ministers whose number would not exceed ten. These Ministers, however, were not popular in the sense that they were not fully responsible to the Federal Legislature Although they did belong to this Legislature as its regular members, yet they were selected and dismissed by the Governor-General who could keep them in the teeth of no-confidence motions, and to whom solely therefore they made themselves responsible. They were in fact the Governor-General's henchmen, to be consulted by him individually or collectively at his will. Their permanent Secretaries having a direct access to the Governor-General, the latter often knew much more regarding the business of their departments than the Ministers themselves knew. Their salary determined by the Federal Legislature, was charged on the revenues of India, and was not subject to the vote of the Legislature. Nor could it be reduced during the term of their office.

The Instrument of Instructions, however, required of the Governor-General to permit these Ministers as much freedom as possible, and while selecting them, to give due representation to the Indian States and the minorities. It was moreover, advisable for him to see that the person's chosen commanded a stable majority in the legislature, so that they could have a smooth sailing in their business. But all these suggestions he was to follow only in his convenience. There was no compulsion whatsoever. A Minister who for any period of six consecutive months was not a member of either Chamber of the Federal Legislature, ceased to be a Minister. The advice tendered by a Minister to the Governor-General was not to be inquired into by any Court of Law.

INSTRUMENT OF INSTRUCITONS

A brief reference to the document of the Instrument of Instructions may here be necessary. For the exercise of the powers detailed above, the Governor-General was given an Instrument of Instructions, which desired of him that (1) he should select only such of the Ministers as commanded a stable majority in the Federal Legislature. He should encourage joint responsibility in them, and be guided by their advice unless the fulfilment of his special responsibilities necessitated otherwise. (2) The budgetary and the borrowing policy followed by him should be such as should not seriously affect the Government's capacity to discharge its financial obligations, nor should it prejudice its credit in the world money markets. (3) He was duly to safeguard the legitimate interests of the minorities. (4) He was to prevent the measures discriminating against the goods of the United Kingdom imported into India; avoiding however, an action, which might affect the competence of the Federal Legislature or the Government in developing their own economic policy. He was to interfere in the country's tariff policy only if he was satisfied that in its main interest it contemplated to injure the interests of the United Kingdom rather than to serve those of India. (5) No action should be taken by the Ministers and no law passed by the Federal Legislature, which might threaten the recognized right or the economic life of an Indian State. It was desirable that the views of the Ministers with regard to the general policy of appointment of Indian officers to the Indian forces or the employment of the Indian forces outside that country be obtained. (7) The Governor-General should encourage joint consultations between himself, the Councillors and the Ministers. (8) He was to exercise a financial control on defence in his discretion, but he was to keep the Federal Finance Department in close touch with such control. (9) He was to encourage consultations to secure common action between the Federation, the Provinces and the Federated States, and (10) For those of the legislative proposals in which the provinces and the Federated States were interested, he was to evolve a suitable method to ascertain their views. (11) He would not stop further discussion of a Bill in the Federal Legislature unless in his view it would endanger public peace. (12) A Bill which aimed at repealing or was repugnant to an Act of Parliament, was to be reserved for His Majesty's approval; and the Governor-General was (13) to further the "partnership between India and the United Kingdom within the Empire...to the end that India may attain its due place among our dominions."

The instruments of Instructions, however, aimed only at the developments on the basis of the principles contained in it, and it was expressly laid down that the validity of an action could not be questioned on the grounds that the instructions in the Instrument, had not been followed.

An Appraisal. "The Federal Government will thus be in reality a one man's rule, unsurpassed in many respects by oriental despotism or modern dictatorship."[3] In fact a close study of the facts clearly reveals that the entire central executive machinery was based on principle which breathed only a dead distrust against Indians and which sought in a way only to cloak what in plain words should have been an almost blank refusal to part with any substance of power.

The Governor-General was not only a pivot of administration, but also a linch-pin of the whole machinery: personification of the Crown, representative of the Home Government and a dictator of India's destinies, all combined in one. He was an arbiter of India's fate, who must be consulted by the Crown while appointing Governors, except those of Madras, Bombay and Bengal. He himself enjoyed vast power of patronage. The appointment of his Councillors, Ministers and that of the permanent secretaries, the financial adviser, the Chief-Commissioners, members and Chairman of the Public Service Commission and others, all this was done by him in his discretion or in his individual judgement. He could appoint a Deputy Governor to administer a part of a province. He appointed Lieutenant-Governors and their executive Councillors with the Crown's approval. He could appoint a Vice President of his Council and President of Council of States.

Then there was his power to make rules for the transaction of Council business and the distribution of the portfolios among the Councillors and the Ministers, his discretionary powers, and those, which he could exercise, in his individual judgement. If his Councillors were simply his handmaids, the Ministers were no better. Their position, as Prof. K.T. Shah observed, was simply "ornamental, without being useful, onerous without ever being helpful to the people. They are supposed to represent responsibility without power, position, without authority, name without real influence."[4] There was the least chance of a direct contact between the transferred and the reserved departments. With only a half-control of their own departments, they were kept perfectly blind to what went on in the reserved ones. And this made the transfer of responsibility only a hoax.

The Governor-General obnoxious responsibility to prevent any grave menace to peace and tranquility of the country, made a mockery of the transfer of the department of Law and Order to the Ministers; just as his special responsibility to protect the interests of the public services made it impossible to run any transferred department according to the wishes of a Minister at all.

Nor were his legislative powers less autocratic. He could stop further consideration of a bill or a clause thereof already under discussion, and could call a joint session to refer the bill to. He could return a bill already passed for reconsideration. He could desire of the Legislature to pass a bill in a particular form, and if the Legislature did not do so he could himself certify it and the bill would became law. He could give his consent to a bill or reserve it for His Majesty's pleasure. The most important of his powers, however, was that of promulgating ordinances and of suspending the constitution, as already discussed.

Hardly could also the Governor-General's financial powers be overestimated. His special responsibility to supervise the budgetary and borrowing arrangements in order that India's credit in the money markets of the world was not prejudiced, was purposely left undefined. A Financial Adviser was appointed to help him in this respect, but the former not being Minister or a Councillor, could hardly comprehend the national policy. Nor was his advice binding on the Governor-General, who could also override the decisions of the majority of the Ministers in this respect. He controlled 80% of the budgets; without his recommendations no proposal for appropriation of money or revenues could be made and in emergency he could authorize expenditure of any amount of money he desired. All this, indeed, was significant.

In the judicial sphere too, his powers were no less strong. He could alter the jurisdiction of a High Court, could appoint additional Judges to it for a specified time, and could make an interim arrangement if the office of a Chief Justice or that of a High Court fell vacant.

Nor were the Governor-General's powers confined only to the Centre. He enjoyed supervisory powers over Provinces, and was to direct the Governors in the exercise of their discretionary powers, in their power of individual judgement and in matters where a prior sanction was required for a bill to be brought in the Provincial legislature. The Governor-General's powers to maintain general peace and tranquillity all over the country, reduced provincial autonomy in many respects to a farce. He could alter the boundaries of any Province, and could take any one of them under his direct control. He had the power to confer titles of honour, personal or hereditary, on a person belonging to any part of the country.

Then the Governor-General controlled the army. Defence of the country was his concern and the External Policy was his business. President Lowell was not incorrect when he observed that the "Governor-General or Viceroy of India and the Czar of Russia are sometimes said to be the two great autocrats of the modern world". Mr. Winston Churchill himself admitted that the

"Governor-General was armed with all powers of Hitler or Mussolini."

FEDERAL LEGISLATURE

The Act proposed to set up a bicameral Federal Legislature in the country to consist of an Upper House known as the Council of States and the Lower House known as the Federal Assembly.

Council of States

The total membership of the Council of States was to be 260. Forty per cent of these seats, or 104 of them, were to go to the Indian States; distributed among them in groups or individually on the basis of their respective importance as shown by dynastic salutes and other such things. Hyderabad, with its population of 14.4 million and a salute of 21 guns, was thus to get 5 seats. Mysore, with its population of 5.6 million and 21 guns salute, ranked next, getting 3 seats. Patiala, Bikaner and Udaipur got two seats each, with a respective population of 1.6, 0.9 and 1.6 million and with the respective salute of 17, 17 and 19 guns. Nabha with a population of .3 million and a salute of 13 guns got 1 seat. So did Alwar, but with .8 million of population and a salute of 15 guns. The representative of the States were to be nominated by the rulers so long as the democratic system was not introduced in them.

The British India was to get the remaining 156 seats, of which 6 were to be nominated by the Governor-General, 75 elected by the Hindus in General Constituencies, 49 elected by Muslims, 4 by Sikhs, 7 by Europeans, 2 by Indian Christians, 1 by Anglo-Indians, 6 by women and 6 by Scheduled Castes. Distribution of the seats among the Provinces was based on several considerations such as population, commercial importance and historical importance. Bengal, Madras and the United Provinces thus got 20 seats each; while Bombay, Bihar and Punjab got 16 each. Next came the Central Provinces and Berar with 8 each; then Assam, Orissa, N.W.F. Provinces and Sind with 5 each; and finally Delhi, the British Baluchistan, Ajmer-Marwara and Coorg getting 1 seat each.

Representatives of the Council of States were so be elected directly on a very narrow franchise. They were remain in the Council for 9 years, one-third of them retiring after every three years. The Council was thus a permanent body.

Federal Assembly

The Federal Assembly or the House of Assembly was the Lower Chamber consisting of 375 seats. Of these, 125 or one-third were to be filled up by the representatives of the Indian States, the remaining 250 seats going to the British India. Here again, the representatives of the States were to be nominated by the Princes, while those from the British India were to be elected.

Distribution of the seats among the States was made roughly on the basis of population, but the number of seats deserved by the most populous States was slightly reduced so as to provide as many States with a separate representation as possible. Hyderabad thus got 16 seats, Mysore 7, Pataila 2, one seat going each to Nabha, Bikaner and Alwar.

The criterion of population was not, however, applied to the Provinces among which the distribution of the seats was made as arbitrarily for the Assembly as for the Council. Bengal with its population of 50.1 million was thus treated at par with Madras with 44.2 and the United Provinces with 48.4, each getting 37 seats. And then, the distribution of seats among the different interests in the British India was such as secured 82 seats to the Muslims, 8 each to the Indian Christians and the Europeans, 6 to Sikhs, 4 to Labour, 7 to Landlords, 9 to women and 105 were kept general to be filled up by the Hindus and the other communities which got no separate representation—the scheduled classes also being included in the list.

Strangely enough, the elections to the Assembly were indirect as against direct elections to the Council; the argument forwarded by the Joint Committee being that direct elections in a country with a large population of 350 million would involve either an unduly large Legislature or unwieldy constituencies, both of which were evils to be avoided. Thus the seats allotted to the Hindus, the Muslims and the Sikhs in each Provinces, were to be filled up by the representatives of these communities in the respective provinces, each community voting separately in accordance with the system of proportional representation by means of a single transferable vote. The system for the scheduled classes was different. Here the persons declared eligible candidates in the primary elections of the last general elections to a Provincial Legislative Assembly, would choose four persons for each of the seats allotted to them in that Province. The persons so chosen would then contest the seats in the general electorate. In the case of Europeans, Anglo Indians, Indian Christians an women, their respective representatives in each Province would constitute and electoral college for the whole of the British India, which could then fill its allotted seats in the Federal Assembly.

The Assembly thus constituted was to have a life of five years, but the Governor-General could dissolve it earlier.

Legislative Powers

When the question of the distibution of legislative powers between the Federal Legislature on the one hand and the Provincial Legislatures on the other, came up for discussion in the Round Table Conference, certain difficulties cropped up. The Liberals desiring to strengthen the unity of the country desired that the residual powers should be vested in the Centre as in Canada, while the Muslims desiring a greater autonomy for the Muslims Provinces insisted that these be invested in the Provinces as in the United States of America. The suggestion ultimately adopted was that the respective powers of both, the provinces and the Centre shoud be so exhaustively enumerated that almost nothing is left for the residuary field. The actual examination of the matter, however, showed that there were certain subjects which could neither be declared exclusively Central nor Provincial. The result was the preparation of three lists: (1) the Federal list which included the subjects like Defence, External Affairs and Currency; (2) the Provincial list consisting of the subjects such as Education, Public Works and Irrigation and Canals and (3) the Concurrent list which was divided into two parts, the one consisting of the subjects such as Criminal Procedure and Contracts and the other part consisting of subjects such as Trade Unions. Industrial Disputes, Inland Waterways and Electricity. In case of conflict between the two the Federal law was to prevail on the Provincial Law.

The Federal Legislature, however, could legislate for a Federated State or a Province with the prior consent of a Ruler or a Governor, as the case may be. After the declaration of emergency by the Governor-General again, the Federal Legislature could legislate on any matter in the Provincial List. In the case of the Chief Commissioners Provinces, however, the Federal Legislature could legislate on any subject at any time.

In the case of the States, no separate lists were prepared. The Federal Legislature could legislate on the subjecsts ceded to the Centre in the Instrument of Accession. The ceded subjects, however remained only concurrent, in the sense that the States could still legislate on them till the entire field was not covered by the Central laws.

The Act enumerated certain special limitations on the legislative powers of the Federal Legislature. Thus, it could pass no Act affecting the Crown and Royal family; affecting the Army Act, the Air-force Act and the Naval Defence Act; affecting the Act itself and affecting the Governor-General's discretionary powers or an Act or ordinance promulgated by him. It could not pass a law discriminating against the British companies, shipping aircraft, etc. operating in the Federal territories. Certain bills required a previous sanction of the Governor-General when they could be brought in either Chamber. No bill passed by both the Chambers could become an Act unless assented to by the Governor-General, and a bill assented to by him could be disallowed by His Majesty. The Governor-General could ask the Legislature to pass a particular Bill, and if it refused, he himself could certify and make the Bill to become law. He could summon or prorogue any Chamber or dissolve the Assembly. In the case of differences between the two Chambers, he could summon them in a joint meeting in which the questions would be determined by majority of both the Houses present and voting.

In its executive powers, the Assembly could elect its Speaker and Deputy Speaker and the Council could elect its President and Vice-President, from their respective members. These presiding officers were to have only a casting vote when there was an equality of votes. While a presiding officer of the Council had to vacate his office in the event of his ceasing to be its member, that of the Assembly could carry on even after the Assembly's dissolution, till the first meeting of the new Assembly. All these presiding officers could, however, be removed by a majority vote of their respective chamber on a notice of fourteen days. The two houses were also empowered to make rules for regulating their respective conduct of business.

Besides, the executive authority could be censured in their Chamber by way of moving resolutions and adjournment motions or by questions and supplementary questions. The Federal Assembly had certain additional powers in the sense that it could move a vote of no confidence against the Council of Ministers and thus remove them in normal circumstances. The Governor-General, however, was empowered to make rules to regulate the procedure of the two Houses in matters related to his discretionary powers or those exercised in his individual judgement. He could also make rules prohibiting the discussion such as of the personal character of the rulers of the Indian States. He could make rules for the procedure regarding the joint sittings of the two Houses. While making these rules, however, he had to consult the President and the Speaker. The Legislative had no power to discuss the conduct of a judge of the Federal Court or of a High Court in the discharge of his official duties

The Financial powers of the two Houses were slightly different, for the financial Bills had first to be brought to the Assembly and then to the Council. But on the whole the financial powers of the Federal Legislature were very much limited. The Governor-General was to cause an annual financial statement to be laid before the Houses. But the expenditure chargeable on the Federal revenues was not subject to vote. This made the Federal Legislative powerless on at least 80% of the expenditure. The remaining 20% of the expenditure was to be submitted in the form of demands for grants, first to the Assembly and then to the Council. A grant refused by the Assembly, however, could still be submitted to the Council if the Governor-General so desired. And a grant reduced by Assembly, was to be submitted to the Council in its reduced shape, unless the Governor-General directed otherwise. The Council too could reject or reduce a grant. But in all cases the Governor-General had the power to restore a grant rejected or reduced.

The Two Chambers. In their mutual relations the two Chambers enjoyed coordinate and equal powers, except in the finance bills, which, as already referred to, could originate only in the Assembly. With this exception any bill could originate in either Chamber, and it could be presented to the Governor-General only if both the Houses had passed it. A bill passed by one Chamber but rejected by the other lapses. So did a bill passed by one but amended by the other, if they did not approve of the amendment. The Act empowered the Upper chamber to grant supplies. This power to this Chamber, it may be remembered, was not granted by the Act of 1919. In order to resolve the differences between the two houses, the Governor-General could call a joint meeting, in which the decisions were taken by a majority vote of all the members of the two Chambers, present and voting.

An Appraisal. There was much that could be said against the composition and powers of the two Chambers. The 40% members of the Upper House and one-third of those of the Lower Chamber being the nominees of the Indian Princes sufficient dead-weight was attached to the Federal Legislature so as to make its progress fatally slow. The distribution of seats among the Provinces was not made entirely on the basis of population. The so-called historical and geographical importance was given due consideration, which in other words signified a consideration being given to the factors like loyalty to the British Crown. Nor was the introduction of the class interests and the communal interest very fortunate. Not only were the people divided into communities and classes, the division was carried to the very home and hearth when the women were given a separate representation. The distribution of seats among the different communities also was not equitable. The Muslims forming only 26% of the population of the British India, were thus given 33% of the seats belonging to the British India in both the Chambers.

Another unfortunate future was the introduction surprisingly of direct elections in the Upper Chamber and indirect election in the Lower Chamber. It was indeed against all common sense. This introduction of indirect elections to the popular Chamber was a rare example of its type all over the world. And then, the indirectly elected house was made dissoluble, while the directly elected house was indissoluble. An abnormally long term of office of nine years given to the members of the upper house was preposterous. It was bound to make the elected members irresponsible.

Nor can one overlook the evil effects that the indirect elections to the lower chamber were bound to entail. Members to this house were to be elected by the provincial assemblies, the provincial and communal politics of which was bound to have its bearing on the Federal Assembly. Those who fought elections on provincial issue were most likely to weaken the national spirit so badly required in the Centre. The system of proportional representation by means of a single transferable vote was bound to create factions in the provincial legislatures. It would also increase corruption, for only about eight provincial electors could elect a member to the Federal Assembly, and a majority of them could easily be brought over by men of means.

The argument that direct election to the Federal Assembly would make constituencies too unwieldy, seems absurd in the light of our experience in independent India. And then, while the indirect election had many disadvantages, the advantages of the direct elections could hardly be overestimated. The educative value of the direct elections, as we have experienced after our independence, was alone a merit high enough to secure a credit for the direct elections, if the British were really interested in the welfare of India.

The co-equal legislative powers of the two Chambers was a snag in the whole Constitution. It would make the conservative upper house perhaps strongest of all the second chambers of the world. The limitations placed on the legislative powers of the Federal Legislature generally, were serious and merited a naked condemnation. The Governor-General's power to make laws independent of the Legislature in case the latter refused to follow his instructions was no less unfortunate. In the event of a deadlock between the legislature and the executive, the latter under the accepted democratic norms had to dissolve the legislative and arrange for fresh general elections, But the principle followed here was unique the like of which was difficult to find in the constitutional law and practice of Great Britain herself.

Then the Federal Assembly was given no complete control even over those Ministers which belonged to it and were supposed to be responsible to it. The restrictions placed on the legislature, such as that against discussing the Governor-General's discretionary powers, also deserved nothing but condemnation. Nor did the financial powers of the legislature deserve an appreciation. About 80% of the expenditure was placed clearly beyond its powers and on the remaining 20% too its powers were limited. Against the refusal of a grant by the Assembly, an appeal could be made to the Council. And the Governor-General himself could restore a cut imposed by the lower house. Although a provision was made that a money bill could originate only with the Assembly, in the actual practice its powers were no better than those of the Council.

The Other Federal Organs

The Federal Court. In a constitution where autonomous units come together to form a Central Federal Government, an independent Federal Court has to be provided for to decide disputes between the units. The Act of 1935 provided for such a Court in India.

The Federal Court of India was to consist of not more than six judges besides the Chief Justice, unless His Majesty increased the number on an address being presented to him by the Federal Legislature through the Governor-General of India. The minimum number was to be three; the decision for the actual number being left to the Governor-General.

The qualifications required of a person to be eligible for appointment as a judge were that he should have been (1) at least for five years a judge of a High Court of a Provinces or of a Federated State, (2) or at least for ten years a barrister of England or Northern Ireland, (3) or at least for ten years a member of the Faculty of Advocates in Scotland, (4) or at least for ten years a pleader of a High Court of a Province or of a Federal State, In order to be eligible for appointment as the Chief Justice, the minimum qualification was fifteen years as an advocate, as barrister or a pleader. In the event of a temporary vacancy, the Governor-General could appoint an acting Chief Justice from among the Federal judges.

A judge, after his appointment, could continue working up to the age of 65 years. But he could resign his office earlier and could be removed by His Majesty on the recommendation of Judicial Committee of the Privy Council, on ground of his misbehaviour or infirmity of body or mind. Their salaries were to be fixed by the King-in-Council, which were to be charged on the Federal revenues, were not subject to the vote of the legislature, and could not be reduced during their tenure of office.

Jurisdiction of the Federal Court was threefold, i.e., original, appellate and advisory. The original jurisdiction lay in disputes between, the provinces, or between one or more provinces and the Federal Government, "round any question of facts or of law". The appellate jurisdiction lay over the decisions of the High Courts of the Provinces and of those of the Federated States, provided that the High Court concerned certified that the case involved an interpretation of the Government of India Act, 1935, or an Order-in-Council. Appeals from the States were also subject to the approval of the Ruler of the State and to its terms of the Instrument of Succession. No appellate jurisdiction was given to the Federal Court in civil and criminal cases. But a provision was made that the Federal Legislature could confer an appellate jurisdiction on the Court, in the evil cases in the High Court, which involved an amount of not less than Rs. 50,000. Passing an Act with the previous sanction of the Governor-General, could do this.

The Governor-General could also seek an advice of the Court on any point of law. The advice was tendered in an open court, and the procedure followed in such matters was like the one followed in original suits. Lawyers from the parties' concerned were to appear before the Court and only then was the advice tendered. It was not obligatory for the Governor-General to accept the advice so tendered, though it would not always be easy for him to reject it.

In all matters, the court sat as a bench and took its decisions by a majority vote; the dissenting judges, if any, being permitted to give their dissenting judgement. The Court was to sit in Delhi and carry its proceedings in English.

Besides its judicial business, the court was also to prescribe rules and procedure which it was to follow in its business, and which the lower courts were to follow in the British India as well as in the Federated States. Besides, a judge of the Federal Court could also be entrusted by the Governor-General with some extra work to be done by him in his individual capacity.

The Federal Court of India was not, however, the final court of judgement in this country. An appeal could be carried to the Privy Council even without leave from it, in cases which involved (1) disputes with regard to the extent of the Federal authority on the subjects ceded to it by a State in its Instrument of Accession; (2) disputes with regard to the application of Federal law in a federated State; and (3) interpretation of the Act or of an Order-in-Council where judgement was given in the original jurisdiction. In all other cases, leave of the Court was necessary.

It was on 1 April 1937, that the Act was put into effect in the Provinces, and it was from December 1937 that the Federal Court started functioning. But since no Indian State federated with the British India and since the federation was never set up in the country at all, the number of judges appointed, besides the Chief justice, was only two, and with this minimum the Court continued working.

The judges of the Federal Court thus constituted, owed their appointment to the Secretary of the State for India, a foreign authority, and under these circumstances, as K.T. Shah observes, it was quite possible that they should "quite unconsciously perhaps lean in favour of the class or power that gives them place, and their importance in the scheme of life."[5] Another defect in the scheme was that the appellate jurisdiction of the Privy Council in India was kept intact, and the final juridical authority was not vested in the Federal Court, as it is required in a Federal Constitution.

Yet, it may be said, the institution of this Court with powers that were given to it, indeed was a turning point in the history of our judicial development. Sir Maurice Gwyer, the first Chief Justice of India, remarked while inaugurating the Court. "Independent of Governments and the Parties, the Court's primary duty is to interpret the Constitution. It would be its endeavour to look at the Constitution, not with the cold eyes of an anatomist, but as a living and breathing organism, which contains within itself, as all life must, the seeds of future growth and development. Its canons of interpretation would not hamper the free evolution of those constitutional charges for which the law provided no sanction, but in which the political genius of a people can find its most fruitful expression."

With the introduction of the Federal Court the inter-provincial disputes began to be considered on the national basis, and this in no insignificant measure helped in consolidating the nationalistic tendencies in the country.

Moreover, guided and presided over by an eminent authority of high moral character, it established a firm tradition of the highest judicial authority working independently of the highest executive authority in this country. By declaring the "Defence of India Rules" as *ultra vires,* the Court effectively exhibited during the Second World War what an independent judicial authority could do to protect the liberties dear to a people. There were several other instances of this type in which the ruthless executive authority was sought to be based on rationalism and logic, and not in few the Court succeeded thereby creating an excellent record of impartial and efficient working.

The Court continued to work till 1950, when it was transformed into Supreme Court of India.

The Federal Railway Authority. This was another federal body, which was to consist of 7 members three of whom were to be nominated by the Governor-General in his discretion, and the remaining four to be appointed by him on the advice of the Ministers. Its president was to be nominated by the Governor-General from among the 7 members, and their salaries determined by him in his individual judgement. The members selected for appointment were to be well versed in matters of industry, commerce and trade.

The Railway Authority thus constituted, was not included in the list of the reserved subjects to be controlled by the Governor-General in his discretion. Nor was it placed under the control of the Federal Ministers, except for matters connected with the safety of passengers and the welfare of the employees, for which again previous sanction of the Governor-General was needed to interfere. The Federal Legislature too was given no power in the matter. The authority was to be a corporate body capable of suing and being sued.

The body was to control and administer the State railways and the railways by the private companies. It could also enter into contracts with private persons in connection with certain matters auxiliary to the railways, such as workshops, forests, iron mines, etc. It could lay down the details of its own procedure and rules for its conduct. Generally, however, it was to take its decisions by a majority vote; the President enjoying a casting vote in case of a tie. A representative of the Governor-General could participate in its proceedings and discussions, but enjoyed no right to vote.

In the institution of this body, the distrust of the Indians was thus more clearly exhibited. It was to deal with a vital matter in the life of the nation such as the means of communications, but it was placed entirely outside the popular control. The purpose was to protect the vested British interests in this country and to secure the foreign bond-holders from the interference of the Indian leaders. But luckily, the railway authority envisaged by the Act never came into existence nor did India try to follow this provision after her independence.

Reserve Bank of India. Although finance was transferred to the control of a popular Minister, yet the Governor-General was given a special responsibility to see that the financial stability and credit of the Federal Government were maintained; and financial stability and credit of a government are intimately linked with currency and exchange, for the control of the latter and the allied matters the creation of a Reserve Bank was provided for.

The Bank was to be managed by a Board of 15 Directors, besides the Governor-General. Eight of the Directors were to be elected by the shareholders, the remaining to be nominated by the Governor-General who was also to enjoy full powers in his discretion to fix their term of office, salaries, etc. He could also supersede the Board and liquidate the Bank. No bill dealing with coinage, currency and the Bank could be introduced in the Federal Legislature, except with the Governor-General's prior consent, which would be given in his discretion. The Bank came into existence in 1935.

Financial Adviser and Advocate-General. Besides, the Act provide for the appointment by the Governor-General acting in his individual judgement, of these two officers. Their salary was to be fixed by the same authority during whose pleasure they were to hold their offices. The function of the Financial Adviser was to advise the Governor-General and the Federal Legislature in financial matters, while that of the Advocate-General was to advise them in legal matters and perform such functions as assigned by the Governor-General. The Advocate-General could also address any of the Federal legislative chambers, though he had no authority to participate in the general political life of the country.

STATES AND THE FEDERAL GOVERNMENT

As already stated, while it was made compulsory for the provinces to join the Federation, the States were declared independent sovereign units to join the Federation in their free option. If the ruler of a State desired to join the Federation, he had to sign an Instrument of Accession, mentioning clearly therein the subjects the control of which he was prepared to cede to the Federal Government. The States joining the Federation were to have 104 seats out of the total number of 260 in the Council of States, and 125 out of the total number of 375 seats in the Federal Assembly. The State representatives in the Central Legislature were to be nominated by the respective rulers themselves. The position of the States in the Federation was made strong, for it was laid down that the Federal constitution could be amended by the British Parliament alone, but that no fundamental amendment could be introduced except with the unanimous consent of the acceding States.

Relations between the Centre and States

It may here be repeated, the States being created as independent sovereign units, the Governor-General had to deal with them in two capacities–firstly, as the Governor-General of India in which position he had an authority to deal with a State with regard to the matters the control of which had been ceded in the Instrument of Accession; and secondly, as the representative of the Crown, in which position he had to deal with the sovereignty as divided between the Indian States and the Paramount Power. But, it may be said, as S.M. Bose observes: "Although the division of sovereignty between Indian States and the Paramount Power gives to their mutual relations a 'quasi-international' character, the States do not retain an amount of independent sovereignty which brings them within the definition of 'persons' in international law."[6]

The States, in fact, enjoyed a qualified sovereignty. They had thus to honour an international agreement entered into with a foreign power by the Government of India. Internally, the Crown had an exclusive jurisdiction over a European British subject in every State. So was it in the case of certain territories like the railway lands and cantonments. In cases like a ruler's minority, the Paramount Power could assume the entire jurisdiction temporarily. The Crown had full responsibility against external and internal aggression, for which the Indian troops in a State had to be maintained by the ruler. The Crown could also interfere with the internal administration of a State. The decision regarding procedure and salutes due to a ruler also rested with the Crown. And in all these matters, whether the States joined the Federation or not, the Governor-General could exercise a due authority in all of them as the representative of the Crown.

With those States, which joined the Federation, however, the Governor-General together with the other Central institutions of the Federal Government of which he was the head, had certain additional responsibilities to fulfil. In the legislative field thus, the jurisdiction of the Central Legislature in a State was to extend to those matters the control of which had been ceded by it in its Instrument of Accession. And in the executive field, the Federal authority was to extend to those matters with regard to which the Central Legislature had the powers to legislate, provided that a ruler had not reserved to himself in the Instrument of Accession a part or whole of the executive power with regard to a matter the legislative power on which had been handed over to the Centre. In so far as the Central executive authority was accepted in the Instrument of Accession, the ruler concerned would help and not hinder in the exercise of that power. In case he failed, the Governor-General could issue him the required instructions. But in the event of his disobeying even those instructions, the Governor-General had to appeal to Paramount Power, the Crown, he himself having no further powers to deal with the matter.

In the judicial field appeals could be taken from the High Court of a federated State to the Federal Court. This could, however, be done only within the sphere agreed to in the Instrument of Accession, and the decision of the Federal Court had to be communicated only through the ruler. The Federal Court having no direct relation with the State High Courts, its decisions were only in the form of recommendations to a ruler.

A Review: The position given to the States in the Federation was obviously such as would prove only reactionary against any democratic development in the country. The form of accession to the Federation was entirely for a ruler to decide. The people of a State had no voice in it. The State representatives in the Federal Legislature were to be nominated by the rulers, but they were to sit with those elected directly or indirectly by the people in the British India, and enjoy equal powers with them. In the Federal Assembly, the States had a solid bloc of one-third votes, which aided by the communal and vested interests in the House was bound to support the British authority and strangle every popular and progressive movement.

The Federal scheme guaranteed many more advantages to the States if they joined. Their internal sovereignty was secured and the Central jurisdiction was limited only within such sphere as was agreed to in the Instrument of Accession. For ten years after the inauguration of the Federation, the States were to have an exemption from direct taxation. The Federal Court enjoyed its jurisdiction in a State only through its ruler, and the administration of the Federal laws in the States was entrusted entirely to the care of the rulers themselves. The Governor-General had to protect the rights and dignity of the Princes. The Paramountcy rights hitherto exercised by the Governor-General-in-Council were now vested in the Crown. The Governor-General was now to exercise these in his discretion, "in so far as they came within the Instrument of Accession; the rights outside the Instrument will be exercised by His Majesty's representative." The external and internal defence of the States was fully guaranteed by keeping the Defence Department directly under the Governor-General.

The position of the States was distinctly better than before. Thus, while the State representatives in the Federal Legislature had every opportunity to exert their influence in the purely British Indian matters, the provincial representatives had no such opportunity with regard to State matters. The States were given voice in the determination of tariff, and the tributes paid by them were to be gradually remitted. The rulers and the subjects of the federated States were eligible for any civil office in the British India, and these offices could even be given to the unfederated States if the Governor-General so desired. The disputes between States and the Central Government, between the States and the Provinces and between the States themselves, hitherto decided by the Governor-General-in-Council, were now to be judicially decided by the Federal Court, from which an appeal could be carried to the Privy Council. The federated States were also given the right to avail themselves of the services of the High Commissioner for India.

The best and the most reactionary power given to the federated States, however, was that any one of them could block a further development of the Constitution, thereby postponing the complete independence of India for an indefinite time. For it was laid down that no important amendment could be introduced in the Constitution except with the unanimous consent of all the federated States. It was lucky the contemplated Federation never came into being.

A General Appraisal of the Federal Scheme

There are three characteristic features of a Federal Government i.e. (1) written constitution, (2) division of powers between the Centre and the units, and (3) the provision of a supreme judicial authority which should decide disputes between the units and the Centre and between the units themselves. All these features were provided for in the Federal scheme envisaged by the Act. Yet, however, the scheme lacked the essence of a true Federation, missing completely almost everything that was necessary.

The essence of a true Federation lies in the fact that (1) the units constituting it must be uniformly independent in their individual existence and they should come together of their free will to form the constitution, and (2) both, the Centre and the units, should be completely independent of each other in their respective spheres, the Federal Government having only coordinate powers with its components.

Now judging the Federal scheme of 1935 under this standard, we discover in it certain features, which were aptly described by Sir Abdul Rahim, President of the Federal Assembly, as "wholly unnatural, artificial and unknown to any constitution." First, thus, the units coming together were not similar in their political character and traditions. Despotic rulers who were extremely jealous of permitting any political rights to their people, controlled the Indian States; while the Provinces coming together to form the Federation enjoyed certain democratic rights and their people were of progressive character. Equality and homogeneity of the component units are a necessary basis in a true federation, but both these features were lamentably lacking in the scheme.

Nor were the units coming together independent in their individual existence. A true federation presents a process of unification, but here a strange phenomenon was exhibited when the existing unitary system was broken up into units and they were arbitrarily considered as independent in their individual existence. But no right was given to them to frame their own constitution, nor were they permitted a sufficient power to amend the constitution. And after making them into so-called independent units, the union established among them was not voluntary, but compulsory. There existed no free will of the Provinces; they are simply huddled together to form the Federation.

Nor were the Provinces left with an independent power in their respective spheres. The special powers of the Governor-General and the Governors made a mockery of their autonomy. The three lists, Federal, Provincial, and Concurrent were drawn up to divide the legislative powers between the Centre and the Provinces, but the residuary powers were left with the Centre which could legislate even over the Provincial list in the event of two or more Provinces requesting for the purpose. The resources assigned to the Provinces were not expensive, and they were not bound to crack before their expanding requirements. But the financial position of the Centre on the other hand was made strong, and its resources were wider than the tax jurisdiction given to it.

The consideration given to the states on the other hand was unproportionately great. The States were given full freedom whether to join the Federation or not; and in the event of joining, what subjects to surrender to the Federal control. In their representation to the Central legislature also, with their one-fourth of the total British Indian population they were granted 33 ½ % seats in the Lower House and 40% in the Upper. Their representatives were to be nominated by their rulers, but they were to enjoy equal rights with the elected members from the British India. It was no wonder that even the Muslim League saw in it "a clear attempt to buttress feudal elements to hold in leash progressive and nationalist forces." According to Jawaharlal Nehru: "Till recent years little was heard of the treaties of States or paramountcy. The rulers knew their proper place...But the growth of the national movement in India gave them a fictitious importance, for the British Government began to rely upon them."

But with regard to the States too, no uniformity was maintained, for each one of them was to decide for itself regarding the subjects it was to surrender to the Federal control, and hence the accession differed with regard to important matters.

Nor was the scheme fortunate in respect of the anomalous dualism that was created in the Federal authority. The British Crown controlled one part of the Federation, while the Indian Legislature controlled another part of it. Such a Federal structure was never heard of. And then, considering the enormous powers and special responsibilities of the Governor-General, in a strictly technical sense the very term 'federation' was a misnomer. If at all the structure envisaged was federal, the Governor-General's power made it unitary in spirit. Indirect elections to the Lower House and direct elections to the Upper, which was a highly aristocratic body, was also hardy in keeping with the federal spirit. Nor could one appreciate a chain of safeguards, which disfigured the whole scheme. The Federal Legislature was not completely free even in the functions assigned to it. "The Governor-General's powers as to the budget and the estimates, his powers to the interference in legislation, his extraordinary powers and special responsibilities," observed Mr Jinnah, "left nothing for the Legislature to do." Eighty per cent of the expenditure was beyond its control, and on the remaining 20 per cent too the Governor-General could restore the cuts imposed by it.

Yet greater sham was the not-very-enviable position given to the Ministers. Defence and Foreign affairs were kept entirely outside their purview. The State Railways were excluded from their concern. They were henchmen of the Governor-General; and though members of the Federal Legislature, they were not fully responsible to it.

The Constitution, with its 321 sections and ten schedules as outlined in the Act of 1935, was perhaps the longest and the most complex in the world. Some of the problems dealt with were hardly constitutional at all. And the yet greater snag in it was that the Federal Legislature in any important respect could not amend it. The amending powers lay only with the British Parliament, and even that could not amend it in certain respects unless the federating States unanimously agreed to it. In other words, ruler of a single State, howsoever small, could hold up the progress of the whole of the country in this way, and even the Paramount power made helpless before him. In a true federation, even the autonomous constituents of it are free to amend their respective constitutions without violating the federal principles. But no such power was given to the Provinces.

It could not, therefore, be denied that the federation was largely evoked by the desire to evade the issue of granting a responsible Government to India. The Muslim League resolution of 11-12 April 1936 said: "All India Federal Scheme of the Central Government…is most reactionary, retrograde, injurious and fatal to the vital interests of British India vis-à-vis the Indian States." "The Provincial scheme of the constitution," the resolution continued," be utilized for what it is worth in spite of the most objectionable features in it." The Congress Working Committee resolution of February 1937 also said: "The Congress had entered the Legislature not to cooperate with the new constitution of the Government but to combat the Act and the policy underlying it."[7]

PROVINCIAL AUTONOMY

Apart from the Indian States, there were three types of territorial units in India as defined by the Government of India Act, 1935. The first was the Chief Commissioner's Provinces such as Delhi and Ajmer-Marwara, in which the Chief Executive authority was the Chief Commissioner who was appointed by and responsible to the Governor-General-in-Council. The second type was the provinces, the total number of which, after separating Burma from India and after the creation of the two new Provinces of Orissa and Sind, was eleven. Within certain provinces then, there were certain territories termed as Excluded and partially Excluded areas. These areas constituted the third type of territories, and they being considered backward, not fit for a responsible government, were excluded from the control of the popular Ministers and placed in the hands of the respective Governors. But with the exclusion of these areas, in the eleven provinces as mentioned above, the provincial autonomy was said to have been introduced. It would be desirable to study here the machinery of the provincial autonomy in some details, so as to judge for ourseleves as to the type of the provincial autonomy that the Act introduced.

A true provincial autonomy, as it is generally understood, is a type of Government which is free from external control and dominance and which is internally responsible to a popularly elected legislature. Application of this two-fold test may show us clearly whether the Provincial autonomy was a true autonomy or a mere farce.

External Control

The sort of freedom the provinces enjoyed from an external control, may better be judged from the executive, legislative and the financial relations that the Act envisaged between the Centre and the Provinces.

The Executive Relations. So far as the executive relations between the Centre and the Provinces were concerned, the Act of 1935 was a distinct improvement on that of 1919 with regard to the Provincial interests. Under the old system, all the executive power that the Provinces enjoyed was understood to have been delegated to them by the Government of India, which could interfere in the Provincial administration to any extent, though in practice this was rarely done, at least in the departments transferred to the popular Ministers. The Act of 1935, however, introduced a major change in this respect. With one stroke it sought to break the old unitary system in which power devolved from the Centre to the provinces; and replaced it with a federal structure in which autonomous units come together of their free will to form a federation. The old provinces which were mere agents of the Central Government, were now for the first time converted into individual units enjoying separate legal authority. But after doing this the Act showed no patience, and instead of waiting to see whether the provinces did join in'a Federation of their free will, the Federation was imposed upon them. So far, however, it was not much awkward, for the provincial executive authority was fully established on all those matters on which the provincial legislatures were competent to legislate. The real trouble came when certain precautionary restrictions were imposed on the Provinces, which ultimately converted the Provincial autonomy into a sham.

The Act thus provided that the provincial executive authority would be so exercised as not to violate a Central law applicable to the Province; nor was it to be so exercised as to impede the process of the Central executive authority; Governor-General would have the powers to direct a Governor to discharge such duties as his agent as he may desire to assign him; the Governor-General could also direct a Governor as to the manner in which executive authority was to be exercised so as to prevent any grave threat to the peace and tranquility of India or a part thereof; a Governor when acting in his individual judgement or in his discretion was to abide strictly by the instructions of the Governor-General or the Central Legislature could, by the consent of a Governor, impose duties and confer powers on the provincial government or its officers with regard to the Central subjects, in which case, however, all the cost would be borne by the Centre; in the event of a provincial government refusing to carry out the directions given by the Federal Government, the Governor-General could in his discretion issue orders to the Governor in this connection, which would have to be carried out even in opposition to the popular Ministers; and an Inter-Provincial Council could be recommended by the Governor-General to the Home authorities to deal with the disputes and matters of common interest of some or all the provinces, or the Federation. Such, thus, were the restrictions imposed on the provinces, but still they were told to have been given the provincial autonomy.

Legislative Relations: Nor were the provisions better with regard to the legislative relations between the Centre and the provinces. Three lists of subjects were provided for, i.e., the Federal List on which the Federal Legislature had the full powers to legislate as it desired; the Provincial List on which the provinces were empowered to legislate; and the Concurrent List on which both the Centre and the provinces were competent to enact laws. The lists were sought to be drawn so exhaustively that the residue would be negligible. The residuary powers were assigned neither to Centre nor to the provinces.

It was then provided that in the event of a conflict between the Central and a Provincial law with regard to a subject in the Concurrent List, the Central Law was to prevail. There was nothing wrong in this provision. But this did not leave the provinces entirely unwatched by the jealous Central eyes in their Provincial List. For here in many of the subjects it was made obligatory that the assent of the Governor-General be secured before a bill could be introduced in the provincial legislature. And further, whereas in a true provincial autonomy, in the event of doubt whether a particular subject belongs to Centre or to the provinces, it is the Federal Court which decides the matter here these powers which were essentially judicial by nature, were assigned to the Governor-General. Further, it was also provided for, that in case of a grave emergency the Federal Legislature would have the complete authority to legislate on any subject of the Provincial List.

Financial Relations: The Act of 1935 introduced certain radical changes in the financial position as laid down in the Montford Reforms of 1919, and conferred in a large measure a financial autonomy on the provinces. Under the old system, the provinces had no free powers to impose taxes or to raise loans on the security of their revenues. The sources of revenue now were divided as follows: (1) There were certain taxes, including land revenue, excise duties, etc., which were to be levied and collected by the provinces. (2) Certain taxes including currency and coinage, import and export, etc., were to be levied and retained by the Centre. (3) Certain of them, including those on salt, non-agricultural income, etc., were to be divided between the Centre and the provinces. (4) Certain taxes, including terminal taxes on goods or passengers carried by rail or air and duties with regard to the property other than agricultural land, were to be levied and collected by the Centre, but assigned to the provinces. The provinces were authorized to borrow on the security of their revenue. And for the maintenance of the financial stability and credit of India both at home and abroad, the necessity for the establishment of a non-political authority like the Reserve Bank of India was recognized. The Reserve Bank of India Act was thus passed by the Federal Legislature, whereby the Bank was established, the constitution, etc. of which has already been discussed.

Thus, the financial powers given to the provinces were far-reaching. Yet, the system introduced was not entirely satisfactory. Certain restrictions in respect of borrowing continued on the provinces, and the sources of revenue assigned to the provinces were neither sufficient to meet their requirements, nor were they sufficiently expansive so as to help the provincial developments. The latter defect was realised from the outset, when a provision was made in the Act for the payment of subventions or grants-in-aid from the federal revenues to the deficit provinces. Later on the Niemeyer Award laid down the rates at which this aid was to be given.

Internal Responsibility

The sort of Government supposed to be internally responsible to the Provincial Legislature and best be comprehended by studying the executive and the legislative machinery introduced by the Act in the Provinces.

Executive Machinery: The old dyarchical form of Government introduced in the provinces by the Act of 1919 was abolished, and in its place the Act of 1935 sought to introduce a full provincial autonomy. Whereas previously the Centre delegated the executive powers to them enjoyed by the provinces, now the provinces as well as the Centre drew their powers from the Constitution and in their respective sphere the former were no more subordinate to the latter. The provincial executive authority, as drawn from the constitution, extended to all those subjects on which the Provincial legislatures had powers to legislate. This power was vested in the Governors, who could exercise it either directly or through a council of popular Ministers.

The Governor: Governor was the Chief Executive authority of a province, who in the case of Bengal, Bombay, and Madras was to be a public man of repute and appointed by the Crown on the advice of the Secretary of State for India. The Governors of the other provinces were to come from the Civil Services of India, and appointed on the advice of the Governor-General. The usual term of office of a Governor was five years, while his total emoluments varied in different Provinces. Thus while the Governor of a Presidency drew an annual salary of Rs. 1,20,000, that of Orissa drew Rs. 66,000 while that of the Punjab Rs. 1,00,.000. The annual allowances of the Governor of Bengal besides his salary amounted to Rs. 6,07,300, while that of the Punjab Rs. 1,41,200. No provincial legislature could alter the salary of a Governor.

Executive Powers: The powers of a Governor were wide and vast and extended to all the different spheres of provincial activities. The executive powers of a Governor consisted of three different categories, i.e. those exercised in his discretion, without consulting the Ministers; those exercised in his individual judgement, where the Ministers were to be consulted but their advice not necessarily to be followed; and those exercised on the advice of the Ministers.

The discretionary powers of a Governor with regard to which he was to work under the control of the Governor-General, could roughly be divided into 32 types, the more important of which were as follows: (1) At the outset, it was the Governor himself who was to decide in his discretion whether a particular matter came under his discretionary powers or not. (2) He was to appoint, summon and dismiss the Ministers and determine their salaries till the provincial legislature fixed them. (3) He was to preside over the cabinet meetings; (4) was to make rules for the convenient transaction of the executive business and (5) was to check crimes aimed at overthrowing the Government. (6) He was to summon or prorogue the legislature and could dissolve the lower House. (7) He could stop discussion on a bill or a clause thereof; (8) was to decide whether an item of expenditure was votable or non-votable; (9) could summon the two Houses, in case of a bicameral legislatures, to a joint sitting and (10) could qualify in certain respects a person disqualified from contesting election to the legislature; (11) Chairman and the members of the Public Service Commission of the Province were to be appointed by him. (12) And an extraordinary discretionary power that of passing Governor's Acts, besides those of issuing ordinances and making regulations with respect to the administration of the excluded and the partially excluded areas etc., a detailed reference to which follows.

The worst, however, was the Section 93 of the Act, which defined his discretionary powers in the event of a breakdown of the Constitution. If the Governor was satisfied that a situation had arised in which the provincial government could not be carried on as according to the provision of the Act, he could assume to himself all or any of the powers exercisable by any provincial body except those exercised by the Provincial High Court. A proclamation issued in this respect had to be communicated to the Secretary of State for India, who was to lay it before both the Houses of Parliament. The proclamation was to remain in force for six months, but could be extended by the Parliament for a period of twelve months from the date on which it should have expired. In no case, however, could it remain in force for more than three years; though later an amendment introduced into this provision by the Parliament allowed the proclamation to continue in force till after the war. The proclamation was to be issued with the concurrence of the Governor-General, and it could be revoked or varied by a subsequent proclamation. Any Act passed by the Governor during the period of a proclamation, was to have force till the end of two years after the expiry of the proclamation.

Section 52 of the Act defined the special responsibilities of the Governor in connection with which he was to exercise the powers in his individual judgement. These special responsibilities were:

(1) safeguarding of the legitimate interest of the minorities;

(2) protection of the civil servants from inequitable treatment;

(3) prevention of any grave menace to the peace and tranquillity of the province or a part thereof;

(4) protection of the British subjects against any discrimination;

(5) safeguarding of the rights and dignity of a ruler and prevention of the measures which discriminate and interfere with the rights of the neighbouring State;

(6) securing of peace and good government in the excluded and the partially excluded areas;

(7) securing the execution of the orders of the Governor-General given to him in his discretion; and

(8) keeping the Governor-General informed with regard to the conduct of irrigation in the Province: this being a subject of special interest to the Secretary of State as laid down in the Act.

(9) Besides, the Governor of the Central Provinces and Berar had certain special responsibilities with regard to Berar and Hyderabad.

In order to enable the Governor-General to see that none of his special responsibilities was overlooked, the Minister and the Secretary in charge of a Department were required in the Act to keep him informed of the relevant matter.

A special reference may here be made to his responsibility No. (2) above. The civil services were placed completely under the control of the Governor who determined their transfers, promotions, leave, punishment, etc. The appointment, dismissal, etc., and the salaries and allowances of his own secretarial staff were also determined by him. And the entire expenditure charged on the above was exempted from the vote in the legislature.

The rest of the powers were to be exercised by the Governor on the advice of the Ministers. But the Ministers themselves being appointed and dismissed by him, here too, the exercise of his personal whim could go to any extent.

Legislative Powers: The legislative powers of the Governor directly as well as through his control of the provincial legislature, were as great as his executive powers. Thus he could summon or prorogue a house and could dissolve the Legislative Assembly; could address them jointly or separately; could call a joint meeting of the two Houses in the event of some differences between them; could make rules for the conduct of their business, in consultation with their respective presiding officers; could send messages to them with respect to some Bill under discussion; could stop discussion on a Bill if he was satisfied that the Bill or any clause or an amendment thereof was likely to endanger public peace and tranquility; could prohibit the discussion or questions with respect to foreign affairs or with respect to an Indian State or the conduct of the ruler or members of the ruling family thereof and his assent being necessary for a Bill to become law, he could withhold it or return the bill for reconsideration or reserve it for the significance of the pleasure of His Majesty. Introduction of Bills in the legislature on many of the subjects required his previous sanction.

Of his direct powers of legislation, the more interesting was that of passing a Governor's Act. He could send the draft of a Bill to the legislature requiring it to pass, but if the legislature failed to do so within a month, the Governor could certify the Bill to become law. Although the legislature and the Ministry were completely free from every responsibility in connection with such an Act, the Act had exactly the same force as the one passed by the legislature.

Then the Governor also had the powers to issue Ordinances, which were to be of two types, i.e., those issued when the legislature was not in session and the Ministry desired them to be issued on its own responsibility, and those issued by the Governor in his discretion or individual judgement with respect to which the Governor himself was responsible.

Financial Powers: Nor were the Governor's financial powers of a less significance. The estimates and the demands were prepared and presented in the legislature under his orders and recommendations; he determined the charges on the revenues of the Province were determinded by him, and he had the powers to pass a rejected demand and to restore a cut in it.

Instrument of Instruction: For the proper exercise his powers in discretion and individual judgement, the Governor was issued an Instrument of Instruction, which was prepared by the Secretary of State and approved by both the Houses of Parliament. Any subsequent change in the Instrument also required a similar approval of the two Houses. The instructions in the Instrument, however, had no legal force, and if a Governor contravened any one of them, he was not answerable for it in a court of law. The main purpose of the Instrument was to enable the development of certain healthy constitutional conventions.

Although the Act empowered the Governor to appoint or dismiss the Ministers in his discretion, the Instrument advised him to appoint them in consultation with the person who commanded a stable majority in the legislature. Representation of the important minority communities in the Ministry was advisable, and so was the fostering of joint responsibility among the Ministers. He was also advised to see that the Ministers collectively commanded the confidence of the Lower House.

The Council of Ministers: To assist and advise the Governor, a Council of Ministers was provided for by the Act. The Governor from among the members of the Provincial legislature appointed the Ministers and they held their office during his pleasure. He could also preside over their meetings in his discretion. The Ministers were not, however, under an exclusive control of the Governor, unconcerned with aspirations of the legislature. For it was provided that the legislature could remove them by passing a vote of no confidence, though it could not increase their salaries during the term of their office. Besides, the Instrument of Instructions also advised the Governor to appoint the Ministers only in consultation with the person who was likely to command a stable majority in the Legislature. He was also advised to encourage a collective responsibility among them. It was, however, a misplaced advice to the Governor to see that the representatives of important communities were included in the Ministry as far as possible. For in many ways it ran counter to the spirit of joint responsibility.

The Act laid down no definite limit with regard to the total number of Ministers in a province. The number varied from Province to Province, the maximum in actual practice being 12 in Bengal and the minimum 3 in Orissa. There was no provision for a Parliamentary Secretary, yet in most of the Provinces they were appointed from among the members of the majority party to assist the Ministers in the parliamentary and administrative problems and to prepare a reserve of trained persons to hold the office of Ministers in the future. The Congress fixed the salary of a Parliamentary Secretary at Rs. 250 per month in the Provinces where it formed ministries.

An Appraisal: Thus, as it is clear, if the provincial autonomy was a mere farce with respect to the external control, it was much more so internally with regard to the executive machinery. In theory the British Parliament and the Secretary of State were said to have been relieved of all controlling authority in the provinces, but in practice, Lord Zetland the Secretary of State admitted in 1937: "The Parliament of this country reserve to itself a potential measure of control in a certain limited and clearly defined sphere–the special responsibilities of the Governors." The Governor's powers in discretion and individual judgement were under the control of the Governor-General who himself in turn being controlled by the Secretary of State, the latter's powers of interference in the provinces could hardly be overestimated.

In the provinces, the Governor sat as a powerful autocrat with his powers so wide and vast that they could cover effectively any department of provincial activities he desired. His powers of appointment and dismissal of Ministers and distribution of portfolios among them were no doubt a misfit in a provincial autonomy, but his powers to preside over the cabinet meetings struck at the very root of it. In the Instrument of Instructions certain healthy provisions were made, but the advice to him to see that the important communities got a representation in the Cabinet, was unfortunate. It was good that he was advised to encourage collective responsibility. But that was not sufficient. Collective responsibility should have been made a legal obligation as in a true provincial autonomy it should be. It was good that the salaries of the Ministers were to be fixed by a legislative action, but the provision that the legislature could not alter the salaries during the Minister's term of office, was hardly conducive to the development of a responsible Government.

Some of the Governor's powers such as that of safeguarding the legitimate interests of the minorities and that of the prevention of any menace to the peace and tranquility of the Province, were so vaguely worded and so mischievously provided for, that they acted as a smoke-screen behind which the Governor could sit always ready to swoop and snatch away any measure of responsible Government that the Act permitted. The Laws and Order was transferred to the control of a popular Minister, but the reservation with the Governor of the power of prevention of grave menace to peace made this transfer a simple hoax. Nor could the transfer of Law and Order mean much when the police was sought to be removed from an effective control of the Minister. For the Sections 56, 57 and 58 made it compulsory that no Police Role or Act could be repealed or amended except with the previous consent of the Governor.

Nor was his responsibility towards the civil services a happy provision. When the civil officers were not under an effective control of the Ministers, when these officers had direct approach to the Governor to inject him with the venom of doubt in the efficiency and capability of the Ministers, one can imagine what sort of responsible Government it would have been.

The Governor's powers to control legislation and the legislature, his power to make Governor's Acts, and his financial powers whereby he could decide the votable and the non-votable items, pass a rejected demand or restore a cut imposed by the legislature; they all were misfit in a responsible Government. But the worst in this respect was the Section 93, which empowered him to assume to himself all, or any of the administrative powers by declaring the Constitution to have broken down. In the light of these facts, it would not be an exaggeration to say that the provincial autonomy was nothing but the autonomy of the Governor, whose very dignity being shrouded in traditions; his direct influence on the administration could not be overestimated.

The Instrument of Instructions to be Governor was well aimed at. Such a document had been extensively used in the Dominions to grant them a practical autonomy. But this, in case of the Dominions, had been possible only because there an amendment in the document did not necessitate an approval by the Parliament. In the case of India however, the Parliament distrusted even the Home Government, lest it should facilitate the development of a responsible Government in the provinces. For, an amendment in the document necessarily required a definite approval of the Parliament.

Provincial Legislature: The Act provided for a legislature in every province, which in the cases of Assam, Bengal, Bihar, the United Provinces, Bombay and Madras was to consist of His Majesty, represented by the Governor, and of the two Chambers, i.e. the Legislative Council and the Legislative Assembly. In the other provinces, it was to consist of the Governor as above, and of only one Chamber i.e., the Legislative Assembly.

Legislative Council or the Second Chamber: The introduction of the Second Chamber was much resented by the Indians who argued that it would necessarily be dominated by the members who represented only vested, conservative and reactionary interests which would impede the progressive legislation in the country. Moreover, they argued the necessary safeguards against hasty action by the legislature were already provided in the Governor's powers in discretion and individual judgement, and the Second Chamber would serve no additional purpose. Nor would it be easy to find out for this Chamber the members who should be qualified to act as elder statesmen.

It was due to these reasons, perhaps, that Montagu and Chelmsford had rejected the system of bicameral legislature in 1919. But the Act of 1935 rediscovered certain merits in it and introduced in some provinces, as mentioned above. The arguments in its defence were: it would secure the services of some who otherwise would not care to contest for its membership; the representation of some vested interests, such as landlords and the other capitalist interests was necessary; the safeguards in the shape of the Governor's special powers could not be so effective in the normal times as the Second Chamber would be, and it would secure an expert mature knowledge which would be a counterpoise to the over-enthusiastic national progress.

These arguments did not appeal to the Indians at that time, but astonishingly enough the bicameralism has been retained in some provinces in the free India for the reasons perhaps that now better qualified persons are available to serve the purpose of the Second Chambers; the experience of the aristocrats, capitalists, etc. should not be let go waste entirely; and the Second Chambers should be retained till the experience definitely proves their futility. Now these chambers are being abolished in one Province after another.

Composition and Rights: The Legislative Councils of the different Provinces varied in size. Thus, while in Bengal the membership of the Council was to be between 63 and 65, in Bombay it was to be between 29 and 30, in Madras between 54 and 56, in Assam 21 and 22, in Bihar 29 and 30 and in the United Provinces between 58 and 60. The Act provided for some of the seats in the Councils to be filled up by the Governors by nomination. In Bengal, for instance, the Governor was to nominate between 8 and 10 members to the

Council. The remaining members however, were all to be directly elected, except in the case of the Councils of Bengal and Bihar where about two-fifths of the members of the Council were to be elected by the members of their respective Legislative Assemblies in accordance with principles of proportional representation by means of a single transferable vote. The council was a permanent body, one-third of its members retiring every third year.

The strength of the Legislative Assembly also varies from province to province. Thus the total membership of the Assembly of Bengal was 250, of Bombay 175, Madras 215, Assam, 108, Bihar 152, United Provinces 288, Central Provinces and Berar 112, Punjab 175, Sind and Orissa 60 each and of the North-West Frontier Provinces it was 50. The official blocs in the Assemblies were completely done away with and all their seats were now to be filled by direct elections. The life of the Assembly was to be five years, unless dissolved earlier by the Governor.

The evil of communal representation in both the houses was rather further extended under the recommendations of the notorious Communal Award of Ramsay MacDonald, given in 1932. Under this award, the separate representations were given to as many as 17 different communities and sections, i.e. (1) the General seats for mainly the Hindus, but including also some of the communities like Parsis which got no separate representation; (2) the General seats reserved for the scheduled castes, as under the Poona Pact already referred to (scheme of the Poona Pact was the only modification introduced in the communal award); (3) Muslims; (4) Sikhs (in Punjab and NWFP); (5) Europeans; (6) Indian Christians; (7) Anglo-Indians; (8) Backward areas and Tribes; (9) Women (General); (10) Women (Muslim) (11) Women (Sikh); (12) Women (Indian Christians); (13) Women (Anglo-Indians); (14) Labour; (15) Landlords; (16) Commerce and Industry; and (17) Universities. Thus, a Hindu could vote only for a Hindu, Muslim only for a Muslim and so on. And this division was carried to every house where a husband could vote only for men and a wife only for women.

Each House elected its own President and Deputy President from its members, called respectively Speaker and Deputy Speaker in the case of Legislative Assembly. These presiding officers were to conduct and guide the proceedings and exercise a casting vote in case of an equal division. No person could be a member of both the Houses or of a Provincial Chamber and of a Central one at the same time. Every member had a full freedom of speech, of asking questions, etc. Salaries and allowances of the members were to be fixed by the legislature itself. A Minister had a right to address either of the Chambers, but could vote only in the one of which he was a member. Similarly the Advocate

General could also sit in either house and participate in the proceedings, but he had no right to vote. The Governor was to see that he called the session of each House before the lapse of six months from the last day of its previous session.

Franchise Qualifications: Franchise and qualifications were not defined by the Act itself. They were to be laid down in an Order-in-Council, which generally adopted in this connection the recommendations of Franchise Committee presided over by Lord Lothan. Property qualifications which was essentially the basis of franchise in the Act of 1919, was retained, but to this were added the educational qualifications and certain special qualifications which aimed at enfranchising about 10 per cent of the Scheduled Castes people and at expanding the women electorate from 315,000, to 6,000,000. Generally the franchise qualifications were high and only the privileged persons like title-holders, the Ministers, the Judges of the High Courts, the Senators of a University, the retired, pensioned and discharged members of His Majesty's regular military forces and others having certain minimum property qualifications, and educational qualifications such as being at least a matriculate, were entitled to vote or stand for elections. Again, a person must have attained the age of 21; he must have been a resident of a constituency where he votes for certain minimum period such as 180 days in Bombay and 120 days in Madras; he must be a British subject or a subject of a State and he must be a Muslim in the Muslim constituency, Sikh in the Sikh constituency and so on. In the University constituency only a senator or a graduate of seven years standing could vote.

The franchise qualifications varied in details, from province to province, those for the Council were much higher than those for the Assembly. Yet, however, there was a general extension of franchise with the result that in place of only 3 per cent who were previously entitled to vote, now as much as 14 per cent of the population of the British India acquired this right.

Legislative Powers: The powers of the provincial legislation can be discussed under three categories i.e. legislative, financial and executive. In its legislative powers, the provincial legislature could make laws on all subjects included in the Provincial and the Concurrent Lists. The Provincial List included the subject of local importance such as Local Self-Government and Public Health; while the Concurrent List included the subjects both of the Provincial and National interest such as Insurance, Unemployment and Criminal Law.

There were, however, certain limitations on the legislative powers of the provincial legislature, such for instance as that it could not legislate on matters which affected the sovereignty and suzerainty of the Crown; nor could it enact laws discriminating against the British subjects or against the British commercial interests. In case of a conflict between the Provincial and the Federal Laws on the Concurrent List, the Federal Laws were to prevail whether passed before or after the Provincial Law.

Then, the previous sanction of the Governor-General was required if the Legislature desired to make laws on a matter affecting an Act of Parliament extending to the province; an Act or Ordinance passed by the Governor-General in his discretion; the Governor-General's freedom to act in his discretion or in his individual judgement; and the procedure for criminal proceedings in which European British subjects were concerned. And the previous sanction of the Governor was necessary in matters, which affected any Act, or Ordinance passed by him in his discretion, and in those, which related to the police force.

The legislative procedure was the same as adopted in the British Parliament. Either House could originate a Bill other than the money Bill. A money Bill, however, could originate only in the Legislative Assembly. Before one House sent a Bill to the other, the Bill had to pass through three readings, and if the Second House passed the Bill in a similar manner without an amendment, or with such amendments as were acceptable to the first House, the Bill was presented to the Governor for his assent. The differences between the two Chambers could be removed in a joint sitting called by the Governor in his discretion.

After a Bill was passed by the legislature and presented to the Governor for his assent, the legislature had once again to face certain limitations on its powers. Thus, (1) if the Governor gave his assent to the Bill presented to him, the Bill became law, but in case he withheld his assent the Bill died and the labour of the legislature went waste. (2) The Governor could also return the Bill to the legislature recommending it to consider certain measures and present it to him once again. (3) He could reserve the Bill for the consideration of the Governor-General, and the latter could give his assent or withhold it or return the Bill to the legislature for reconsideration or reserve it for the approval of His Majesty. (4) If the approval of His Majesty of the Bill reserved for his consideration was publicly notified within twelve months of the presentation of the Bill to the Governor, the Bill became Act, otherwise it died. (5) Even the Acts passed with the assent of the Governor or of the Governor-General, could be disallowed by his Majesty within twelve months of such assent.

Financial Powers: Before the commencement of a financial year, the Governor could cause the Annual Financial Statement to be laid before the Chamber or Chambers. The statement had separately to show the sums required to meet the expenditure charged on the provincial revenues, and the sums required to meet other expenditure not so charged. A sum required for the discharge of the Governor's special responsibilities, if any, had to be shown separately.

The expenditure charged on the provincial revenues, consisted of the following items: (1) salaries and allowances of the Governor and the expenditure relating to his office; (2) the debt charges and the expenditure incurred in raising loans, etc; (3) salaries and allowances of the Ministers and the Advocate General; (4) salaries and allowances of the Judges of the High Court; (5) expenditure with regard to the excluded areas; (6) expenditure required to satisfy the judgement awarded or decree of a Court and (7) any other expenditure so charged by the Act. All these items, except the first, could be discussed by the legislature, but none of them was subject to its vote. The other expenditure was submitted to the Legislative Assembly in the shape of demands for grants and this was subject to vote. The Assembly could refuse a grant or reduce it, but it could not transfer it or increase it.

There were certain very serious limitations on the financial powers of the legislature: (1) the proposals for expenditure could be initiated only by the executive, no private member could do this; (2) on the sums charged on the provincial revenue, the legislature had no right to vote; the Governor's salary and allowances could not even be discussed. The exclusion of the salaries and allowances of Ministers from the legislature's vote, was hardly in accord with the true parliamentary procedure. (3) On the votable expenditure too, the Governor could restore any rejection or cut imposed by the legislature. And (4) the legislature could not, without the previous recommendation of the Governor, consider a Bill or an amendment thereto, with regard to (a) regulating the borrowing of money, (b) imposing or increasing, a tax, and (c) increasing an expenditure or charging it on the provincial revenue.

After the legislature completed its voting on the different demands, a schedule was authenticated by the Governor by his signature, specifying (1) grant passed by the legislature; (2) those refused or reduced, but restored by him for the proper discharge of his responsibilities; and (3) the expenditure charged on the provincial revenues. The schedule was now laid before the Assembly, but it could not be discussed by it. All the expenditures for the year had to be made strictly in accordance with this Schedule, for any increase of expenditure the passage under the same procedure of a supplementary statement being necessary.

Executing Powers: The Provincial Ministers were virtually appointed and removed by the Legislative Assembly, for it could pass a no-confidence vote or defeat some major piece of legislation introduced by the Ministry and thus oust it. Besides, both the Chambers could put questions and supplementary questions; pass resolutions suggesting a particular course of action; move adjournment motions to draw the Government's attention to a matter of an urgent public importance and make rules regulating their own procedure. By most of these methods it could make the life of the Ministers precarious.

Here again, however, there were certain limitations on its power. Thus, the Governor could stop the further consideration of any matter which he in his discretion felt to be affecting the discharge of his special responsibilities with regard to preventing any grave menace to the peace and tranquility of the province. The legislature could not discuss the conduct of any judge of a High or Federal Court in the discharge of his duties. The Governor could regulate its business with regard to the matters which affected his functions in discretion or in individual judgement in connection with matters as securing of timely completion of financial business, the relations with a foreign State or Prince; personal conduct of an Indian Prince or of a member of his family; tribal or excluded areas, except with regard to the estimate of expenditure. All this the Governor did in his direction after consulting the presiding officers.

An Appraisal: Thus, the provincial legislature envisaged in the Act of 1935, was much better than that under the Act of 1919. The size of the Chambers was considerably increased, the system of direct election was introduced, and the nominated non-officials were completely done away within the Assembly, though a small number of them was retained in the Council. The franchise qualifications were lowered and the members enjoyed a greater freedom in their criticism and control of the executive, and the Ministry could even be removed by a no-confidence vote of the Assembly.

Yet, much was left to be desired. The association of the King Emperor as an integral part of the legislature was an anomalous feature. The Second Chamber, a citadel of reaction, was thrust on six provinces against their desire. The Ministers were given no power to demand and force the dissolution of the Assembly. The communal and class representation was extended and some communities were given an under representation. The Muslims, thus with their 7.1 and 14.8 per cent population respectively in Madras and U.P., were given 13 and 27 per cent seats in respective legislatures. The Europeans with their population only of less than 1.35 per cent, got as many as 3 per cent seats in the provincial legislature. The franchise qualifications, though lowered, were still very high, so that as much as 73 per cent of the adult population got no right to vote. The exclusion of certain matters from the powers of legislation and the necessity of securing a previous sanction of the Governor-General and Governor for the introduction of certain classes of legislation in the provincial legislatures, together with many other limitations on the legislative, financial and executive powers of the legislature, made the provincial autonomy a mere farce. A major part of the provincial expenditure was declared non-votable, and even the expenditure that was subject to vote made only a mockery of the legislature's authority. For any cut or rejection of the demand could easily be restored by the Governor. The Governor's powers to regulate the conduct of the legislature and exclusion of the Police Department and the Superior Services from the legislature's power of control; this was all unfortunate. The greatest snag, however, was the Governor's legislative powers which lay embedded in the bottom, but which could at any time make the progress of the legislature impossible.

Thus, the system of provincial autonomy, whether considered from the viewpoint of external control or from that internal responsibility, fell far short of perfection. Though a considerable progress was made, yet the goal of complete provincial autonomy lay far ahead.

A DUAL POLICY

Willingdon followed a dual policy of repression and politico-economic reforms, as will be revealed by the following account.

Press Act of 1931

Mr Gandhi started the Second Non-Cooperation Movement in 1930 as we have already seen. This year once again brought about a great excitement and daring adventure into the Indian political life. The Indian Press did not play an inconsiderable part and to curb its freedom a new enactment was brought forth which was passed in the name of the Press Act of 1931.

This Act (i) made it necessary for the keeper of a press and publishers of newspapers to deposit a security with the Government (ii) a new declaration for a printing press was to be granted only after depositing a security of Rs. 1,000 to Rs. 10,000 as the magistrate may fix; (iii) this security could be forfeited by a state government in cases of objectionable printing; (iv) a provincial government could also forfeit certain publications and authorize the customs officers to detain packages containing them. Against the cases of such forfeiture, however, applications could be made to the High Court, which could set aside such a forfeiture. (v) The Act also laid down the penalties, which could be imposed on those who published a newspaper or kept a press without depositing a security.

The powers conferred on the provincial governments with regard to the newspapers and presses under this Act obviously were wide. Not a few printers and publishers suffered under this Act. Thus, the *Liberty* of Calcutta was called upon to deposit a security of Rs. 6,000 a good part of which was later on forfeited. Similarly the printer and publishers of the *Bombay Chronicle* had to deposit Rs. 3,000 each for having published an objectionable article written by one Mr Horniman.

Foreign Relations Act of 1932

Yet another Press legislation followed in 1932 when Willingdon's Government passed the Foreign Relations Act to punish such publications, which interfered with or affected the maintenance of good relations between His Majesty's Government and the government or the governments of the friendly foreign states. This Act was necessitated by a repeated interference of the Indian newspapers into the administrative affairs of the neighbouring states.

Indian States Protection Act, 1934

This Act was passed to prevent the newspapers from criticizing the administration of the princely states of India and to deal with the bands or organizations working on semi-military lines to spread disaffection in these states. The Act obviously was aimed at preventing the people of the states from catching up with the nationalist movement in India.

Sind: While using his diplomacy and stiffness to meet political agitation, Willingdon did not overlook the need for constitutional reforms. There had been a demand for separation of Sind from the Bombay Presidency. The Muslims at the Round Table Conference had repeated this demand, and they wanted that Sind should be set up as a full-fledged province. A Committee was appointed to devise a scheme for the purpose and constitute Sind into an independent province with its own Governor, Legislature and a Secretariat.

North-West Frontier Province: His more important reforms however lay in the North-West Frontier Province, which in 1930 had been a storm centre of the Red-shirt movement. Promises to extend the benefits of the reforms of 1919 had been made but their fulfillment had been delayed till Willingdon took up the matter. Although complete calm had not yet been restored in the Province, electoral rolls, voters lists, etc. were drawn up, elections were held and the benefits of dyarchy were extended in the midst of the doubts that people there lacked traditions of responsibility, had not yet fully come under the influence of the modern civilization and were unaccustomed to the exercise of power. A complete change in the atmosphere took place, and normal conditions were restored in a province, which was considered to be most dangerous.

Kashmir Troubles: Willingdon's Government had to face a prolonged period of upheaval in Kashmir where fall in the agricultural prices had brought about disaffection among the Mohammedan peasantry. Majority of the landlords, businessmen and merchants being Hindus, the economic grievances of the poverty-stricken Muslims soon adopted religious overtones and suddenly a holy war was proclaimed which all the generosity and large-heartedness of the Maharaja of Kashmir failed to stand. Muslims *jathas* started appearing from Punjab and the North-West Frontier Province "to fan the flames of raving incendiarism and to unchain the blood-hounds of murder; Muslim fanatics all over the country actively sympathized with the action of their co-religionists in the Hindu state; Muslim journals, the more fanatical of them, accounted in flaring headlines and with scarcely hidden joy the progress of butchery and the achievements of a fratricidal war."[8] At the request of the ruler Willingdon dispatched a strong military detachment to control the situation. There were rumours that the Government wanted to depose the Maharaja. Obviously in these circumstances a heavy loss of Muslim life would have repercussions on the Muslim politics in the country; but on the other hand if the Government did not succeed in restoring order, the Hindu suspicions would be strengthened. A direct conflict with the fanatical Muslim *jathas* had to be avoided and the British troops worked under the strictest orders to act as a moral force as far as possible. Within six months peace was restored and both the Muslim grievances and Hindu fears were allayed. The Maharaja was persuaded to inaugurate a Legislative Council based on a wide franchise and to declare an extensive amnesty.

Economic Reforms: Willingdon gave his attention to the economic reforms as well. Several practical measures were adopted to ameliorate the condition of peasants in India. A coordination of agricultural crops with the world requirements in order to help the development of foreign trade was insisted upon. An Indian delegation was sent to the Imperial Economic Conference at Ottawa to secure favourable trade terms for the Indian agricultural produce. Extensive retrenchments were made in the military budget and several other measures undertaken by Willingdon brought about a considerable improvement in trade and industry. Willingdon was able to remark with pride. "The reduction in imports may signify that India is relying more on her industrial production, and this combined with the increase in the favourable balance of payments can be interpreted as signs of strength in the intrinsic position of India...Our position remains one which compares favourably with that of any other country."

Foreign Relations: Willingdon had to face sudden difficulties on the undemarcated frontier between Burma and China where the semi-administered tribes often disturbed peace and created international complications. The Viceroy made use of the services of His Majesty's representative in China. Conversations with China were started and certain principles were evolved on the basis of which the international boundary could be demarcated. As a result of this a long-standing disagreement between Burma and China was brought to a close.

There were certain disturbances at Kashgar under the Chinese authority. There was a serious revolt and the Tongan rebels attacked His Majesty's Councillor. The property of the Indian merchants settled in the town was plundered and a large number of them started fleeing to take refuge in India. Willingdon's government immediately moved, the Chinese government tendered an apology for the neutrality of the Consulate having been violated. Measures were taken to protect the interests of the Indians in the Chinese Turkistan and thus an international complication was avoided.

In 1933 His Holiness Dalai Lama of Tibet died. His death created the possibility of an international rivalry to secure ascendancy in that country. The Regent appointed pending the reincarnation of the Dalai Lama however, turned to be as friendly towards the British as the Dalai Lama had been, and thus any possibility of a foreign influence hostile to the British getting a lodgement in Tibet was avoided.

Some difficulties arose in the Government of India's trade relations with Japan which were controlled by the Anglo-Japanese Commercial Convention of 1905. This happened when there was a sudden depreciation of the Yen resulting in India being dumped with cotton-goods at rates very much lower than even those at which raw cotton in India could be procured. The prevailing tariff duty could not protect the Indian interests with the result that the Government, besides introducing some tariff changes, took a bold step to denounce the Anglo-Japanese convention. Fresh negotiations with Japan were started which resulted into another Convention and Protocol being initialted by the two parties in April 1934. As a result of this the trade friction between India and Japan, which had become quite serious, was brought to an end. The Indian textile interests were given due protection and stable markets for the Indian raw-cotton in Japan were secured.

Frontier Troubles: Some disturbances broke out in the North-West Frontier Province where in 1933 the Upper Mohmands made a sudden attack from their semi-independent territory on Halinzai, one of the tribes loyal to the British. There was a possibility that the trouble might spread all over the frontiers. The Governor took speedy action and troops were dispatched which dispersed the hostile Lashkars.

The troubles in the Mohmand areas were, however, only a prelude to the large-scale disturbances, which soon broke out in Bajaur, further to the northeast.

Here the things were not so simple, for the villages were inaccessible and direct action was more or less impracticable. After a full consideration of the whole matter, notices were issued to certain individuals to surrender the offenders whom they had been harbouring. Offers of rewards were also made. But when this produced no effect, an air-action was authorized. There was much criticism in England that the innocent people were attacked from the air and large scale destruction of property and human lives was brought about. Lord Willingdon however explained the whole matter and assured his critics that there was only one village which in the present case had been attacked, and even there before the actual bombardment was done, due warnings had been given and the people had almost all of them vacated their houses. Consequently the losses suffered by the people were rather economic than human. Be that as it may, as a result of the severe action taken by the Government peace in the area was restored once again.

Willingdon retired from India in 1936. Immediately after his arrival in England he was raised to a Marquessate. In 1941 he led a trade delegation to South America and occupied several other important offices before he died on 12 August 1945. "His good health, good will and good nature gave him a happy life which he always enjoyed, working to the end."[9]

NOTES

1. See Punniah, *Constitutional History of India*, pp. 352. etc.
2. Nehru, *op. cit.*, p. 297.
3. Ahmed, Z.A., *Indian Federation*, p. 43.
4. Shah, K.T., *Federal Structure*, p. 223.
5. Shah, K.T., *Federal Structure*, p. 389.
6. Bose S.M., *The Working of Constitution in India, A Commentary on Govt. of India Act*, 1935, pp. 38-39.
7. See Philips, *The Evolution of India and Pakistan*, pp. 201-235; Sharma J.S., *op. cit.*, pp. 505-589.
8. Trench, Victor, *op. cit.*, p. 222.
9. Mersey, Viscount, *op. cit.*, p. 144.

6

Marquess of Linlithgow 1936-1943

PROVINCIAL AUTONOMY IN OPERATION

Victor Alexander John Hope, the eldest son of John Adrian Hope, First Marquess of Linlithgow and Seventh Earl of Hopetown was born on 24 September 1887. He was educated at Eton and in 1908 succeeded to the titles of his father. In 1911 he married Doreen Maud, the daughter of Sir Frederick Milner, the Seventh Barronet. He became Civil Lord of Admiralty in 1922, Deputy Chairman of the Conservative Party in 1924 and in 1926 he was appointed Chairman of the Royal Commission on Agriculture in India. He worked in this office till 1928 when he was made G.E.C.I.E. and Knight of the Thistle. When a Joint Select Committee of the two Houses of Parliament was set up to prepare the way for the Government of India Act 1935, Linlithgow was appointed its Chairman. This was an important job, and when in 1936 Willingdon retired from India he was supposed to be the natural successor.

Linlithgow took oath of his office on 18 April 1936 and immediately thereafter he gave his broadcast to the people of India. In the broadcast he said: "Now speaking to you in your homes with those you love about you, I wish you to know that as I promised my true allegiance to His Majesty and dedicated myself to the service of India, I was conscious that I spoke not only for myself but also for you all. I am confident that everyone of you will wish, on this solemn occasion, with me to pledge yourself anew to the service of your motherland and of your fellowmen." He also had a few words for the children of India to whom he said: "Children! I speak to you as your King-Emperor's Viceroy and as your friend. Remember that when you grow up it will be with you that the honour of your country will rest." Then, "God has indeed been good to me for he has given me five children. But among my children I have no favourite."[1] The broadcast was in English, which at his suggestion was immediately repeated in Hindi. This gesture of the Viceroy was much appreciated by the people.

It was in the time of Lord Linlithgow that the Act of 1935 was put into force.

The Princes of India having refused to join the Federation, the federal part of the constitution had to be kept in abeyance. The Part III of the Act, dealing with the subject of provincial autonomy, however, was put into operation, and the system of provincial autonomy was inaugurated on 1 April 1937. The interval between the passage of the Act and the inauguration of the provincial autonomy was used in the preparation of electoral rolls, delimitation of constituencies etc., and the holding of elections.

Of the different parties, which contested the elections, the Congress did so not with a view to working the constitution but in order to wreck it. The League, however, decided to accept the provincial scheme "for what it was worth," though it rejected the federal part of the Act. The liberals although dissatisfied with certain parts of the constitution, also decided to give a fair trial to it. The Justice Party of Madras and the others too followed suit, and thus the first elections under the new constitution of 1935 turned out to be a lively affair.

The results of the elections were interesting. The Congress contested as many as 1161 seats and won 711 of them, securing an absolute majority in five of the eleven provinces, i.e. Madras, Bombay, C.P., U.P. and Bihar. In three of the provinces, it was returned as the largest single party. The Muslim League, on the other hand could secure only 51 seats out of the 482 seats reserved for the Muslims all over India. It polled only 4.8% of the total Muslim votes, proving thereby that it did not as yet possess that strength which it secured in a couple of years that followed. The Congress Muslims won 26 seats, while 41, 40 and 35 of the seats in Bengal went respectively to the three Muslim parties of the Province, i.e. the Independents, the Muslim League and the Praja Party; and 106 of the 175 seats in the Punjab went to the Unionist Party which was a coalition of the Hindus, Muslims and the Sikhs dominated by the Muslims; the remaining Muslim seats going to the other splinter groups. The Liberals were routed, and so was the Justice Party of Madras, although it had controlled the legislature since 1922.

The Congress had contested the elections with a view to wrecking the constitution. But once it secured so grand a success at the polls, a second thought began and majority of its members led by Dr. C Rajagopalachari, Dr Rajendra Prasad and Sardar Patel, began to advocate the acceptance of office.

Some of the most important leaders like Jawaharlal Nehru, however, opposed this idea, and ultimately Gandhi had to propose a compromise formula which laid down that the Congress would agree to form Ministries in those provinces where it had a majority, provided that the Governor-General gave a clear assurance that the Governors of the provinces would not use their special powers, and in day-to-day administration they would act only on the advice of Ministers.

The matter came under the consideration of Lord Linlithgow who, however, refused to give any such assurance, with the result that the Congress refused to take office. The Governors invited the leaders of the second largest parties in their respective provinces to form Government. The interim non-Congress ministries were thus formed but they having no complete hold over the legislatures, failed to run a smooth Government. In the meanwhile, the negotiations with the Governor-General went on, who ultimately issued a statement to the effect that although no legal assurance could be given, there was no doubt that under the spirit of the Act, "it would be distinctly discourteous to Governors if they interfered with their Ministers in matters over which the law gave the latter full control and with which the Governors were under no legal obligation to interfere."[2] Clearly, the statement did not meet the Congress demand categorically, yet Mr. Gandhi discovered in it a basis of raepprochment, and the interim ministries having resigned, the Congress formed Government in six provinces in October 1937, with a view to "combating the new Act on the one hand, and of prosecuting the constructive programme on the other."[3] The next year a Congress-led coalition was sworn in Assam, and in the meanwhile the League Ministry having been defeated in the N.W.F. province, the Congress assumed office there as well. The remaining three Provinces of Bengal, Punjab and Sind got coalition Ministries in which the Congress had not part to play.

Working of Autonomy

It may be interesting to examine how the provincial autonomy worked. The Congress Ministries assuming office in eight provinces, continued to work till October 1939 when they resigned on the war issue. The details of this will be discussed in the following chapter. A non-Congress Ministry assumed office in Orissa towards the close of 1941, and another such Ministry was formed in N.W.F.P. in 1943. But in the remaining Congress-majority provinces, the Governor's regime continued under Section 93 till the fresh elections in 1946 restored the popular Ministries again. In the non-Congress provinces of Bengal, Punjab and Sind also the provincial autonomy flourished for as many as ten years.

Role of Governors: In the eight conrgess provinces during the period the provincial autonomy was in force, the Governors, as Mr Gandhi himself testified, behaved themselves more or less in a constitutional manner. Except in four cases, the legislation passed by the provincial legislatures received the Governor's assent, and the Civil Services gave their due support to the Ministers in the fulfilment of their programmes. This does not, however, mean that during this period there were no constitutional crises in the Congress provinces at all. In fact, there were quite a few crises of this type, which, however, were happily overcome. A short reference to some of them would be interesting.

In Orissa thus, the Governor proposing to proceed on leave, the Chief Secretary to the Government was proposed to be raised to the Acting Governorship. The Congress ministry of the province, supported by the Congress High Command, objected to the subordinate official being raised above its head and prepared to resign. The Governor getting his leave cancelled, however, saved the situation.

In the Central Provinces the Governor rather went out of the way to safeguard as essential principle of Cabinet solidarity. Here Dr. N B Khare, the Chief Minister desired two of his Ministers to resign their office so as to enable him to reconstitute the Ministry. The Ministers refused on the plea that they had received no such instructions from the High Command, with the result that the Chief Mnister himself put in his resignation. The Governor intervened and dismissing the dissenting Ministers, invited Dr Khare to reconstitute the Ministry. This was a healthy action on the part of the Governor, but he perhaps did not act from good motives. The Congress High Command blaming the Governor for an attempt at dividing the Congress ranks took a disciplinary action against Dr Khare himself and replaced him with Pt. Ravi Shankar Shukla. This was a lesson to the Governor that he should not try to be too active whether to help or to harm.

In the United Provinces and Bihar, again, a crisis developed in February 1938 when the Congress Governments took up the question or releasing the political prisoners in order to fulfil their promises. The Governor saw in this a grave menace to peace, and the Governor-General intervened by issuing orders against this step under Section 126. This was a challenge to the Ministries, which put in their resignation as a protest. G.B. Pant, the Chief Minister of U.P., wrote in his resignation letter thus: "It is unconceivable that release of no more than 50 political prisoners, some of whom were merely boys when they were convicted, and several of whome have undergone long terms of imprisonment and are due to be released within a few months in the usual course, can be a grave menace to peace and tranquility of any province in

India. We have every reason to believe that they have abjured the path of violence. The jail authorities have a similar impression... We have discussed this question on numerous occasions with Your Excellency." Moreover, the interference of the Governor-General in the affairs of an autonomous province was also taken a serious exception to. Here, again however, the situation was timely saved as a result of compromise between the Congress High Command and the Viceroy Lord Linlithgow, whereby it was agreed to that the release would be effected gradually after considering each case on merit. Obviously it was only a face-saving device for the Governor and the Viceroy.

U.P. Crisis and Pirpur Report. A more serious and more interesting crisis, however, developed in U.P. At the time of assuming office in the Congress-majority provinces, it was proposed that in these provinces the Congress should enter into coalitions with the Muslim League so as to win their cooperation. The matter was taken up as a test case in U.P. where the provincial branches of Congress and League entered into negotiations under the instructions of their respective High Commands. The U.P. Congress expressed its willingness to enter into the Coalition provided (1) that the Muslim League group in the province worked under the control of the Congress High Command and not separately and (2) that the Muslim League Parliamentary Board in U.P. dissolved itself and stopped putting candidates in the future elections. These obviously were harsh conditions and amounted almost to a dissolution of the U.P. branch of the League.[4] But they were not strange if we consider that the Congress was in an absolute majority in the Province, and it was only an out-of-the way offer so as to create a good will in the League. Moreover, if the coalition was formed without these conditions, the Congress, as Mr Jawaharlal Nehru observed, feared an intrigue "with the Government over the heads of the other Ministers...There would have been no binding cement, no common loyalty, no united objective, and individual ministers should have looked and pulled in different directions."[5] The negotiations, however, failed and the Congress formed the Ministry in U.P. on its own.

The League began to hunt for imaginary grievances of a discriminatory treatment towards the Muslim minority in U.P. A list of such supposed Congress atrocities was drawn up by Mr Jinnah and in pursuance of the League's resolution of 20 March 1938 a Committee was appointed under the Raja of Pirpur (in U.P.) to investigate into the matter. After its eight months' hard labour the Committee submitted its report which proving the Muslim grievances as correct, charged the Congress among other things, of (1) a discrimination against the Muslims in services, (2) inadequate subsidies to the Muslims schools, (3) propagation of Hindi with official support, and interestingly enough, (4) the Government's permission for the singing of 'Bande Matram' which had previously been banned by the British authorities and (5) the use of the Congress flag on the public buildings. The report concluding that the British rule was better for the Muslims than the Congress rule, sent a bitter wave of disgust into the Congress. The Congress offer to submit the case for verification to the Chief Justice of India, an Englishman, was rejected and Mr Jinnah countered it with the proposal that a Royal Commission of Judges presided over by the Law Lord of the Privy Council be rather appointed for the purpose. The Congress expressed its willingness to do so, but the Viceroy and the Governor being sure that the League's allegations were nothing but an irresponsible fabrication, interfered and let the matter drop. This was another instance of the Governor's acting in a responsible and dispassionate matter.

The part played by the Governors in the non-Congress provinces, however, differed. Here the Governors made a more active interference in the administrative affairs, and during the War particularly the office of the Ministers became precarious. In Sind thus in 1938, Allah Baksh the Chief Minister having surrendered his title Khan Bahadur as a protest against the war policy of the Government, the Governor dismissed him even though he commanded a stable majority in the legislature. There were as many as five changes in Sind during 1937-43, and in 1946 the Governor called the leader of the largest party to office even though coalition having a stable majority in the Assembly existed. Again, in Bengal the Chief Minister Fazalul Haq was forced by the Governor to resign just when the voting on grants in the budget session was on. And in 1945, when the then Chief Minister was refused a vote of grant, the Governor still kept him in office by compelling the speaker to adjourn the House. In all the three provinces of Bengal, Sind and N.W.F., by keeping most of the Congress members behind the bars the Governor kept the League Ministers in power, even though they did not command a majority in the Assemblies. The Governors, in these provinces, had a pro-League leaning and Mr Shayama Prasad Mukherjee, a Bengal leader, was not incorrect when he said that it was better that the Governor of the province rather sat on the League benches.

In Punjab the Governor's hold went to such an extent that though the Chief Minister absented himself on a private business for as many as six months, the Governor appointed no substitute even in an acting capacity. Sir Sikandar Hayat Khan, the Chief Minister of this province, rather openly acknowledged the merit of the Governor's mature guidance in day-to-day problems, and the Governor took liberty with him to such an extent that when sounded regarding the release of the political prisoners in U.P. and Bihar, he informed the Governor-General that the Chief Minister of the province had advised him against such releases lest peace and tranquility of the province should be disturbed. When questioned in the Assembly, Sir Sikandar denied having ever tendered such an advice.

It is obvious thus that the Governor's interference in the non-Congress provinces often went to an obnoxious extent. That was perhaps the reason that when the Governor's rule was imposed in the Congress provinces in 1939, in the non-Congress provinces the Ministries still went on working.

Working of Ministries: The working of the Ministers in the Congress as well as in the non-Congress provinces proved on the whole satisfactory. In the Congress provinces only the leaders of the majority party were invited to form Ministries. In the non-Congress provinces although the Governors chose the Chief Ministers, they did the job well. The power of the distribution of portfolios belonged to the Governors, but they established a healthy convention in this respect by permitting rather the Chief Ministers to exercise this power. The Ministers continued in office so long as they enjoyed the confidence of an Assembly, and resigned when a vote of no-confidence was passed. The Ministry in Assam rather established a wholesome convention by resigning when the Assam Assembly rejected an important piece of legislation. It did not insist on a regular vote of no-confidence. The principle of collective responsibility was also evolved, and minorities were given due representation in the Cabinets. An exception in this respect existed in Orissa where no capable Muslim Congress members could be found for inclusion in the Ministry. The Orissa Muslims waited on the Governor and protested against this, but the Governor acted wisely and while assuring them that their interests would not suffer, he refused to interfere in the Ministry. The regular Cabinet meetings in the Congress province were only formal. For, under the Constitution they had to be presided over by the Governors in whose presence it was difficult to discuss the policy matters. The Ministers therefore had usually already taken decisions in their private meetings before they met under a Governor's Chairmanship. In the non-Congress provinces, however, the regular Cabinet meetings presided over by the Governors were more than formal. For, here the Governors played an active role in the executive functions, of which nobody made a secret. The Chief Ministers like Sir Sikandar Hyat Khan of Punjab rather welcomed it.

Another healthy convention developed during this period was the appointment of Junior Ministers, usually known as Parliamentary Secretaries, though not provided for in the Act. A Parliamentary Secretary was different from a Permanent Secretary who belonged to the Public Services and worked as the administrative head of a Department. The Parliamentary Secretary was a member of the legislature and belonged to the party in power. His duty was to assist the Minister under whom he was appointed. In the coalition ministries these secretaries provided a valuable and reliable support in the legislatures to the parties in power. The practice, which followed the model of England, was considered good for the reason that it provided a suitable opportunity for the would-be ministers.

Civil Services: The part played by the Civil Services under the Ministers also proved almost satisfactory. The appointment, dismissal, conditions of service, etc., of the superior services were placed under the control of the Secretary of State-in Council, and on their insistence they were granted certain additional safeguards in the Act so that they may work comfortably under the new set-up. Yet, however, there were three categories of them. First were those who resigned at the introduction of provincial autonomy, the second continued in order to create trouble for the Ministers and third were those who really desired to cooperate. The example of the second category could be found in the Chief Secretary of the United Provinces who issued an order to the administrative officers that the orders of the Government were to be executed only when countersigned by one of the Secretaries. The firm action of Mr G B Pant, the Chief Minister, however, brought him round, whereafter the Services all over India realised their position and began to adjust themselves under the changed environments, although it was not always easy for them to work under the national leaders some of whom had often been ill-treated by them. The Services often complained of over-interference by the Ministers in the day-to-day working of their departments. And this was not very much less often correct, explaining correctly the subservient position of the Services to which they almost adjusted themselves.

Congress High Command: The ministers themselves in the Congress provinces worked under the control and guidance of the Congress High Command, which had been set up in March 1937. This consisted of three persons, i.e., Dr Rajendra Prasad, Sardar Vallabhbhai Patel and Maulana Abul Kalam Azad who formed Parliamentary sub-Committee of the Working Committee of the Congress. Mr Coupland criticizes the activities of the High Command saying that, "the Unitarian policy of the Congress violated provincial autonomy and responsible government."[6] But this criticism seems to be uncalled for. A central controlling authority over the provincial Congress Ministers was a necessity if some uniformity of standard and behaviour was required in the Indian administration to be maintained. Moreover, this alone could facilitate the development of the parties on national lines and there was nothing unusual in it if the examples of the countries such as the United States of America, Canada and Australia were considered.

The Provincial Cabinets, thus, went on working almost smoothly till 1939 when in the Congress provinces they resigned and the essential principles of the Cabinet system began to recede to the background. The Assam Chief

Minister thus continued in office even though defeated in the Assembly. In a House of 60, the Orissa Chief Minister had a command only over 14, yet nothing unbecoming was seen in his being continued in office. On the other hand the Chief Minister of Bengal and that of Sind were forced to quit even though they had solid majorities at their back. Nor was now the principle of collective responsibility respected as much as before. For if a Chief Minister resigned, it did not make it obligatory for his colleagues in the Cabinet also to do so.

Achievements: Yet, for so long as they worked, the popular ministries did quite a commendable job of all-round development. The development of primary education was undertaken and a literacy campaign was launched to educate the adults. Several steps were taken for rural development. Agrarian legislation was undertaken, efforts were made to remove the curse of moneylenders and relieve the peasantry of debt. Loans were forwarded for the development of land, marketing facilities were developed, the famine relief business was put on a more efficient footing and irrigation developed. In the field of industries too, a commendable contribution was made. The cottage industries were encouraged and loans were forwarded for the development of other industries such as that of the manufacture of electrical goods. A start was made in the Congress provinces towards the gigantic work of making the whole of India dry which involved a loss of an excise revenue of as much as 18 crore rupees. Bombay and Madras were more active in this respect, although the attitude on the whole was cautious. Nor was the development in the political field overlooked. The panchayat system was encouraged in the villages and the Congress ministry of Bombay took a courageous step, supported fully by the legislature, by restoring to the original owners the land that had been confiscated by the British imperialists to punish those who had participated in the Civil Disobedience Movement. The Madras Ministry also showed a great courage by ordering the removal of the statue of the notorious General Nail from a public place. And the lines followed by the Congress were also adopted by the Non-Congress Ministries, which also gave quite a good account of themselves. The very "psychological change was enormous" writes Jawaharlal Nehru, and "an electric current seemed to run through the countryside...the fear of the police and secret service agent vanished...and even the poorest peasant added to his feeling of self-respect and self-reliance."[7]

There were, however, certain defects in the working of the Ministries. There was thus a tendency towards over-spending the income. The majority rule was often enforced without an effort to seek a compromise with the minority opinion. And not unoften, the legislation done was hasty, the bills drafted lacked the required quality and they had later to be amended. Yet, as Coupland writes:

"The Congress had at least become a constructive force in Indian politics...Now it has shown that the power of its great organization and the disciplined enthusiasm of its members could be put to a more practical purpose."[8] Moreover the practical experience which the popular minister got during this period, proved useful in the days to come.

THE 'AUGUST OFFER' AND THE CRIPPS MISSION

The 'August Offer'

It was on 3 September 1939 that the Second World War broke out in Europe. As early as April 1939 when the British sent a contingent of Indian troops to Aden, the Congress warned them against imposing a war on India and against using "Indian resources in a war without the consent of Indian people." The warning, however, fell on deaf ears and in August more Indian troops were dispatched to Aden, Egypt and Singapore. And now came a bombshell when without consulting the Indian leaders, Linlithgow declared India to be a belligerent country. The steps were also being contemplated to amend the Government of India Act, 1935 in order to concentrate all powers in the hands of the Government of India so as to curb the liberties of the people.

The reaction of the Congress was sharp, and on 14 September it declared in a resolution: "India cannot associate herself in a war said to be for democratic freedom, when the very freedom is denied to her, and such limited freedom as she possessed is taken away from her...If Great Britain fights for the maintenance and extension of democracy, then she must necessarily end imperialism in her own possessions...A free democratic India will gladly associate herself with other free nations for mutual defence against aggression and for economic cooperation." What the Congress demanded in concrete terms as her condition for cooperation, was a declaration: (1) promising that India would have full freedom to frame her Constitution after the war, and that (2) the British should immediately establish a popular Government in India.[9] The liberals supported the Congress by demanding that the Government should replace "the present form of Central Government by a government responsible to the people," while the Muslim League seeing no harm in the declaration of the aims of war, demanded that the Congress should be given no assurance without their consent.

Congress Resignation

The demand of the Muslim League suggested a way to the Viceroy, Lord Linlithgow who, in order to beat the Congress with the old weapon of 'divide and rule', started giving a series of interviews to the representatives of every conceivable class, interest and community to demonstrate a bitter lack of unity among the Indians. This provoked even Mr Attlee, the leader of the Opposition in the Commons to criticize Linlithgow as being out of touch with realities and as lacking 'imaginative insight.'[10] The Viceroy consulted as many as 52 persons and ultimately came out with his statement of 17 October 1939. In this White Paper the Viceroy said: (1) It is the declared policy of the government "that the partnership between India and the United Kingdom within our Empire may be furthered to the end that India may attain its due place among" other Dominions. (2) The Government would re-examine the whole scheme of India's Constitution after the war is over. (3) It was not possible to make an immediate transfer of substantial power, but when this is done, (4) the advice and assistance of all the parties will be taken. The minorities need not worry. And (5) a "Consultative Group" consisting of the representatives of the important communities and interests would be set up to help the Viceroy in the conduct of war.[11]

The declaration, as obvious, was a mischievous attempt at dividing the Indians. It repeated the old promise of Dominion Status for India as ultimate aim, but in the immediate time the Congress could be granted nothing better than a membership of a "Consultative Group." In other words, as Gandhiji observed: "The Congress has asked for bread and it has got stone." The Congress Working Committee considering the demand as evasive, called upon the Congress Ministries on 1 October to resign. The resignations were immediately submitted and in November the Viceroy proclaimed the application of section 93 in the eight Congress provinces where the resignations had taken place and where now the Advisers' regime were set up.[12]

Talks Re-opened

The Viceroy, however, could not remain completely oblivious of the popular demands, and re-opened negotiations with some of the Indian leaders such as Mr Gandhi, Dr Rajendra Prasad and Mr Jinnah. On 2 November 1939 he wrote to Dr Prasad and Mr Jinnah, reminding them of what he had told them during discussions. He said: (1) As an *ad hoc* arrangement during the War, the representatives of the Congress and of the League, together with those of one or possibly more of other important groups, could be included in the Viceroy's Council. The privileges and obligations enjoyed by these members would be identical with those enjoyed by the existing members and the entire arrangement would be within the scheme of the existing law. (2) This could, however, be done only if the Congress and the League agreed between them on some scheme of Government for the provinces. But Dr Prasad replied to the Viceroy on 3 November to declare first "the war aims without which it is impossible for the Congress to consider any subsidiary proposal. We are anxious to settle the communal question, but this should not be dragged and made to come in the way of declaration of Indian freedom." Mr Jinnah's reply on the other hand, was different. The Viceroy's proposal had encouraged communal approach to the question, and he insisted in his letter dated 5 November that (1) no declaration shall, either in principle or otherwise, be made without the approval of both, the Hindus and the Muslims. He went even beyond this and insisted on an assurance that (2) His Majesty's Government would try and meet all reasonable national demands of the Arabs in Palestine and (3) the Indian troops would not be used outside India against any Muslim power or country. The Viceroy did not find Dr Prasad' proposal acceptable. Mr Jinnah's first two points were, however, promised a sympathetic consideration, but no guarantee could be possible on the third, though here too precaution would be taken to respect the feelings of the Indian Muslims. It is clear, however, the Viceroy and the Congress pulled towards different directions. While the former's effort was to give a communal turn to what was purely political, the latter insisted on keeping communalism and politics apart. A deadlock was thus created, and no further progress in the talk was possible.[13]

In the meanwhile the Congress ministries in the province having resigned, Jinnah's heart reverberated with joy and on 2 December 1939 repeating the charges of the Pirpur Report against the erstwhile Congress Governments, he called upon the Muslims of India to observe a "Day of Deliverance" on 22 December. The Muslims all over India, were to hold meetings and everywhere pass the resolution saying that "the Congress Ministry both in the discharge of their duties of the administration and in the legislatures have done their best...to destroy Muslim culture, and have interfered with their religious and social life, and trampled upon their economic and political rights...thereby created an atmosphere which spread the belief amongst the Hindu public that there was established a Hindu raj." The resolution was to express "deep sense of relief at the termination of the Congress regime in various provinces and rejoice in observing this day as the 'Day of Deliverance' from tyranny, oppression and injustice and urge upon the Governor of the province, in which the meeting was held, to enquire into the legitimate grievances of the Musalmans...and redress the same at the earliest moment."[14]

Annoyed to bitter extent by Jinnah's attitude, Mr Nehru wrote to Mahadev Desai: "There is a limit even to political falsehood and indecency but all limits have been passed." The general opinion held in the Congress ranks was that the Viceroy himself was responsible for the development of this communal frenzy and callousness in Mr Jinnah.

The middle of 1940 saw the war situation taking a worse turn. Holland, Belgium and Denmark fell before Germany and Norway seemed to be on her last legs. The British forces themselves had sustained a crushing defeat at Dunkirk and the whole of Great Britain was being strafed by bombers. The very existence of democracy was at stake when Mr Gandhi's heart throbbed out in sympathy for the British and he declared on 1 June 1940: "We do not seek our independence out of Britain's ruin. Mr Jinnah's activities were also taking a serious turn. In March 1940 the two-nation theory was proclaimed and the Muslim League forwarded its demand for Pakistan. Mr Jinnah was also carrying on negotiations with the Viceroy and there was a possibility of the League developing a strong hold on the Government in the absence of the Congress. It was due to these reasons that the Congress Working Committee meeting at Poona offered on 7 July 1940 to "throw its full weight into the country and whole-hearted cooperation in men and money," provided that (1) the Government acknowledged that independence was the goal of India and that (2) it immediately established a provisional National Government at the Centre.[15]

In the meanwhile, however, a ministerial crisis occurred in England. Mr Churchill, a rank conservative, replaced Chamberlain as Premier; Amery replacing Lord Zetland as the Secretary of State for India. Mr Churchill frankly declared that Atlantic Charter in which the Allies had promised to restore Self-Government in all the countries, did not apply to India. He in fact had absolutely no compunction in declaring that he "had not become His Majesty's first Minister to preside over the liquidation of the British Empire."[16] The Viceroy, however, was authorized to make a more concrete offer to the Indians for their readiness to cooperate.

A statement consisting of new proposals was issued on 8 August 1940 and hence has been known as the "August Offer' of the Viceroy. The statement made out the following points: (1) The Dominion Status was the British objective for India. (2) The Government accepted for the first time the demand that the framing of the new Constitution was "primarily the responsibility of Indians themselves, and should originate from Indian conceptions of the social, economic and political structure of Indian life." (3) Immediately after the war, "with the least possible delay," the Government would set up "a body representative of the principal elements in India's national life in order to devise the framework of the new Constitution." (4) The new constitutional scheme, however, would be built "within the British Commonwealth of Nations" and in it a provision would be required for the "due fulfilment of the obligations which Great Britain's long connection with India has imposed on her and for which His Majesty's Government cannot divest themselves of responsibility." (5) A full weight would be given "to the views of minorities in any revision" of the existing Constitution. (6) The Viceroy would immediately invite "certain number of representative Indians to join" his Executive Council. (7) He would also "establish a War Advisory Council which would meet at regular intervals and which would contain representatives of the Indian States and of the other interests in the national life of India as a whole." (8) The Government hoped for a full cooperation of all the parties and communities so that India secured an equal and free partnership in the British Commonwealth of Nations.[17]

An Appraisal

The August Offer was a definite advance over any of the declarations so far made by the British authorities. In the Viceroy's declaration of October 1939, while a promise for the re-examination of the whole scheme of constitution after the war was made, the right of the Indians themselves to draft their constitution was not conceded. But now it was definitely declared that the framing of the new constitution was "primarily the responsibility of Indians themselves." The Dominion Status after the war was also promised. The proposals regarding the Executive Council and the Advisory Council also made an effort to accommodate the public aspirations to some extent.

Yet, the proposals fell too short of what the Congress demanded. Mr Churchill in fact had already declared that the Atlantic Charter did not apply to India and therefore the Viceroy's declaration could not be expected to depart from the fundamental principle of this declaration. First, no definite time limit was prescribed for the grant of the Dominion Status after the War. Secondly, the "body representative of the principal elements in India's national life in order to devise the framework of the new constitution" was promised, but it was not made clear whether this body was to be a full-fledged Constituent Assembly or simply another Round Table Conference. Thirdly, it could be anybody's guess as to what the British actually meant with regard to a provision in the Constitution for the "due fulfilment of the obligations which Great Britain's long connection with India has imposed on her." Fourthly, the promise to give a full weight to the views of the minorities was in a way an acceptance of the League's demand that no political progress in India could be made without the consent of that party. In fact a veto in this connection seemed to have been given to the League. The British desire to perpetuate their hold over India was discernible and for this the bogey of the communal division in India was sought to be made a full use of. The Congress lost all its faith in the British statesmanship and cynicism began to develop with reguard to the very concebtion of "Dominion status within the British Commonwealth. The observation of Mr Nehru that his conception was now "as dead" as a door nail," was significant.[18] Little wonder, the Congress rejected the offer outright.

On the other hand, however, while exhilarated on the British assurance that no future constitution could become final without their consent, the Muslim

League too found reasons to reject the offer. For according to them "the partition of India was the only solution of the most difficult problem of India," but the August Offer gave no assurance with regard to this.

The Liberals neither accepted ncr rejected the Offer. Their policy emanated from three arguments. First, they held, the British policy was vague with regard to certain important matters. Secondly, they desired a time limit to be set for the grant of Dominion Status without caring whether a particular community agreed or not. And thirdly, the Indian Members in the Executive Council should be party leaders.[19]

THE CRIPPS MISSION

The 'August Offer' failed to satisfy the aspirations of the people. Even leaders like C. Rajagopalachari and Jawaharlal Nehru, who were in favour of an active help to the British in their War efforts, turned against them, and the all India Congress authorized Mr Gandhi to start Civil Disobedience again. In view, however, of the critical war situation, instead of launching once again a mass Civil Disobedience Movement Mr Gandhi adopted a novel practice of agitation, which was called Individual Civil Disobedience. Under this, the individuals were to be selected by Mahatma Gandhi personally. An individual thus selected would give a notice to the District authorities informing them that he was going to dissuade the people from giving help to the Government in the War, which was thrust on India without her consent. And thereafter he would start his activities by addressing public meetings and by other methods.[20]

The novel Movement was started in November 1940 and Vinobha Bhave got the distinction of being selected as the first Satyagrahi. He gave a due notice to the authorities and actually addressed an anti-war public meeting before he was arrested and put behind bars. Other arrests followed in quick succession. Mr Nehru found his way into prison in October 1941, and after him almost all the top-ranking Congress leaders together with others were arrested one by one. There was no need of waiting till one addressed a public meeting. The individuals were taken into custody on the very receipt of a notice. The total number of persons thus arrested, was estimated at about 30,000. "Among them were six ex-Premiers of provinces, twenty-nine former Ministers and 290 members of provincial legislatures."[21]

Some people criticized this action of Mahatma Gandhi when the British were engaged in a life and death struggle. Sir Sikandar Hayat Khan termed the action as "stabbing the British in the back." But those who criticized the action did not suggest a better alternative for showing resentment against the British effort to trample under their feet the legitimate rights and aspirations of the

Indians whom, outside their country, they were using for the protection of these very rights for others. Nor could it be said that the Congress leaders were less alive to the war dangers, or that they did not understand the necessity of not embarrassing the allied nations under such a situations. It was, in fact, only because of these reasons that when the British attitude towards the Indians required a forceful agitation, only a mild and symbolic movement was started.

For a time the British Government did not seem to worry much. But as the number of the arrests mounted, the reports of the agitation and comments appeared daily in the press, the attention of the people began to be diverted from war, and therefore the British apprehensions grew and they began to think of placating the public opinion.

Council Expansion

It was perhaps due to this reason that the Viceroy's Executive Council was expanded and the Advisory Council, in terms of the August Declaration, instituted in October 1941. Adding five more Indian members who now occupied eight seats in all raised the total number of the members of the Executive Council. But all this was hardly of much significance. The Congress and the League having refused the Council's membership, only Dr Ambedkar represented an organized party, the remaining members enjoying the credit only of being the 'yes-men' of the Viceroy. These members were responsible to the Governor-General and not to the Legislative Assembly. They were appointed and dismissed by the Governor-General and were allowed no powers to be envied. External Affairs, Defence, Home and Finance–all these departments remained securely in the hands of the British, and the unimportant departments, together with some created just newly to serve the Defence requirements were handed over to the Indians. The public opinion obviously could not thus be placated.

The Release

And now, after only about a month had passed since the Executive Council's expansion, all of a sudden came the release of almost all those who had been imprisoned as *Satyagrahis*. Nobody could understand why the Government did this. But some people said it was to win public sympathy for the new Councillors who were looked upon as renegades. This seemed correct. For the proposal for release was actually, initiated by three of the new Indian members of the Viceroy's council. The Viceroy had to agree to save an awkward situation, though Mr Churchill did not want to give an impression that Mr Gandhi and party had won and agreed only after a warning, "give in, when you lose India don't blame me."[22] If it was so, the Satyagraha which had created the public opinion, was having its effect. Be that as it may, the Congress leaders saw in this action of the Viceroy no element to rejoice at, and while C. Rajagopalachari favoured suspension of the movement only as a political strategy, the Mahatma desired it to continue. Ultimately, however, the matter was referred to the A.I.C.C. to decide.

War and its Effects

In the meanwhile the war situation worsened. Japan entered the war dramatically on 7 December 1941 by pouncing on Pearl Harbour. Indo-China, Indonesia and Malaya fell before her forces like skittles and the closing days of February 1942 brought a bang of the inevitability of Burma's fall.[23] The war thus knocked at very doors of India, and Mr Churchill, the apostle of the imperialistic exploitation of India, admitted in plain words, that the British had "no assured means" for India's defence. With the Indian leaders, however, the case was different. Means or no means, it was impossible for them to see that if the British imperialism went, its place was taken over by the Japanese fascism, which was still worse. The Congress thus decided to suspend the Satyagraha Movement, relieved Mahatma Gandhi of its leadership at his own request on 30 December 1941 at Bardoli and brought Jawahar to organize the country for defence.

Outside the Congress, however, Mr Gandhi expressed his determination "to continue my mission whether I am alone or assisted by an organization or individuals," and the Congress Working Committee Resolution of 30 December 1941, at Bardoli, also asked the Congressmen in their individual capacity to "render him full assistance in the presentation of this mission, including the offering of civil disobedience." Officially, however, the Congress did not agree that non-violence could help in all situations, national or international. Relieving Mr Gandhi of its leadership, the Congress resolution declared: "While there has been no change in Britain's policy towards India the Working Committee must nevertheless take into full consideration the new world situation that has arisen by the development of war into a world conflict and its approach to India. The sympathies of the Congress must inevitably lie with the people who are the subject of aggression and who are fighting for their freedom. But only free and independent India can be in a position to undertake the defence of the country on a national basis and be of help in the larger causes that are emerging from the storm of war. The whole background in India is one of hostility and of distrust of the British Government and not even the most far-reaching promises can alter this background, nor can a subject India offer voluntary or willing help to arrogant imperialism which is indistinguishable from fascist authoritarianism."[24]

But this did not mean that the Congress satyagraha activities so far went in vain. The Government attitude in fact and already softened as revealed repeatedly by their efforts to placate the public opinion. And now, if the worsening war situation led the Congress to suspend its movement, it also moved the imperial authorities at Home towards the advisability of immediately announcing political concessions to the Indians to win their active sympathy for the War efforts.

The Indian Liberals

In March and July 1941, Non-Party Leaders Conference was held at which Sir T.B. Sapru, a past President of the All-India Liberal Federation presided. In these conferences resolutions were passed which demanded that to keep the sympathies of India in the war activities the Central Executive Council should immediately be turned into truly National Government, popular Governments should be restored in provinces, India should be represented in the War Cabinet in England and should be consulted like other Dominions in important matters. A telegram to this effect was sent to Mr Churchill who then was at Washington, which besides Mr Sapru, was signed by some other important leaders of India some of whom had already been on the Viceroy's Executive Council. This telegram was given considerable importance by the British Government, and it paved the way for sending a Mission to India.[25]

Contact with Japanese

The so-called quisling activities in India also effected the situation. Lord Linlithgow wrote to Mr L.S. Amery, the Secretary of State for India on 21 January 1942: "Recent report from military authorities in eastern India is to effect that there is a large and dangerous potential 5th Column in Bengal, Assam, Bihar and Orissa, and that indeed potential of pro-enemy sympathy and activity in eastern India is enormous. Sarat Bose has been a lesson. The activities of U Saw and Tin Tut (a senior civil servant occupying a very responsible position) are another and a grave one."[26]

Sarat Chandra Bose, as referred to by the Viceroy Linlithgow above, had, "with his brother Subhash Chandra Bose, been a leader of the Forward Bloc, a group formed by members of Congress in Bengal who disagreed with the orthodox policy of the party. Though expelled from Congress in October 1940, Sarat Bose continued to lead the Congress Party in Bengal Legislative Assembly. On 11 December 1941 he was arrested and detained under the Defence of India Rules. The Government of India announced that they were satisfied that there had been contact of such nature between him and the Japanese as to render his immediate apprehension necessary."

U Saw, Prime Minister of Burma, and his Advisor U Tin Tut, on the other hand, "were arrested on their return journey from a visit to Britain and America." The announcement issued from 10 Downing Street on 18 January said: "From reports received about the movement of U Saw after his goodwill mission to this country it has come to the knowledge of his Majesty's Government that he has been in contact with Japanese authorities since the outbreak of war with Japan. This fact has been confirmed by his own admission. His Majesty's Government have accordingly been compelled to detain him, and it will not be possible to permit him to return to Burma."[27]

Enlightened Opinion in England

On 18 December 1941 a letter was published in *The Times*, England from Sir George Schuster M.P. who had served as Finance Member of The Viceroy's Executive Council and Dr Edward Thompson, the historian. This letter urged "a fresh start in India", a representative Cabinet in the Centre and coalition Governments in the Provinces.[28] Among Englishmen, however, the man who had the greatest sympathy for the cause of India was Mr. Clement Attlee, Lord Privy Seal in the War Cabinet till 10 February 1942. It was in fact at his suggestion that the Cripps Mission was sent to India. His views expressed in the Cabinet and outside make an interesting reading and we are tempted to quote at length from his memorandum on the Indian Political Situation dated 2 February 1942. "I have read with interest the memorandum by the Secretary of State for India and the telegram of the Viceroy, but I am unable to accept the conclusion that nothing can or should be done at the present time. This seems to me to result from a dangerous ignoring of the present situation….India had been profoundly effected by the changed relationship between Europeans and Asiatics, which began with the defeat of Russia by Japan at the beginning of this century…The reverses which we and the Americans are sustaining from the Japanese at the present time will continue this process…The gallant resistance of the Chinese for more than four years against the same enemy makes the same way. The fact that we are now accepting Chinese aid in our war, and are necessarily driven to a belated recognition of China as an equal…makes the Indian ask why he, too, cannot be master in his own house…Similarly, the success against the Axis of a semi-oriental people, the Russians, lends weight to the hypothesis that East is now asserting itself against the long dominance of the West…Increasingly large contribution in blood and tears and sweat made by Indians will not be forgotten and will be fully exploited by Indians who have not themselves contributed. The Secretary of State thinks that we may weather the immediate storm by doing nothing; but what of subsequent storms? Such a hand-to-mouth policy is not statesmanship… educated Indians do accept British principles of justice and liberty. We are condemned by Indians not by the measures of Indian ethical conceptions but by our own, which we have taught them to accept…crude imperialism of the Viceroy…is fatally short-sighted and suicidal…and now is the time for an act of statesmanship…; A renewed effort must be made to get the leaders of the Indian political parties to unite. It is quite obvious from his telegram that the Viceroy is not the man to do this…Lord Durham saved Canada to the British Empire. We need a man to do in India what Durham did in Canada…There is no virtue in delay or in mere dilatory action…My conclusion therefore is that a representative with power to negotiate within wide limits should be sent to India now, either as a special envoy or in replacement of the present Viceroy, and that a Cabinet Committee should be appointed to draw up terms of reference and powers."[29]

World Opinion

Nor did the pressure of the world opinion make a less contribution. The Japanese attack on Britain and America in the Far Eastern Theatre had convinced President Roosevelt that in order to give an effective fight to the Japanese, India had to be turned into a base for which an active cooperation of the Indians was necessary.[30] Generalissimo Chiang Kai-Shek of China, the leader of one of the major powers participating in the war as recognized after the Japanese intervention, suddenly visited India in the spring of 1942. And during this visit he showed no lack of frankness in appealing to the British to concede India's demand. How Chiang's visit caused a flutter at 10 Downing Street in London is revealed from Churchill's letter of 3 February 1942, in which he made his effort to lessen the importance of the Congress leaders whom the Generalissimo wanted to see. In the letter addressed to the Generalissimo, Churchill thus said: "It gives us all the greatest pleasure to know that Your Excellency would visit India…With regard to your seeing persons like Mr Gandhi and Mr Nehru, who are in a state at least of passive disobedience to the King Emperor, this you will readily see is a matter which requires very grave consideration…In any case, if you begin seeing the leaders of Indian Congress Party it would be necessary that you should also see Mr Jinnah representing 80,000,000 Muslims, and representatives of the 40,000,000 depressed classes and of the Indian Princes who rule over 80,000,000 to whom the Imperial Government is bound by solemn treaties. I must point out that the Congress Party, although successful some years ago in the Provincial Elections, in no way represents the martial races of India who are fighting so well."[31]

Again addressing Linlithgow in this connection on 3 February 1942 Churchill remarked: "We cannot possibly agree to Head of Foreign State intervening as a kind of impartial arbiter between representatives of King

Emperor and Messrs. Gandhi and Nehru. I hope indeed that when he has seen you and members of your Council he will not wish to have discussions with parties mentioned...In no circumstances must he be allowed to see Nehru, as you apprehended, by getting off at Allahabad or wherever Nehru may be. There could be no possibility of such meeting remaining secret and nothing would be more likely to spread pan-Asiatic *malaise* through all the bazaars of India."[32]

Dr Evatt, Australia's Foreign Minister, also urged the British to move, and so did several of the members of the British Parliament. The pressure on Mr Churchill thus mounted till 8 March 1942 when Rangoon fell and a serious urgency was added to the matter. Three days after this event Mr Churchill ultimately did feel the ground moving from under his feet, and he announced that Sir Stafford Cripps, the Lord Privy Seal, Leader of the House, a well-known Socialist, a man who had just succeeded in bringing Russia into War on the side of the Allies, who had already twice visited India, was popular with the Indians and was a personal friend of Mr Nehru, would go to India to break the Indian deadlock.[33]

These were thus, the circumstances, which led to the softening of the British attitude towards India and to the sending of the Cripps Mission.

Sir Stafford Cripps arrived in Delhi on 22 March 1942, and immediately started his discussions with the Governor-General and the Councillors. The leaders of different parties met him and consultations and discussions went on for twenty days. In these discussions Mr Nehru and Maulana Azad represented the Congress, Mr Jinnah represented the League point of view, untouchables were represented by Dr Ambedkar and M C Rajah, Hindu Mahasabha represented by Savarkar, and the Liberals by Sir T B Sapru and Jayakar. Besides, the other splinter communities and interests and the Princes of India were also consulted. The people thought Sir Cripps had brought with him some deadlock-resolving proposals and had the authority to take final decisions. But here again, as the time passed, the hopes began to founder and totter and ultimately they died. Cripps failed to resolve the deadlock.

PROPOSALS OF THE CRIPPS MISSION

The proposals which he brought with him and which were discussed with the Indian leaders, fell under two categories: (A) Those concerned with long-range arrangements and (B) those, which related to the interim or immediate arrangement.[34]

Long-term Proposals

(1) Creation of a new Indian Union with a Dominion Status, associated with the United Kingdom and other Dominions by a common allegiance to the

Crown, but equal to them in every respect, in no way subordinate in any aspect or its domestic or external affairs.

(2) Setting up of a constitution-making body immediately after the end of the war. The constitution-making body shall be composed as follows, unless the leaders of the principal communities agree upon some other form before the end of the war: (a) "Immediately upon the result being known of the provincial elections which will be necessary at the end of hostilities, the entire membership of the Lower Houses of the Provincial Legislatures shall, as a single electoral college, proceed to the election of the constitution-making body, by the system of proportional representation. This new body shall be in number about one-tenth of the number of the Electoral College." (b) "Indian States shall be invited to appoint representatives in the same proportion to their total population as in the case of the representatives of British India as a whole. These members will have the same powers as the British Indian members."

(3) The British Government undertakes to accept and implement forthwith the Constitution framed by this body subject to the following conditions. (a) If a province of India is not prepared to accept the new Constitution, it shall have the right to retain its present constitutional position, though it will be free to accede even subsequently if it so desires. (b) The non-acceding provinces will be authorized, if they so desire, to prepare a separate Constitution of their own, by a procedure analogous to the above. They will enjoy the same full status as the Indian Union will. (c) A treaty will be negotiated between His Majesty's Government and the constitution-making body. The treaty will cover all necessary matters arising out of the complete transfer of responsibility to Indian hands, such as the protection of racial and religious minorities in accordance with undertakings given to the British. No restrictions will, however, be imposed on the powers of the Indian Union to decide in the future its relationship to the other Member States of the British Commonwealth–which in other words means that the Union could secede from the Commonwealth if it so desired. (d) The States would be free to adhere to the new Constitution or not. In the latter case, revision of the existing treaty arrangements as according to the new situation, will be necessary.

Immediate Arrangement

The British Government will retain the control of Defence "as part of their world war effort," for the interim period. But they would invite the leaders of the principal parties to immediately and effectively participate in the "counsels of their country, of the Commonwealth and of the United Nations."

An Appraisal. The Cripps proposals were a definite advance over the August Offer, first, because they were more concrete and precise. Secondly, the country was given a definite promise of full Dominion Status. Thirdly, the freedom to secede from the British Commonwealth was offered. Fourthly, the new Constitution was to be framed entirely by the Indians. The "August Offer" invited the Indians only to discuss principles and methods of drafting a new Constitution, but the present proposals offered a definite plan for establishing a constitution-making body after the war, in case the Indians themselves failed to prepare a plan of their own before the end of the hostilities. In other words, even if the Indians did not agree on a constitution, that would be no excuse for the British to continue; India would get her freedom in one or more units. Fifthly, the minority parties like the Muslim League drew a greater satisfaction from it, for the principle of Pakistan was conceded.

Still, however, the proposals had several defects because of which they failed and none of the political parties of India offered to accept them. The Congress Working Committee in its resolution of 11 April 1942 thus rejected these War Cabinet proposals for the following reasons: (1) The proposals related principally to the future, upon the cessation of hostilities, while the Committee held that "only a free and independent India can be in a position to undertake the defence of the country on a national basis." (2) While the future independence may be implicit in the proposals, accompanying provisions and restrictions were such that real freedom "may well become an illusion." Even the "constitution-making body is so constituted that the people's right of self-determination is vitiated by the introduction of non-representative elements" from the States. (3) While the representation of an Indian State in the constitution-making body was fixed on a population basis, the people of the State had no hand in choosing those representatives, nor were they to be consulted at any stage while decisions vitally affecting them were being taken. The ninety millions of people in the Indian States were in fact treated only "as commodities at the disposal of their Rulers." (4) The freedom given to the States to opt out of the Union was unfortunate. "Such States may in many ways becomes barriers to the growth of Indian freedom, enclaves where foreign authority still prevails, and where the possibility of maintaining foreign armed forces has been stated to be a likely contingency and a perpetual menace to the freedom of the people of the States as well as of the rest of India." (5) The acceptance before hand of the novel principle of non-accession for provinces was also a severe blow to the conception of Indian unity, and was an apple of discord likely to generate growing trouble in the provinces, and which could well lead to further difficulties in the way of the Indian States merging themselves into an Indian Union. Though the Committee was not in favour of compelling the people of any territorial unit to remain in an Indian Union against their declared and established will, yet there was no doubt that it was wedded to Indian freedom and unity.

The Muslim League, on the other hand rejected these proposals for some different reasons. It is said Mr Jinnah drafted a resolution for the League for the acceptance of the proposal, but waited for the reaction of the Congress. When the Congress rejected, he tore up this resolution and brought a new one, which brought out the following criticism. The League Working Committee's resolution of 11 April 1942, while expressing their gratification that the possibility of Pakistan was recognized by implication by providing for the establishment of two or more independent Unions in India, regretted that (1) the proposals "embodying the fundamentals are not open to any modification and therefore no alternative proposals are invited." (2) The main object of His Majesty's Government as adumbrated in the preamble of the draft Declaration was the constitution of one Indian Union, the creation of more than one Union being relegated only to realm of remote possibility, and was purely illusory. (3) The constitution-body was proposed with the primary object to creating one Indian Union; therefore it was unfair to the Muslims to compel them to enter such a constitution-making body, when the League had finally decided that the only solution of India's constitutional problem was the partition of India into independent zones. (4) The Muslims right hitherto enjoyed by them to elect their representatives by means of separate electorates was not provided for in the case of the elections to the constitution-making body. (5) Though the principle of Pakistan was conceded, yet the method laid down was such as to negate this object, for in the draft proposals the right of non-accession had been given to the existing provinces which had been formed from time to time for administrative convenience rather than on communal principles which would be necessary for the creation of Pakistan. (6) With regard to the Indian States, it was a matter for them to decide whether to join or not to join or form a Union (7) With regard to the treaties to be negotiated between the Crown and Indian Union or Unions, the proposals did not dedicate as to what would happen in case of disagreement on the terms between contacting parties; nor was there any provision made as to what would be the procedure when there was a difference of opinion in negotiating a revision of treaty arrangements with the Indian States in the new situation. And (8) the proposals were not definite with regard to the interim arrangement.

The Depressed Classes also rejected the proposals. Their reasons were that they got no necessary safeguards for their interests; that the scheme had to be rejected or accepted as a whole, there was no scope for negotiations; that the following comment of the Declaration on the 'August Offer' was unnecessary and was an attempt to stand on prestige. The comment was that "the present declaration is intended not to supersede, but to clothe these general declarations with precision and to convince the people in India of the War Cabinet's sincere resolve."

Among other Parties, to the Liberals the proposals were against the integrity and security of India. The Hindu Mahasabha rejected them for they implied Pakistan in them. The Sikhs were afraid that the Muslim majority in the Punjab might opt for Pakistan, in which case the Sikhs would be compelled to secede from India against their wishes.

The most important point of criticism, however, on which almost all the parties agreed, though for different reasons, was that the proposals pertained only to the future and no immediate satisfaction was sought to be given to the people. Mr Gandhi is said to have interestingly remarked that the entire scheme brought by Cripps, was a sort of 'post-dated cheque on a failing bank." The words 'failing bank' aroused the indignation of some Englishmen and Gandhi denied having uttered these words at all. Yet there was no doubt that the Mission had been sent only under the stress of the war circumstances, and the proposals, as Prof. Laski observes, "looked more like a counter-move against Japan than a recognition of Indian claims, at any rate to many important Indians."[35]

Then the proposals were vague in many respects and did not seem to have been made after a thorough study of the matter. The position with regard to the states was not well defined. Nor was a procedure laid down for the provinces, whereby they could decide whether to accede to the Union or not. Sir Cripps said, if the proportion of the majority in a provincial legislature voting to opt out of the Union was less than 60 per cent, the minority had the right to ask for a plebiscite of the adult male population. This means a majority of 60 per cent and possibly of less in the case of plebiscite, could tread over the rights and aspirations of as much as 40 per cent of the population and decide their fate as it liked. Nor did the Act give a serious thought in this connection to the Sikhs in the Punjab, who would be driven by the Muslim majority like dumb cattle.

Then, the distribution of seats in the provinces under existing Constitution was based on narrow franchise, communal reservation and separate electorates for the provincial legislatures. Since these legislatures were to elect members to the constitution-making body in the Centre, the provincial defects were bound to be reflected in the Constituent Assembly, thus making it difficult to produce a good work.

His Majesty's Government was to accept the Constitution drafted by this body provided that India signed a treaty with the British to cover "all necessary matters arising out of a complete transfer of responsibility from British to Indian hands." But, as pointed out by the League, no provision was made as to who would decide the cases of differences in this connection. If it was his Mayesty's government which could decide, then India surely was not a completely independent nation.

The whole scheme, in fact, as Prof. Laski observes, "was carried out far too hurriedly...And it had about it...something of the British habit which Mr Kingsley Martin has well described as art of forgiving generously those we have grievously wronged."[36] "It is said beyond measure," observed a friend of his, "that a man like Cripps should allow himself to become the devil's advocate."[37]

Besides the inadequacy of the proposals, the way they were sought to be implanted in India was also a factor leading to their failure. Sir Cripps earned a very high reputation for his having brought Russia to join the Allies in the war. His persuasive manners and his old contacts with India had raised high hopes in his capability for handling the Indian problem. But in actual practice his haste, vagueness and shifting position dashed all hopes to the ground. When he for the first time explained the proposals, the picture painted by him was very rosy, thus wrote Maulana Azad, the then President of the Congress. "The net result of the proposal was," writes the Maulana, "that in place of the majority of British Members in the existing Executive Council, there would be an Executive Council composed of Indians alone. British officers would remain as Secretaries, but not as members of the Council." The system of Government would not, however, be changed before the war. Immediately after the war the whole question of Indian independence would be taken up. Further that in the Executive Council so constituted, the Viceroy would function as a constitutional head like the King in the UK; and that though the India Office would remain, the position of the Secretary of the State would be like that of the Dominion Secretary in respect of other Dominions. Cripps gave all these clarifications to the Maulana in the first interview. But in the second interview he went back on almost all these assurances. With regard to the Executive Council, for instance, in the second interview he could only hope that the Council would, "even during the war, work like a Cabinet."[38] With regard to Defence, if Cripps was after all hesitations, prepared to appoint an Indian Defence Minister, the powers of his Minister were to extend only to such matters as the social arrangement for foreign missions, the canteens, printing, stationery, etc., and not to real defence matters.

Maulana Azad was in fact perplexed as to why Cripps changed his position in this manner. The Maulana may here be quoted at length: "One possible explanation is that Sir Stafford had hoped to persuade the Congress to accept the proposals, even though there was no change in the basic situation, by his persuasive powers and pleasant manners. That is why he had initially given categorical assurances in order to create a favourable first impression. When, however, the proposals were examined in detail and he was subjected to cross-examination, he felt that he must be cautious and refrain from raising hopes, which he was not in a position to satisfy. An alternative explanation is, that during this interval, the inner circle of the Government of India had started to influence him. The Viceroy and his entourage constantly surrounded him. It was perhaps inevitable that their point of view should at least partially colour his vision. A third alternative explanation is that during the interval, messages had passed between Delhi and London, and the British War Cabinet had sent him fresh instructions which made him feel that if he went too far he might be repudiated." The speech of Lord Halifax, an ex-Governor-General of India and the then British Ambassador to the USA, delivered on 7 April 1942, it may be mentioned, was significant. He threatened that in case of the failure of the Mission, India would have to go without the transfer of any power at all.

Maulana Azad concludes by saying that it "may well be that all the factors mentioned above had contributed to bring about a change in the situation." But commenting on Cripps, he writes: "Cripps was essentially an advocate and as such he was inclined to paint things in a rosier colour than as warranted by facts... I heard later that in Moscow also, he had occasionally exceeded his instructions in a similar manner."[39]

Nor did Cripps seem to have shuddered from going down to the extent even of levelling slanderous charges against Congress and its President when he found that his proposals were not finding favour with them. He accused them of trying to secure the assistance of Louis Johnson, President Roosevelt's personal representative in India. When there was an adverse comment on the proposals in some papers which generally expressed Congress point of view, Cripps offended Maulana Azad by saying that 'the Hindu Press' had not welcomed the proposals, instead of saying that a section of press had not done so. "This reference to the Hindu Press," writes the Maulana, "appeared very odd to me. It also occurred to me that perhaps he was putting the emphasis on the Hindu Press because I am a Muslim."[40]

In fact the whole attitude of Cripps towards the Indian press was stiff, and Prof. Laski comments: "It was psychologically disastrous for Sir Stafford to go to India in a 'take it or leave it' mood, and, on his return practically announce that we washed our hands of the offer. That was bound to make it look...propagandist's art among our allies who contrasted American relations with the Philippines against the British relations with India."[41]

NOTES

1. Glendevon John, *The Viceroy at Bay, London*, 1971, pp. 22-23.
2. Linlithgow, Marquess of, *Speeches and Documents,* pp. 80-81.
3. See Sitaramayya, *op. cit.,* pp. 51-71.
4. "This proved to be fatal error–the prime cause of the creation of Pakistan –but in the circumstances it was very natural one." Writes Penderel Moon, *Divide and Quit*, pp. 15-16.
5. Nehru, *Autobiography*, p.371.
6. Coupland, *India, A Restatement,* p. 161.
7. Nehru, *Autobiography,* p. 378.
8. Coupland, *op. cit.*, pp. 165-68; Sharma. J.S., *op. cit.*, pp.502-588.
9. Norman Dorothy, *Nehru The First Sixty Years,* his statements, speeches etc., I, pp. 643-46.
10. Glendevon, John, *The Viceroy at Bay,* London, 1975, p.155.
11. Norman, Dorothy, *op. cit.*, I, pp. 650-60.
12. Sitaramayya, *op. cit.*,II, pp. 124-44.
13. Viceroy's Statement of 5, Nov. 1936 etc., Sitaramayya, *op. cit.*, II, pp. 145-49.
14. Sri Prakasa, *Pakistan Birth and Early Days*, pp. 5-7; Coupland, *Indian Constitutional Problem,* Part II, pp. 184-85.
15. *Indian National Congress Resolutions,* pp. 74-75.
16. Norman D.,*op. cit.*, II, p.128.
17. Linlithgow, *op. cit.,* pp. 250-52
18. Norman Dorothy, *op. cit.*, II, p.38.
19. For further details *see.* Gwyer and Appadorai (ed.) *Speeches and Documents on the Indian Constitution,* Vol. II; Indian Annual Register, (1940), II, p. 244.
20. See Norman D., *"Gandhi to Nehru" op. cit.*, II p. 43.
21. H N Brailsford, *Subject India,* p. 59.
22. Glendevon, John, *The Victory of Bay,* pp.208 12.
23. Sir R. Lumley, The Governor of Bombay, thus for instance, wrote to Lord Linlithgow, the Viceroy, on 1 January 1942: "The past fortnight has been marked by anxiety about the war and anticipation of internal political developments. The former has sharpened speculation about

the latter. The Japanese advance in Malaya, the reported exodus from Calcutta and, in particular, the bombing of Rangoon have been followed by with anxious attention, and...There is nervousness about the future." Mansergh, Nicholas & Lumby, E.W.R., *The Transfer of Power,* 1942-7, I p.1.

24. Mansergh and Lumby (Ed.), *op. cit.*, I, pp. 879-884.
25. *Ibid.,* pp. 4-5.
26. *Ibid.*, p. 48.
27. *Ibid.,* (foot notes), p. 49.
28. *Ibid.*, p.54.
29. Mansergh and Lumby, *The Transfer of Power,* 1942-7, I, 1970, pp. 110-112.
30. *See* Sen, Dhinendranath, *Revolution by Consent*, p. 215.
31. Mansergh and Lumby, *op. cit.*,I. p, 113-114.
32. *Ibid.,* I. p. 114.
33. *See* Azad, Maulana A.K., *India Wins Freedom,* p.47.
34. Stafford's proposals were published on 30 April 1942. Sitaramayya, *op. cit.,* II, pp. 313-15.
35. *See* Laski Herald J., *Strategy of Freedom.*
36. Laski, *op. cit.,* p. 354.
37. For further details *see* Gwyer & Appadorai, *op. cit.*, II.
38. Azad, Maulana A.K., *India Wins Freedom,* pp. 48-51.
39. Azad, A.K., *op. cit.*,pp. 52-53.
40. *Ibid.*, pp. 54-55.
41. Laski, *op. cit.*, p. 362. *See* for further details, Sharma J.S., *op. cit.,*pp. 589-613.

7

The Quit India Movement

The Circumstances

Cripps proposals were suddenly withdrawn on 11 April 1942. The whole drama of Cripps Mission to India seemed to be only a propaganda move without any intention of acceding to India's demands. That it was so, was frankly admitted by the Secretary of State for India in a letter dated 10 June 1942. He wrote to the Viceroy: "Cripps Mission...has by now receded far into the background of his (Churchill's) mind. For him, the main thing about it has been the good effect in America; for the rest, he isn't interested, really disliking the whole problem as much as ever before,"[1] But the public opinion could not be befooled even in England, and exasperated at the attitude of B.B.C. also, Linlithgow wrote to the Secretary of State: "I have been very much disturbed by the prominence lately given to Nehru and Gandhi's utterances in the B.B.C. oversea broadcast...it creates a world-wide impression that Nehru and Gandhi are entitled to speak for all India and our natural and only successors...I would suggest...that if it is not possible...to debar the B.B.C. from giving any (such) publicity...in the same way as...news from any enemy source, such matter should be subjected to the closest scrutiny and that minimum publicity should be accorded to it."[2] While before the outside world, then, the British might have been able to paint a dark picture of India, a divided house unfit for immediate freedom; within India the Cripps Mission resulted only an utter frustration and disgust. The Congress efforts to reorganize India for an effective fight against the Japanese menace received a severe jolt and the general mass of people fell into a dull despondency, which could prove utterly harmful to the country. Maulana Azad comments thus: "There was great bitterness against the British which at times was so intense that they did not think of the consequences of Japanese conquest of India." To Jawaharlal, therefore, it seemed necessary "to convert the sullen passivity of the people into a spirit of non-submission and resistance, though that non-submission would be to begin with against arbitrary orders of the British authorities it could be turned into resistance to an invader. Submissiveness and servility would lead to the same attitude towards the other and thus to humiliation and degradation."[3]

In the meanwhile the Japanese danger to India had increased and their attack on Bengal seemed imminent. Mr. Gandhi somehow developed the belief that if the British immediately left India there would be no reason left for Japan to attack this country. It was therefore proposed that a 'Quit India' resolution should immediately be passed by the Congress, for as Gandhi told Louis Fischer: "There is no half-way house between withdrawal and non-withdrawal. It is, of course, no complete physical withdrawal that I ask."[4] The demand was only for an immediate transfer of power to India failing which the Congress would launch a non-violent movement against the British. Gandhi perhaps believed that with Japan knocking at the very doors of India, the British instead of taking any drastic steps against the movement would rather try to come to terms with the Congress.

The Congress Resolution

The Congress Working Committee, therefore, met on 14 July 1942 and despite its President, Maulana Azad's view that "a non-violent movement could not be launched or carried out in the existing circumstances,"[5] and that in case a resolution to this effect was passed, the Government would immediately take a drastic action against the Congress leaders, the resolution was adopted. The resolution made out the following important points: (1) The Congress was willing to change the existing ill-will against Britain into a goodwill and make India a willing partner in the war in favour of the Allies, but that was possible only "if India feels the glow of freedom." (2) The communal tangle in India could be solved only if the British withdraw from this country. (3) In making, however, "the proposal for the withdrawal of the British rule from India, the Congress has no desire whatsoever to embarrass Great Britain or the Allied Powers in their persecution of war." As a proof of their sincerity with regard to this, the Congress was "agreeable to the stationing of the armed forces of the Allies in India, should they so desire, in order to ward off and resist Japanese or other aggression and to protect and help China." (4) Should, however, this appeal fail, the Congress would be reluctantly compelled to start a non-violent movement under the leadership of Gandhi "for the vindication of the political rights and liberty." (5) The A.I.C.C. would meet on 7 August and take a final decision in this connection.

The All India Congress Committee meeting confirming the above resolution of its Working Committee, clarified the position further in its resolution of 7 August. It said (1) On the declaration of India's independence, provisional Government representative of all-important sections of the people of India will be formed. (2) Its primary functions would be to defend India together with its Allied powers, and to promote that well-being of the people. (3) The provisional Government would evolve a scheme for constituent assembly, which will prepare a constitution acceptable to all. (4) After yet another appeal to the British for the transfer of power, the Committee sanctioned the starting of a non-violent movement against the British, if necessary, under the leadership of Gandhiji.[6]

Crisis Precipitated

After the Congress Working Committee first passed the resolution, Mr Gandhi told a large concourse of the foreign press on 15 July that if the power was not immediately transferred and if the Congress started its movement, it would be a non-violent revolution against the British. Gandhi was perhaps certain that the Japanese menace being at the very doors of India, whatever was said the Government would precipitate the crisis. But Gandhi's gun misfired as it had done several times before. Shortly after the Press Conference, Mira Ben (Miss Slade, daughter of a British admiral, who had become Gandhiji's disciple and was given this name) was sent to the Viceroy to explain the matter. But it was an utter surprise that the Viceroy refused even to give her an interview when the Congress was talking of a rebellion, violent or non-violent. Gandhi, however, still continued to believe that the Viceroy would not precipitate the crisis and on 8 August 1942, the A.I.C.C. passed its resolution.

But the worst happened as Maulana Azad and Jawaharlal had feared, and as a reaction to the Quit India Resolution of the A.I.C.C. on the morning of 9 August, Gandhiji together with the whole Congress High Command, including Jawaharlal, Maulana Azad, Acharya Kripalani, Asaf Ali, G.B. Pant and others, was bundled into a special train to prison. Gandhiji was in the Aga Khan's Palace at Poona, while the others were taken to the Ahmednagar fort in the Bombay Province. Dr. Rajendra Prasad who for some reason had not attended the A.I.C.C. meeting, was arrested and detained at Patna. They were all condemned to imprisonment till 15 June 1945.

The action of the Congress was not liked by the Muslim League which termed it as a movement directed at coercing the British to hand over the Government to a Hindu oligarchy, and at disabling the British from fulfiling their obligations towards the Muslims. The League directed the Muslims to dissociate themselves from the movement. The Hindu Mahasabha remained lukewarm but refused to court arrest. The Communists feared that the Congress movement would jeopardize the Allies' position in the war. Only the Socialist

Party supported it, but they rather preferred to do so by an underground movement.

On the general mass of people, however, it had an effect of an electric current. The leaders being behind the bars, the movement founded in non-violence began to develop a horribly violent effect, as it was to be expected. Everywhere the students, the workers, the housewives, the businessmen and others rose in protest against such sudden arrest of their leaders. There were processions, meetings and strikes. Life in Delhi, Bombay, Madras, Amritsar and several other cities was paralysed. The Government's retaliation was brutal, to which the people reacted with equal vehemence. But the armless people could not fight for long. The lathi-charges, machine-gun fires from aeroplanes, brutal torture of men and dishonouring and open insult of women, all this silenced the people to an utter helplessness, and the movement went underground.

The Government estimate of the losses, which was said to be exaggerated in certain respects and underestimated in others, showed: 940 persons were killed, 1,630 injured in firing, 60,229 arrested and 18,000 detained. Bombing was resorted to at 6 places, i.e. Patna, Nadia, Bhagalpore, Monghyr, Tamulk and Talchera, and military was called out at 60 places. On the other hand, 318 stations were burnt or destroyed; at 12,000 places telephone and telegraph wires were tampered with: 60 post-offices were completely destroyed, 252 seriously damaged and 633 less badly damaged. There were 59 derailments. The total loss in property, equipment, cash, etc., was of the value of about 44 lakhs of rupees.[7] Among others, the Chanda district of Bengal, Ballasore district of Orissa, the eastern districts of U.P., the whole of Assam, Bihar and the coast-area of Orissa suffered the most brutal atrocities committed by the Government.

Violence Responsibility

Opinions have differed as to who was responsible for all this violence in the midst of intense efforts of the Congress to keep its struggle completely non-violent. The blind followers of Gandhi's logic would say that it was the Government who did it. For had not Gandhi instructed his followers just before his arrest: Let every non-violent soldier of freedom write out the slogan 'do or die' on a piece of paper or cloth and stick it on his clothes, so that in case he died in the course of offering satyagraha, he might be distinguished by this sign from other elements who do not subscribe to non-violence."

But the tragedy is, the words often convey a meaning different from what is thought of, and in this case that is what happened when the words 'do or die' shorn of their context, became a slogan with the people. Moreover, Gandhi himself said that the voluntary courting or arrest would be different this time, and the volunteers would resist arrest, submitting to Government only if physically forced to do so.[8] Gandhi's words that in case of the government's failure to respond, the Congress would start a non-violence revolution, had indeed an immediate effect when instead of bowing down before the Congress demand, as it was expected, the Viceroy even refused to see Mira Ben.

It would not in fact be wrong to say that Gandhi had misread the whole situation, and despite the warning of Maulana Azad he persisted in the belief that the Viceroy would not arrest the leaders and precipitate the crisis. One would have wished that at least after the Viceroy's refusal to meet Mira Ben he would have realised what effect his professions were having on others and what was the Viceroy likely to do if the A.I.C.C. passed its resolution. But this did not happen. It is indeed impossible for an impartial observer to hope that in the event of the Congress talking of non-violent revolution, the Viceroy would wait to discuss the matters peacefully with the leaders. But Gandhi persisted in his theory and even as late as just an hour before his arrest on 9 August he told Mahadev Desai: "After my speech of last night, they will never arrest me."

That the Government had been closely watching the situation and had decided upon a plan of strong action immediately after the 14 July resolution of the Congress Working Committee is revealed from a circular letter the Viceroy addressed to the different Indian Governors. In his letter of 3 August 1942, the Viceroy informed the Secretary of State for India as to how the Provincial Governors had been instructed to follow a two-stage plan to meet the situation created by the Congress resolution. The first stage of the plan was to be followed till the ratification of the Working Committee's resolution, and it consisted of usefully employing the time in propaganda and public opinion inside and outside India, to get a support for strong action. "The ratification of Working Committee's resolution without substantial amendment (and no amendment will be regarded as substantial unless it unambiguously removes threat of mass movement) will mark commencement of second stage. As soon as this takes place Bombay Government will inform Government of India, all Provincial Governments, Chief Commissioners and Political Residents by telegram containing pre-arranged code word. No action will, however, be started until Government of India send all above addresses further telegrams containing another pre-arranged code word which will be the signal for action...On receipt of telegram from Government of India—

(a) Bombay Government will arrest Gandhi and all members of Working Committee who may be in Bombay under Defence Rule 26.

(b) Each Provincial Government will proclaim under Criminal Law Amendment Act, Congress Working Committee, All-India Congress Committees and Provincial Congress Committees operating within its jurisdiction, but not Indian National Congress as a whole. Provincial Governments will also be directed to proclaim other Congress Committees or Committees affiliated to Congress, including those of Congress Socialist Party, against which they consider it essential to take action…

(c) Each Provincial Government will then seize relevant offices and funds and also arrest under Defence Rule 26 all individuals whom they consider competent and likely to attempt to organize and launch mass movement…

If any member of Working Committee abstains from attending Bombay meeting on…lack of sympathy…he will not be arrested immediately but his reaction to the other arrests will be awaited. Any member who is prevented from attending by unavoidable circumstances will be arrested in his province…

Gandhi will be arrested under Defence Rule 26 and will be detained in Bombay Presidency…Mahadev Desai, Mira Ben and Doctor Sushila Nair (Lady Doctor) will be permitted to accompany Gandhi if they voluntarily accept restrictions on communication."[9]

There was in fact also a proposal to deport Mr Gandhi and some of his colleagues to Uganda, Aden or Nyasaland, beyond the reach of the people of India, which, they thought, would help to dispose of the problem probably for good. But the Indian Members of the Viceroy's Council did not agree and the matter had to be dropped.[10]

The worst happened. The leaders were arrested, and this resulted into an uncontrolled mass movement, which was bound to go violent. Clearly thus, Gandhi's failure to read the situation correctly and some of the words which he uttered led to such violence which he himself so much abhorred.

But for all this, Mr Gandhi is not alone to blame. The people of India by their habits formed through centuries are prone to be led by charismatic personalities. Little wonder, one would often hear them say that Gandhiji would bring freedom to India by some superhuman method or a magic. The tragedy, however, lies in the fact that even the great leaders such as Dr Rajendra Prasad, Sardar Patel and Acharya Kripalani should have been so mesmerized in his presence as to have completely laid aside their own judgement. It was unfortunate for Gandhiji that only very few ventured to argue with him freely, for which he should himself perhaps have felt sorry in his silent moments. His decisions in such circumstances often proved faulty and immature. This happened in the Congress Working Committee meeting on 14 July. Besides the Maulana, only Jawaharlal Nehru ventured to disagree with Gandhi in his belief that the Government would not fall with a heavy hand in the event of such a resolution being adopted. All the rest nodded their assent without much argument, believing that what Gandhi held could never be wrong.

Yet, the revolution of 1942 had been a great event in the history of India. Its amplitude can well be judged from J.P. Narain's observation: "The resolution of 1942 occupies the same place in the history of this country as the French and Russian revolutions in the history of their respective countries. The amplitude of the Revolution had no parallel in history. In no other revolution had such vast multitudes taken part."[11] And although it was soon crushed, in its effects it was far reaching. The words 'Quit India' had not been uttered in the Congress resolutions. They were adopted by the people who felt the resolution amounted to this. Yet these words had come to stay. The old talk of Dominion Status was burnt away in the terrible fire of 42, and now a new India was born with 'a new direction to its political life.'

One is tempted to quote at length from a Bombay Congress bulletin dated 9 January 1943 to exhibit the spirit that dominated the times. This may also incidentally prove that the lieutenants of Mr Gandhi did not share his philosophy, even when they understood it. The bulletin said: "Let us admit that the revolution has not been able to attain that pitch, that momentum, which we all expected it would...The gigantic and sweeping mass uprising and mass demonstrations and mass attacks that we witnessed in the beginning of our struggle have slowed down and subsided...We Confess that while numerous centres of usurper administration have been attacked and, in many cases, destroyed, and the war on communications had been carried on with more or less sustained tempo, we have not been, as yet able to paralyse the administration completely. The factories are still working and producing war materials, and other factories which have been producing intellectual slaves are still active: the students have again lapsed into inactivity and drifted into the old rut..."[12]

How the Viceroy himself looked at the 1942 revolution is revealed by his letter to the Secretary of State in which while expressing his irritation at the growing interest of America in the Indian problem he said: "I am engaged here in meeting by far the most serious rebellion since that of 1857, the gravity and extent of which we have so far concealed from the world for reasons of military security...The lives of Europeans in outlying places are today in jeopardy...These are the circumstances in which I am now threatened by visitations from Wendell Wilkie and Sherwood Eddi...My experience of peripatetic Americans which is now extensive is that their zeal in teaching us our business is in inverse ratio to their understanding of even the most elementary of the problems with which we have to deal. My fear now is that these Americans may openly express their wish to see Congress leaders now under detention. Whether they themselves do or do not press for that, I am certain that the Hindu Press, which is always anxious to exploit the possibilities of American intervention in Indian affairs, will proclaim that they ought to see Gandhi and Nehru. Pressure of that nature is bound to be deeply damaging to my government. Moreover such visitors do untold harm by airing their uninformed opinions in interviews and private conversations. "The Viceroy begged the Home authorities to arrest at least for a time this flow of well-meaning sentimentalists from the USA to India, so that we may mind here, what is still, I suppose, our business."[13]

GANDHI'S FAST AND RELEASE

Within a short time after the arrest of the Congress leaders, the situation in the country was brought to normal. And now started a propaganda campaign at the British hands, in India as well as abroad that it was Gandhi who was responsible for all the violence perpetrated in the country. When Gandhi learnt of it, he was perturbed and desired that either he should be tried in a court of law for the charge preferred against him or he should be allowed to clear his position in public. But the Government insisted that the 'Quit India' resolution and some utterances of Gandhi were responsible for violence and unless the 'Quit India' resolution was withdrawn, the Government could not release Gandhiji.

Despite all this, however, Mr Gandhi had some compunctions, and as Maulana Azad writes, for two main reasons he decided to undertake a fast for twenty-one days. These reasons were, that "he had not expected that Government would arrest the Congress leaders so suddenly. He had also hoped that he would get time to develop the movement on non-violent lines according to his own ideas. Both his hopes had been shattered. He accepted the responsibility for what had happened and undertook "the fast as an expiation for the situation."[14]

The fast commenced on 10 February 1943 and after thirteen days his condition became so bad that the physicians attending on him declared that he would collapse within 24 hours unless released earlier. The Viceroy, Lord Linlithgow, however, remained ruthlessly indifferent and in an emergency meeting of his Council got majority of the Councillors vote against Gandhi's release. Only three persons, M.S. Aney, H.P. Modi and N.R. Sarcar voted against the move, and these three gentlemen even resigned from the Council. A non-party Conference held at Delhi, but not attended by the League, demanded an immediate release of Gandhi. But even this had no effect on the

Viceroy who demanded that Gandhi should publicly repent and the 'Quit India' resolution should be withdrawn before the release of Gandhiji could be ordered. The callousness of the Viceroy who had majority of the councillors under his influence, went even to such an extent that it was learnt that sandal wood was collected in the Agha Khan palace for cremation if the worst should happen. It was lucky however, that the calculations both of the physicians and the Government were upset, and Gandhi lived on to come successfully out of his self-imposed ordeal.

There is an account which seems interesting to quote: "On 21st February Gandhi's condition was critical and his death was thought to be very near. From that day forward he suddenly began to improve. By the 25th he was considered out of danger. It was an amazing recovery. Many believed it to be an act of God. Others attribute it to glucose, among them the Surgeon-General, who thought that Mahatma was probably given a stimulant by an attendant whose devotion to him proved stronger than obedience to the rules of fasting which forbade such synthetic support. Whatever the truth of the matter there was a curious circumstance concerning Gandhi's weight. When he began his fast on 10th February he weighed 109 lbs. By the 16th he was down to 97 ½ lbs. On the 24th, when he was well enough to be weighed again, his weight was 90 lbs. But on 2nd March, the last day of his fast, it had gone upto 91 lbs. It has been a most strange sequence of events. From an Indian source the Viceroy heard that the crisis in Gandhi's condition was engineered, while the "leaders" conference was taking place, between Birla House and the Mahatma's entourage: as soon as it was clear that the Government of India were not going to move, a message was sent authorizing the application of stimulants. The whole truth will probably never be known. It may well be that Gandhi himself was unaware of what was done to resuscitate him."[15]

Sir R. Lumly, the Governor of Bombay was rather forthright in his declaration that Gandhi "has, in the result, confounded all medical prophets. The most likely explanation of this feat seems to be, first, that he knows more about fasting than any doctor: and, secondly, that one or other of the non-official doctors gave him glucose to help him through, and possibly more fruit-juice than has been admitted."[16]

During Mr Gandhi's fast President Roosevelt's representative in India was kept by the Viceroy in touch with all developments. The President repeatedly expressed his concern and on 19 February 1943 he wrote to his representative to express to the Viceroy "our deep concern over the political crisis in India. Please express to his Excellency our hope that a means may be discovered to avoid the deterioration of the situation which would be almost certain to occur if Gandhi dies." How the Viceroy himself looked at the possible consequences of Gandhi's failure to survive the fast is revealed from his reply to the anxious enquiry of the American representative, as he wrote to the Secretary of State for India: "Mr Phillips asked me what would happen if Gandhi dies. I replied, six month's unpleasantness, steadily declining in volume: little or nothing at the end of it. After it was over—as it would be over before India was wanted for a major operation of war eastwards—India would be far more reliable as a base for operations. Moreover the prospect of a settlement would be greatly enhanced by the disappearance of Gandhi, who had for years torpedoed every attempt at a settlement."[17]

In the meanwhile, with the efforts to crush the agitation, the search for a suitable solution of the Indian problem continued. The statesmanship of Mr Amery, the Secretary of State for India, is revealed in his letter to Linlithgow dated 19 October 1942. He wrote: "I have no doubt you get as bored as I do with the continuous clamour for some 'initiative' to break the deadlock, some new constructive' policy, by people who have neither initiative nor constructive ideas of their own to suggest, but who feel that somehow, somewhere, there is an "Open Sesame' that needs only to be spoken by you or me to create a united self-governing India throwing itself with undivided enthusiasm into the war...I have always attached the greatest importance to Coupland's work (R. Coupland, *The Future of India*—Oxford University Press, 1943) and only hope that the actual analysis of the constitutional problem in his third volume will come out reasonably early next year. I should be quite glad, too, much as I am opposed to any form of American political intervention, if some American University were to appoint its own Coupland, or even trio of Couplands to study the constitutional problem. The conclusions, good, bad, or indifferent, might at any rate help both Indians and Americans to realise what the problem is...One of the difficulties about an overt initiative on our part has always been the suspicion which would be directed against any team nominated by ourselves. Somehow it ought to come from Indians, but so far neither party leaders nor even Indian students or businessmen seem to have made the slightest attempt to get down to it." Continuing, the Secretary of State suggested in the alternative that a committee of three or four members of the Viceroy's Council itself, all of them Indians, may be appointed "to investigate the possibility of creating an organization of non-official political investigator working under an impartial Chairman such as Judge from one of the dominions. The term of reference might be:

(1) to study and recommend methods in expansion of or alternative to those proposed in the draft Resolution for bringing into existence the kind of constitution-making body that would be most likely to lead to an agreed and workable constitution;

(2) to prepare materials in the form of studies of particular problems bound to engage the attention of the constitution-making body which might serve to facilitate the subsequent discussion of these in that body itself.

...What it would, I hope, do is to stimulate the process of thinking and turn India's mind on to the concrete problem to be settled and distracted from the futile clamour for impossible, because irreconciliable, demands." In another letter of 10 November the Secretary of State even proposed that some acknowledged experts in the American Federal Constitution "should be specifically invited to join force with experts in India in studying the Indian constitutional problem. They and possibly also a Swiss Constitutionalist might be co-opted...and arrangement of this sort would have the advantage of ensuring that the American contribution was made with the full sense of responsibility and would bring American fair and square up against Indian political intransigencies."

The Viceroy however objected to the proposal of Committee of his Council being appointed for the purpose. For he said in his reply that "action on these lines might well cost me my government. I would be known all over India within a week, and from the moment they embark on this enquiry my colleagues selected for the duty would be the target of propaganda and prejudice from every conflicting interest in the country."[18] Otherwise also the whole proposal was dropped.

One only regrets that while forwarding such views the Secretary of State and the Viceroy completely forgot that already once at least the Indian leaders had drafted a constitution, which they would like to have in India. It was the famous Nehru Report of 1928, which the Government decided then completely to overlook.

OTHER DEVELOPMENTS

Wardha Scheme of Education

Of the other developments of the time of Linlithgow, some related to the field of education, The Wardha Scheme of Education came into being in 1936. This scheme was a product of the genius of Mahatma Gandhi who himself appointed an experts' committee to go into the matter as he desired and submit its report. The report thus prepared presented the nation with a scheme of education, which is popularly known as the Wardha Scheme of Education or the scheme of Basic Education, which was put into practice by the Congress ministries under the constitutional reforms of 1935. The scheme secured its best success in Kashmir and Bihar, but the outbreak of the Second World War leading to the resignation of the Congress ministries, checked its progress till a thought began to be given to it anew after India's independence.

The whole scheme revolved around the principle of educating the children on such lines besides developing (a) the mental and intellectual capabilities of the children, (b) develop also their moral qualities, (c) make them capable of earning their livelihood right from the beginning and (d) teach them to produce such articles of art and beauty during their education itself that should pay their way through. Thus, under this scheme, (i) the children are educated through some craft or some other productive work such as carpentry, smithy, spinning, weaving, etc. which should be locally popular. (2) The selected craft is made the centre and around this the whole plan of child's intellectual and moral development is revolved. (3) The commodities thus prepared in the institution, are to be sold out in the market, and it is expected that the income that would thus accrue, would make the scheme self-sufficient in its financial requirements. (4) Under this scheme, the primary education would occupy as many as seven years, (5) a compulsory but free education would be given to all boys and girls of a particular age group and (6) the instructions would be imparted in the child's mother tongue. (7) It was hoped that the scheme would make an all round development in the child-mental, moral, intellectual and professional.

The Sargeant Scheme of 1943

Another scheme came in 1943. It was the Sargeant Scheme of Education prepared by a Committee appointed for the purpose under the chairmanship of Sir John Sargeant the Education Adviser of the Government of India. The scheme was to be put into practice after the end of Second World War.

The Sargeant Committee considered the matter in its details. It liked some of the principles of the Wardha Scheme and adopted them in its report. But it covered not only the primary, but also the secondary education, the university education, technical and physical education.

The Committee recommended that (1) Nursery schools should be opened for the children of 3 to 6 years age group. These schools should be run by women and instead of imparting any instructions, should teach them good social behaviour and other such things through games and friendship among them. (2) For the children of 6 to 14 years' age group, education should be made compulsory and free and should be divided into two parts; (a) part one for children of 6 to 11 years of age, and to be known as the Junior Basic; and (b) part two to be for those students of average calibre who cannot be taken direct from the Junior Basic into the High School Education, this part to be known as the Senior Basic. (3) The children of the age of 11 to 17 years, who have shown a promising progress during the Junior Basic training, and some even of the Senior Basic students who have by now given a better proof of their genius, should be taken into High or Seconday Schools; and (4) about ten per cent of the High School students who have shown an excellent progress during their course of studies, should be taken into the colleges for university examination after completing a three year's degree, course. (5) The cream of the students should be taken for pure and applied research. (6) A National Youth Movement should be started to educate the young men in physical health. (7) University Grants Commisssion should be set up to maintain a good standard of teaching and examination, and salaries of the teachers should be raised to attract the best talent to this profession. The scheme envisaged an expenditure of over 200 crores of rupees. But after the war was over, India having secured her independence, the scheme as such, was never put into practice, though the schemes adopted by independent India did draw upon its best qualities.

India's Sterling Balance

An interesting event of the time of Lord Linlithgow was the development of India's sterling balances. Before the war the balances had been in favour of Britain, but during the war the situation was dramatically reversed. India paid in many ways, men, supplies, etc. with the result that she now became a considerable creditor of England and the Allies. On 14 March 1942 Sir Kingsley Wood put up a note that "unless steps are taken in the very near future to reduce substantially the rate at which these balances are growing, the position will be created of extreme difficulty which will be far beyond the possibility of solution by the resumption of exports. We shall be quite unable to convert these immense sterling sums into gold, dollars or other currencies except very gradually. They will, therefore, have to be blocked and we shall be told that the City of London is obtaining a forced loan from the impoverished Indians or we shall be accused of defaulting on our debt to India. This would be most dangerous politically." It was proposed that Britain's part "should be to supply everything that calls for payment in sterling and India's all that calls for payment in rupees."[19] This is because war requires all resources to be pooled.

Linlithgow was distressed, "at the prospect of India being considered to have played less than her part in war sacrifice," and persuaded the Cabinet to receive his Finance Member Sir Jeremy Raisman for discussion of the matter. It was argued that India being a poor country any repudiation of the debt by England, which was her trustee, would be unreasonable. As a result of such a step the sympathy of the Indian leaders would be lost, more so because even after such sacrifices India remained relatively defenceless against an invader. As a result of the discussions. Raisman was able to extract a promise from the

Chancellor that he would persuade the Prime Minister Churchill, who was then away in the Middle East, that a favourable decision for India should be taken. In the meanwhile the decision was deferred with the approval of the Cabinet. Churchill was however a different man and he was furious when he learnt what had happened in his absence. The Secretary of State Amery wrote to the Viceroy:

"Winston harangued as at great length about the monstrous idea that we should spend millions upon millions for the defence of India, then be told to clear out, and on top of it all owe India vast sums incurred on her behalf. I tried, without much effect, to make him understand that a great deal of this expenditure was for goods supplied to the Middle East and even to this country, that anyhow it was impossible to disassociate the defence of India from the general war effort and say that everything we did in the Far East was simply done for the defence of India…"[20]

Churchill's arguments were indeed strange. India had been declared a belligerent country against her wishes. She fought for the defence of Britain and her Allies and now when the real danger of Japanese invasion as a result of the British follies was at her very doors and the Prime Minister himself had declared that Britain had no ready means to defend her, she was suddenly told that whatever Britain did in the war was done only for her defence and she should meet the expense. The discussions continued and the Cabinet deferred the question only on Churchill's condition that Britain reserved the right to reopen the whole question with a view to a possible counter-claim against India. Linlithgow refused to accept this condition. But in the meanwhile the Congress rebellion in India enraged the Prime Minister yet further and the Viceroy could secure no justice for the country.[21]

Agricultural Problems

The Viceroy had a keen interest in India's agricultural problems. "Gow" which in Hindi means 'cow' is the last syllable of the Viceroy's name, and he within a few days of his arrival in India bought two Hissar bulls at his own expense, to be made available to the cultivators in the neighbourhood of New Delhi for purposes of breeding. He personally visited several Indian villages and in 1937 organised an All-India Cattle Show which proved a great success.

Towards the end of November 1938 the Viceroy held a Conference of Ministers on Agricultural Marketing in which he emphasized the need of an adequate preliminary survey and carefull economic reconnaissance. He pleaded for standardization and explained what he meant by it· "…The marketing officer, who knows the requirements of the ultimate markets and the prices ruling in those markets, is frequently in a position to advise the cultivator that he will increase his prospects of profit by growing some varieties other than that one which seems to possess the highest agricultural advantages...Consider how much loss may be spared to the grower if his marketing organization is able to provide him with very early warning of...a change in demand..."[22]

The Famine

In 1943 a great famine once again shown its ugly face in India and this time made a million and a half of the population of Bengal a morsel under its deathgiving monstrous jaws. Lack of detailed statistics, bad communications, pressure on railway for military traffic, greed of traders and hoarders, difficulty of making the people switch from one diet to another, suspicion of the bona fides of the Government, denial of natural rice supplies from Burma, bad harvests, cyclone, floods and inefficiency of the Government, all these were the causes of this famine. The remedy probably lay in imports, but Britain and the Allies could not spare the shipping. Under the system of provincial autonomy introduced by the Act of 1935, famine was constitutionally a provincial responsibility. For this reason and because of the Viceroy's "obsessive contempt for personal publicity" as the Viceroy's son. Glendevon writes, the Viceroy did not as much as even pay a visit to Bengal.[23]

Be that as it may, the Bengal Famine Enquiry Commission was appointed which submitted its report in September 1945 and expressed its shock at the failure of the Government and of the society to protect such large mass of unfortunate people from the fatal fate. It expressed its astonishment at a complete "moral and social breakdown" in the country, few feeling the responsibility for doing something to save the starving populace.

The Commission recommended that the Central Government should amalgamate the Departments of Food and Agriculture into one. An All India Food Council should be set up to coordinate food administration all over the country. The production of protective food should be increased so as to improve the standard of nutrition. The State should monopolise the procurement and distribution of grains. The agricultural prices should be kept at a fair level so as to serve the interests both of the producer and the consumer. The minimum and maximum price should be fixed up for rice and wheat for the post-war period till the end of at least six years of the war. The Government of India worked on the recommendation to meet the situation of rising prices immediately after the war. The situation was creditably handled, but this happened in the time of Wavell, the successor of Linlithgow.

The Fakir of Ipi

Linlithgow had to face certain problems in the North-West Frontier areas also where the Fakir of Ipi raised a standard of revolt. It was the tribes of Waziristan, which struck this time. Ipi belonged to Torikhel Waziris and was born in 1890. He was Imam of the small mosque at Ipi in 1936. The place was situated close to the road between the Lower Tochi valley and Bannu. John Glendevon writes: "It was rumoured in the hills that he kept two pigs, one representing the Viceroy and the other the Commander-in-Chief. When in a mood to stimulate his morale he would cut a small piece from one or the other or both."[24] Though the first part of this statement may be correct the second part of it seems to be difficult to understand. Arthur Swinson says that the Fakir "was a fanatical hater of all infidels willing at any time to stir up religious passion for his own ends."[25]

It was in 1936 that the Waziri revolt under the leadership of the Fakir of Ipi, who had slowly gathered importance for his hatred of the British, took place. The Mahsuds and the Waziris of Wanna also jumped into the fray, a holy war was declared and by 1937 the British had to put as many as 30,000 troops in the field. The Fakir organised his *lashkars* with great tact and skill. Each man who joined him was to bring his own food sufficient at least for ten days. The Durand Line was in the proximity of the disturbed areas and when hotly pursued it was not difficult for the rebellious man to escape across it to Afghanistan. The Afghan Government secretly sympathized with them, and this made the matter still more difficult for the British. The Fakir "himself was as slippery as an eel. In time he built himself a hide-out in the remote valley of Gorwekht, about a mile from the border; and his lieutenants were always able to give him ample warning of the approach of enemy troops."[26] When all warnings to the Torikhel people to expel the Fakir from their midst fell on deaf ears, an attack was delivered on the Fakir's headquarters at Arsalhot. The resistance soon collapsed but the Fakir himself escaped. After the suppression of the Torikhel the rebellion of 6,000 Bhitannis had to be faced. From here the Fakir moved down to Maddakhel and from there on to the mountainous country to the west of Razmak near the Durand line. The trouble continued and although the tribal people suffered heavy losses as a result of extensive air bombing, the British casualties ran into hundreds killed and thousands wounded. The Fakir could not be captured and he continued his activities bringing about an unrest around Bannu even in 1940. After the partition of India the Fakir still remained at large, a considerable menace to Pakistan as he had been to the British. He died in 1960, when *The Times* honoured him with an obituary: "A man of principle and saintliness...the inspiration of and general of tribal revolt..." Arthur Swinson writes that such an obituary "must have raised many a wry smile in Cheltenham and the arm-chairs of the military clubs."[27]

An Estimate

Linlithgow retired in 1943. As a result of the role he had played in India there was no cordiality between him and Mr Gandhi. On September Mr Gandhi addressed him thus:

"On the eve of your departure from India I would like to send you a word."

"Of all the high functionaries I have had the honour of knowing, none has been the cause of such deep sorrow to me as you have been. It has cut me to the quick to have to think of you as having countenanced untruth (this probably related to Linlithgow's assertion that Gandhi was personally responsible for all the violence that took place in 1942), and that regarding one whom, at one time, you considered as your friend. I hope and pray that God will some day put it into your heart to realise that you, a representative of a great nation, had been led into a grievous error."[28]

There has been much criticism of Linlithgow's political policies in India. He has been condemned for his leisurely manner in which he approached the prices to establish a federation. Linlithgow failed to take the Indian leaders into confidence when he declared India a belligerent country. His attitude towards Mr Gandhi during his fast was too stiff and relentless for which probably the Home Government was to blame more than he. There may be a justification for his policies yet as D.H. Llips and Mary Doreen Wainwright write, "it was during Linlithgow's viceroyalty that the Indian National Congress rebelled, and the Muslim League declared for partition, which events must be accounted failures for a Viceroy charged with the task of applying the Act of 1935, which was to fulfil the British political dream of a united responsibly ruled India."[29]

R.J. Moore writes about Linlithgow: "His want of political insight and constructive imagination gave his somewhat Victorian virtues, the appearance of complacency, pomposity and insensitiveness." Further: "What made Linlithgow belatedly aware of the true nature of the Indian problem was the crystallization of the demands of the Congress and the League, soon after the outbreak of the war, and his subsequent interviews with the party leaders. Even then he was lamentably slow to take effective action, despite the promptings of Zetland. It seems possible that during the early stages of the war an outstanding diplomatist might have developed a formula to solve the Indian problem."[30]

After his retirement, Linlithgow was made a Knight of the Garter. In 1944 and 1945 he was the Lord High Commissioner to the Church of Scotland and continued enjoying several honours and distinctions.

NOTES

1. Mansergh and Lumby, *The Transfer of Power,* 1942-7, Vol.II, p.198.
2. *Ibid.,* 276-77.
3. Azad, *India Wins Freedom,* pp. 71-72.
4. *Ibid.*
5. *Ibid.*, p.76.
6. Norman D., *op. cit.,* II, 120-124.
7. See Govind Sahai, *42 Rebellion,* p.21; Sitaramayya, *op. cit,* II, pp. 376-77.
8. See Azad, A.K., *op. cit.,* p.74.
9. Mansergh and Lumby, *op. cit.,* II, pp.534-36.
10. See, *Ibid,* II., pp. 452-53, 586-87, 595-96, 606-607.
11. Gobind Sahari, *42 Rebellions,* Foreward.
12. Glendevon, John, *Viceroy at Bay,* pp. 249-50.
13. Mansergh and Lumby, *op. cit.,* II, pp. 853-54.
14. Azad, *op. cit.,* pp. 75-76.
15. Glendevon, John, *op. cit.,* pp. 266-67.
16. Mansergh and Lumby, *op. cit.*, II, p.755.
17. Mansergh and Lumby, *op. cit.*, III, pp.687-88, 690.
18. Mansergh and Lumby, *op. cit.*, III, pp 139-42, 229, 262, 270.
19. Mansergh and Lumby, *op. cit.,* I, pp.425-26.
20. Quoted Glendevon, John, *The Viceroy at Bay,* p. 255.
21. See further details, *Ibid.*, pp. 254-55.
22. *Ibid.*, pp. 107-108.
23. Glendevon, John, *op. cit.*, pp. 274-75.
24. Glendevon, John, *op. cit.*, p. 48.
25. Swinson, Arthur, *North West Frontier,* p. 327.
26. *Ibid.,* p. 328.
27. *Ibid.,* p. 332.

28. Glendevon, John, *op. cit.*, pp. 275-76.

29. Phillips and Wainwright (ed.), *Partition of India,* p. 18.

30. *Ibid.*, pp. 80-84.

8

Earl Wavell 1943-47

Son of Major-General Archibald Graham Wavell by Lian Mary, Archibald Percival Wavell was born on 5 May 1883. After getting his education he was commissioned in his father's regiment, the Black Watch in 1901. For some time he served in Africa and was then posted in India. In 1908 he passed into the Staff College and was sent to Russia where he travelled much and learnt the Russian language. In the First World War he served as Brigade-Major in France and then as Liaison officer in the Caucasus and Egypt. He was married in 1930 to Eugenie, the daughter of an army officer. He steadily rose in his rank and was appointed Brigadier-General and Chief of Staff to an Army Corps in Egypt. When the war was over and his ranks were scaled down, he was appointed Major; in 1930 he was made a Brigade; Commander in England; in 1937 he commanded troops in Palestine and was shortly after created K.C.B. He played a considerable important role in the Second World War and was promoted Field-Marshal in 1943. In the same year he succeeded Linlithgow as Viceroy of India.

On 6 May 1944 Mr Gandhi was suddenly released. Three reasons were generally offered for this action of the Government. First, the new Viceroy Lord Wavell who took over from Lord Linlithgow in October 1943, was a man of more accommodating nature. Secondly, after his fast Mr Gandhi did not recover his old health, and in April 1944 he fell seriously ill. The Civil Surgeon of Poona declared that he was not likely to survive the illness, and the Government decided not to risk his death in the prison. Thirdly, the war situation also had changed as a result of the Indian National Army of Netaji Subhash Bose attacking India and actually occupying about 51,000 miles of the Indian territory comprising Manipur and Aishevpur. It was supposed that Gandhi's release would help meet the situation, though he was not actually permitted to meet the members of the Congress Working Committee despite his request.

THE C.R. FORMULA

For a couple of months after his release, Mr Gandhi remained too weak to take any part in politics. But as soon as he felt better, he committed two more blunders. First, in a statement to the *News Chronicle* of London he declared that if the British immediately made India free, the country would voluntarily support the British war effort. It was a surprising statement in the context that throughout the war he had held fast to his view that even if India's very independence depended on her participation in war, he for one would never favour this participation. For he was against violence of any type. This offer, while completely confusing the public opinion in India, won no credit to Gandhi even from the British as he expected. For the victory of the Allies now being almost sure, the British no longer needed India's support. The statement, it was thought, was calculated to win the British sympathy for India, but the bait offered had almost lost its value. Thus, Mr Gandhi announced such a fundamental change in his policy yet the gain was nil. The gun was fired late and amiss.

Secondly, Mr Gandhi started a correspondence with Jinnah in order to reach a settlement regarding the demand of Pakistan. The author perhaps needs to offer no apology in quoting in this connection excellent writing of Maulana Azad at length: "Gandhiji's approach to Mr Jinnah on this occasion was a great political blunder. It gave a new and added importance to Jinnah, which he later exploited to the full,...Mr Jinnah had lost much of his political importance after he left the Congress in the twenties. It was largely due to *Gandhiji's* acts of commission and omission that Mr Jinnah regained his importance...large sections of Indian Musalmans were doubtful about Mr Jinnah and his policy but when they found that *Gandhiji* was continually running after him and entreating him many of them developed a new respect for Mr Jinnah...it was *Gandhiji* who first gave currency to the title 'Quid-a-Azam', or great leader, as applied to Mr Jinnah. When Indian Musalmans saw that Gandhiji also addressed Mr Jinnah as *Qaid-i-Azam,* they felt he must really be so".[1]

Be that as it may, Mr Gandhi started his correspondence with Jinnah. Earlier Mr C. Rajagopalachari had advocated in the Congress the acceptance of the demand of Pakistan. But there being no support for his proposal, he resigned from the Congress to canvass public opinion outside. Not being a member of the Congress Working Committee now, Mr Rajagopalachari had not been arrested when others were. He prepared a definite formula regarding Pakistan and after Gandhiji was released he showed it to him. Gandhi liked this formula and it was on this basis that the correspondence with Jinnah was started. Gandhi met Mr Jinnah in September 1944 and discussed the C.R. formula with him. The C.R. formula consisted of the following clauses:

(1) The Muslim League endorses the Indian demand for independence and will cooperate with the Congress in the formation of a provisional Government for the transitional period. (2) After the termination of war, a Commission shall be appointed for demarcating contiguous districts in the north-west and east of India, wherein the Muslims are in absolute majority. In these areas a plebiscite of all inhabitants will be held on the basis of adult suffrage to decide the issue of separation. (3) It will be open to all parties to advocate their points of view before the plebiscite is held. (4) In the event of separation, mutual agreements shall be entered into for safeguarding defence, commerce and communications and for other essential purposes. (5) Any transfer of population shall only be on an absolutely voluntary basis. (6) These terms shall be binding only in case of transfer by Britain of full power and responsibility to the Government of India.

Jinnah, however, rejected this formula after some negotiation with Gandhi. Gandhi, in his answer to the questionnaire of the Sapru Committee, gave the following points on which the troubles between him and Jinnah arose: (1) Jinnah was the President of the League and considered Gandhi merely, as an individual. (2) Jinnah had no prepared scheme, but insisted that if Gandhi first accepted Pakistan of his conception, only then he would discuss other things (3) Gandhi suggested an authority at Centre acceptable to both the parties, but Jinnah insisted first on complete partition as between two nations, and then agreement between them as on Foreign Affairs, etc. (4) Jinnah wanted two independent sovereign States with no connection between them except by treaty. If any party broke that treaty consequences obviously would be war. (5) Jinnah opposed clause 2 of the C.R. formula which demanded plebiscite of all inhabitants on the basis of adult suffrage. Jinnah would not have the plebiscite of the Muslims, for he thought that the League represented the Muslims of India, and that other communities should have no voice as to Pakistan which was the Muslim's exclusive right wherever they were in majority. (6) Gandhi accepted division as between members of same family, reserving for partnership things of common interest. Jinnah wanted a complete dissolution amounting to full sovereignty in the first instance. Moreover, it was said, Mr Jinnah insisted that (7) all the six Muslim majority provinces of the Punjab, North-West Frontier, Sind, Baluchistan, Bengal and Assam should be included in Pakistan as a whole and that (8) Pakistan should be given a corridor through India. Connecting the Eastern and the Western wings of Pakistan.[2]

The C.R. formula rejected, Bhulabhai Desai, the leader of the Congress Party in the Central Legislative Assembly and Liaqat Ali, then General Secretary of the League, agreed upon a new formula on personal basis.[3] But this formula too was rejected both by the Congress and the League.

In the meantime the Congress leaders, except Mr Gandhi remained behind the bars, and as the time passed the popular resentment on this score mounted. The war situation in Europe improved as the year of 1945 opened but the war against Japan was expected to last for about two years and for this India's good will was essential. For this country was expected to be turned into a major base for the Allied war operations. Little wonder, the American pressure on the British Government for the solution of India's political problem increased. To this was also added the pressure of Russia which desired as early ending of the Indian deadlock. The deteriorating economic condition in India also played its role. The growing class of workers in this country required for the improvement of their lot an immediate attention of the Government. Nor was the condition of the Indian peasantry more enviable in this respect. There was a lack of sufficient food and starvation was rampant in many parts of the country, particularly Orissa and Bengal. The years 1943 and 1944 witnessed as many as 1 ½ million deaths for the lack of food. About 4 ½ millions suffered severely under starvation pangs. These were indeed estimates of the Government itself. But the Indian administration, over-burdened with its war activities, could pay no proper attention to all these problems. In the meanwhile the general elections in England were also approaching. The Labour Party as being incapable of handling the Indian situation blamed the Conservative Government of Mr. Churchill, and unless the Conservatives did something to pacify India, their chances of success at the polls were not supposed to be far from bleak.

It was in these circumstances that Wavell visited Home in the spring of 1945 and had certain urgent consultations on the Indian problems for about a month and a half. During this period the hostilities in Europe ended, and the whole attention of the Allies was diverted towards Japan. This added to the urgency of the matter, and after the Viceroy's return to India, a statement was issued simultaneously in London by Mr Amery, the Secretary of State for India, and in India by Wavell. This statement goes by the name of Amery-Wavell Plan or simply as the Wavell Plan.

THE WAVELL PLAN

The Statement mainly related to the Viceroy's Executive Council with regard to which the following changes were proposed:

(1) The Executive Council would be constituted so as to give a balanced

representation to the main communities, including equal proportion of Muslims and Caste Hindus. (2) For this purpose, the Viceroy would call into Conference a number of Indian politicians who were the heads of the most important parties or who have recent experience as Chief Ministers of provinces together with a few others of special experience and authority. The Viceroy would invite from this Conference a list of names who could be recommended to His Majesty for appointment to the Viceroy's Council. (3) The responsibility for the recommendation of such appointments, however, would continue to rest with the Viceroy whose freedom of choice therefore remained unrestricted. (4) The members of the Executive would be Indians with the exception of the Viceroy and the Commander-in-Chief who would retain his position as War Member. "This is essential so long as the defence of India remains a British responsibility." (5) Nothing contained in any of these proposals would effect the relations of the Crown with the Indian States through the Viceroy as Crown's Representative. (6) If such a cooperation was achieved at the Centre, it was hoped to be reflected in the provinces so as to enable the Governor's Government under Section 93 of the Act of 1935 to be replaced by coalitions of the main parties of the provinces. (7) The External Affairs (other than tribal and frontier matters which had to be dealt with as part of defence of India) would be placed in the charge of an Indian Member of the Executive so far as British India was concerned. (8) If this happens, fully accredited representatives would be appointed for the representation of India abroad. (9) All these changes were to be introduced without making any change in the existing statute law except for one amendment to the 9th Schedule to the Act of 1935 requiring that not less than three members of the Council must have at least ten years' service under the Crown in India. (10) And this, the Statement declared, was the "utmost progress practicable within the present Constitution."

Shortly after the Statement the Congress leaders were released and the Conference as proposed in the Statement, was convened at Shimla. The Conference started with high hopes which, however, were soon dashed to the ground due to a very stiff opposition of Jinnah whose objections to the proposed arrangement were that: It would shelve the issue of Pakistan; it would give the Congress a clear road to national unity, and that the interim arrangement will run for an unlimited period which would enable all the forces for United India completely to jeopardize the Muslim interests. His greatest demand, however, which ultimately sounded the death-knell of the Plan was that the League should have the sole right to nominate all the Muslims to the Council. The Viceroy rejected it saying: "I have to attempt to form an Executive Council representative, competent and generally acceptable." The Congress reaction was that it "cannot recognize the sole right of such nominations by a communal organization nor can it reduce itself as a consequence to a limited communal field."

Thus, the Wavell Plan also came to a naught. The Plan was a definite improvement upon any scheme proposed so far. It reasonably met the aspirations of the progressive Indians for an interim period, but the intransigence of the Muslim League brought its doom. Behind the League, however, it was the British diplomacy which was alleged to be at work. The Conservative Party of England, the critics said, desired to perpetuate the English hold over India by the old method of divide and rule. The whole Plan was said to be an election stunt; that was why the negotiations were abruptly called off only after about a month of the general election. It was aimed at bringing the communal differences of India to the notice of the world powers.

Yet, if the Plan failed, it left behind certain effects, which, though not palatable in every respect, made the political atmosphere of India clearer. The Pakistan issue gathered its importance and the Congress realised that it could not prevent its formation. The controversy over the responsibility of the '42 violence had brought a gloom over the Indian people who doubted if the Congress was going to stick to its 'Quit India' resolution at all. The release of the Congress leaders and unequivocal declarations of Nehru and Patel justifying the violence and expressing their resolve to adhere to the said resolution, cleared the gloom and charged the nation once again with a will to fight. This brought the Congress back into the high estimation of the people and paved the way for its grand success in the coming general elections. This also, in a way, almost exhausted the possibilities of a further progress under the 1935 Act, and thus necessitated its replacement.

CABINET MISSION PLAN

Circumstances

The year 1945-46 witnessed a sort of evolution taking plaçe all over India. Within a short time of the failure of the Shimla Conference, an entirely new India seemed to have taken birth. A wave of enthusiasm, which the release of the Congress leaders sent into every fibre of this country, was obviously, a great cause of it. But yet greater contribution towards this direction was made by two great and historic events, one of them being the INA trials.

The INA Trials

The British had sent a good number of the Indian soldiers to Singapore and Malaya. When these regions fell into the hands of the Japanese, the British officers left these soldiers to their fate. Rash Bihar Bose, a Bengali revolutionary living in Japan as an exile, prevailed upon the Japanese warlords for raising an army of Indian patriots from these prisoners of war. Subhash Chandra Bose escaping from India in January 1941, joined the INA and converted it into a magnificent fighting force. In 1944, this army attacked India and actually occupied a small part of its territories. But soon Japan surrendered and Burma being reoccupied by the British, many of the INA officers fell into the British hands as prisoners. The British wanted to prosecute them, but the Congress objected to it with the argument that these men had been deserted by the British, and had they not organized themselves into INA, they should have been forced to work in the construction of roads etc., thereby helping the Japanese to conquer India for Japan. They rather took up the best course and helped the Japanese when they promised to hand over the conquered Indian territories to the INA (Indian National Army). The British ultimately agreed to try some of these officers in public.

The three of the officers thus, Major Sehgal, Major General Shah Nawaz Khan and Colonel Dhillon, a happy combination respectively of the three communities, Hindu, Muslim and Sikh, were tried in open in the Red Fort. The trials began in November 1945 and the Congress undertaking their defence, a leading Indian Lawyer and leader of the Congress Party in the Central Legislature, Mr Bhullabhai Desai, undertook to act as their Chief Defence and Counsel. All the three, however, were ultimately convicted and sentenced to death. But such was the great public resentment generated during these trials that the Government had to bow and suspend the sentences. This was a great public victory, more significant for the symbolic union in it of the three great communities of India. A great interest in the politics of their country exhibited during this period by public, convinced the British that there had been an all round awakening and the British hold in India could not be perpetuated for long.

Naval Mutiny

Another significant event was the Naval Mutiny in Bombay during this period. Disaffection had spread in the ranks and here too disturbances began to occur on political issues. The story commenced with the mutiny in the RAF at the Dum Dum airport near Calcutta. The hunger strikes in the Royal Indian Air Force and certain cases of indiscipline in the Royal India Army followed. The greatest event however, occurred on 18 February 1946 when the naval officers in Bombay mutinied. "This was the first time since 1857 that a section of the Defence Forces had openly rebelled against the British on a political issue." And all "these developments convinced the British that they could no longer rely on the Armed forces unless the political problem of India was satisfactorily solved."[4]

Labour in Power

Luckily for India, in the meanwhile the general elections in Great Britain brought a sweeping victory to the British Labour Party, which had fought the elections on the issue of granting complete independence to India. The die-hards of Mr Churchill were swept aside and the new Labour Prime Minister Mr Attlee, shortly after assuming power, sent a Parliamentary Delegation to India in the Winter of 1945-46 to report on the Indian Situation. The Delegation was convinced that the Indian freedom could not now be delayed for too long and reported accordingly to the authorities at Home. On 14 February a proposal to send a Cabinet Mission to India was announced and on 15 March 1946 Mr Attlee made a statement in the Commons admitting (1) that in the past both the Indians and the British had committed faults; (2) that the post formula could not be applied to the situation existing in India in 1946; (3) that despite their divisions, all the Indians were united in their desire for independence; (4) that the conception of nationalism had grown so strong in India that it even permeated the military ranks; (5) that if there were some social and economic problems in India, they could be solved by the Indians alone; and (6) that, therefore, the Cabinet Mission was "going to India with the intention of using their utmost endeavour to help her to attain her freedom as speedily and fully as possible."

The proposed Mission consisting of Lord Pethick Lawrence, the Secretary of State (who headed the Mission), Mr. A.V. Alexander, the First Lord of Admiralty and Sir Stafford Cripps, President of the Board of Trade, arrived in Delhi on 24 March and immediately commenced its discussions with the Indian leaders. These discussions, however, could result in no compromise formula and ultimately the Mission had to announce its own Plan on 16 May 1946, which was as follows. This plan was known as long-range plan as against the short-range plan with which we will deal in the following pages.

The Mission ruled out the possibility of the formation of Pakistan, as desired by the Muslim League, for the following reasons: (1) A solution which involved a radical partition of the Punjab and Bengal would be contrary to the wishes and interests of a very large proportion of the inhabitants of these provinces; (2) any division of the Punjab would of necessity divide the Sikhs, leaving substantial bodies of them on both sides of the boundary; (3) the whole of the transportation and postal and telegraph systems of India have been established on the basis of a United India. To disintegrate them would gravely injure the general interest of both parts of India. (4) The Indian Armed Forces had been built up for the defence of India as a whole, and to break them in two would inflict a deadly blow on the long traditions and high degree of efficiency of the Indian Army and would entail the gravest dangers. The Indian Navy and Indian Air Force would become much less effective. (5) The two sections of the suggested Pakistan contain the two vulnerable frontiers in India and for a successful defence in depth the area of Pakistan would be insufficient. (6) A further consideration of importance is the great difficulty, which the Indian States would find in associating themselves with the divided British India. (7) And, there was the geographical factor that the two halves of the proposed Pakistan State would be separated by some seven hundred miles and the communication between them both in war and peace would be dependent on the good will of Hindustan.

A Union of India

Despite all this, the Mission would not blind itself "to the very real Muslim apprehensions that their culture and political and social life might become submerged in a purely unitary India." Keeping in view these facts, therefore, the Mission made the following recommendations regarding the Union of India:

(1)There should be a Union of India, embracing both British India and the states, which should deal with the following subjects: foreign affairs, defence and communications; and should have the powers necessary to raise the finances required for the above subjects. (2) The Union should have an executive and legislature constituted from British Indian and States representatives. Any question raising a major communal issue in the legislature should require for its decision a majority of the representatives present and voting of each of the two major communities as well as a majority of all the members present and voting. (3) All subjects other than the Union subjects and all residuary powers should vest in the provinces. (4) The states would retain all subjects and powers other than those ceded to the Union. (5) Provinces should be free to form groups with common executives and legislatures and each group could determine the provincial subjects to be taken in common. (This means the Muslim majority Provinces could constitute themselves into a group thereby securing the purpose of Pakistan to a limited extent). (6) The constitutions of the Union and of the groups should contain a provision whereby any province could be a majority vote of its legislative assembly call for a reconsideration of the terms of the constitution after an initial period of ten years and at ten-yearly intervals thereafter.

The Mission hoped that the new independent India might, choose to be a member of the British Commonwealth. But ultimately it was a matter for India herself to decide whether to do so or not.[5]

Constituent Assembly

(1) In order to frame a Constitution on the lines suggested above, the institution of a Constituent Assembly was proposed as follows: (a) The Constituent Assembly was to consist of 389 members, 292 of whom were to represent the British India, 93 would come from the Indian States while 4 were to represent the Chief Commissioner's Provinces. (b) The provincial representatives from the British India were to be sent in the proportion of one member for every one million of population. (c) The seats allotted to every province were to be divided between its different communities in proportion to their population. For this purpose only three types of electrorates were recognized, i.e., the General which were to consist of the entire population other than the Muslim and the Sikh; the Muslim and the Sikh in the Punjab. The old system of giving weightage to the minorities was dispensed with. (d) The allotment of seats to the Indian States was also done on the basis of population as above, but the method of the election of the States' representatives was to be decided by consultation for which a Negotiating Committee was to represent the States.

(2) After the preliminary meeting of the Constituent Assembly the provincial representatives were to divide themselves into three sections i.e. The non-Muslim majority provinces of Bombay, Madras, Orissa, Bihar, the United Provinces and the Central Provinces; the North-Western Muslim majority Provinces of N.W.F. Province, Punjab, Sind and the British Baluchistan, and the North-Eastern Muslim majority provinces of Assam and Bengal.

These sections were then to proceed each to settle the Constitution of the provinces included in it, and also to decide whether any group constitution would be framed for those provinces, and if so with what provincial subjects would it deal. Immediately after the new constitution comes into operation, a province would have the freedom to leave a group in which it had been placed. This decision of leaving the group could be taken by the new provincial legislature as constituted after the first general elections under the new constitution.

(3) After this, the representatives of the three sections would meet together with those of the Indian States in order to frame the Union Constitution. In the Union Constituent Assembly, a resolution the distribution of varying subjects between the Centre and the Provinces, or that dealing with a major communal issue, could be raised only if approved by a majority of representatives present and voting of each of the two major communities.

(4) The British Government would implement the Constitution drawn by this Constituent Assembly.

A Treaty

It would by necessary to negotiate a treaty between the Union Constituent Assembly and the United Kingdom to provide for certain matters arising out of the transfer of power.

Interim Arrangements

An interim government having the support of the major political parties would be set up at the earliest. This Government would be handed over all the portfolios including that of the War Member and would be given every help and cooperation by the British.

The States

Regarding the States, the Mission said, after the transfer of power to the British India, it would not be possible for the Crown to retain paramountcy over them, nor was it possible to transfer this Paramountcy to the new British Indian Government.

An Appraisal. The Cabinet Mission proposal of 16 May 1946 are supposed to be an honest effort of the British to solve the tangled political problem of India for which in a way they themselves had been responsible. These proposals sought to give the best satisfaction to all the different elements without sacrificing the essential principles of nationhood. "They offered to the Muslim community," thus observed Lord Wavell himself, "the right to direct their own essential interests, their religion, their education, their culture, their economic and other concerns." The provinces included in sections B and C and the grant of full autonomy to the Sections and freedom to frame their own constitutions, offered to the League the essence of Pakistan; yet, as Lord Wavell observed, the proposals "preserve the essential unity of India which is threatened by the dispute between two major communities; and in especial they remove the danger of the disruption of that great fellowship, the Indian army…on whose strength, unity and efficiency her future security will depend." Then, to "the Sikhs they preserve the unity of their home-land, the Punjab," and they "provide in the special committee, which forms a feature of constitution-making machinery, the best chance to the small minorities to make their needs known and secure protection for their interests."

The proposed Constituent Assembly was to be composed entirely of Indians. Its members were to be elected on democratic principles of proportional representation and on the basis of the strength of population. The communal and class division so mischievously introduced by the Act of 1935, were done away with and communal representation was now confined only to the Muslims and the Sikhs. The system of weightage to the minorities was discarded. And a definite commitment was made that a constitution framed by such a Constituent Assembly was to be implemented.

With regard to the states also, the proposals were a significant advance over all other proposals so far made. According to the Cripps' Plan, it was the Indian Princes who were to nominate the states' representatives to Constituent Assembly, but now the states were to form a Negotiating Committee to negotiate with the British Indian representatives the method of choosing the states' representatives. Obviously, therefore, under these circumstances the states, people were bound to secure a better deal with regard to their representation.

The Union Government was to enjoy full freedom in all subjects except in those which it surrendered to its units. And the Interim Government was to be handed over all the portfolios with an assurance of the best British cooperation.

Yet the proposal had certain defects. Although the rights of the Muslim minority were protected, those of the others like the Sikhs were not given much consideration. In the all India Congress Committee meeting of 6-7 July 1946, Sardar Vallabhbhai Patel particularly "referred to the great injustice done to the great Sikh community…and said that the Sikhs had not been consulted before, were thrown, bound hand and foot, into the 'B' Group…and therefore they were smarting under the sense of a grievance. Further more…the Sikhs were not given the same safeguards and communal veto as had been given to the Muslims."[6]

Although the Constituent Assembly was to be constituted on democratic lines, yet it could not be a true representative of the people, for the system of adult franchise was not introduced. Then the proposal regarding the grouping of the provinces was vague and both the Congress and the League interpreted it differently. The Sectional Assemblies were first to frame their own constitutions and those of the provinces included respectively in them, and then they would meet to frame the Constitution of the Union. The more progressive elements saw in this an attempt to put the cart before the horse. In this way, while on the one hand, the Central Constituent Assembly was to become a playing-ground of the parochial interests, on the other the provinces would lose their hard-earned autonomy; for the Provincial Constitution was to be determined by the Sectional Assembly, and the provinces like the Congress Majority Province of N.W.F. in the 'B' Group and that of Assam in the 'C'

Group were bound to have their interests severely injured at the hands of the communal majority of the League in their respective Sectional Assemblies.

Nor was the proposal regarding the lapse of the British Paramountcy over the Indian States very fortunate. This Paramountcy was not conferred on the Indian Union and the states were given full freedom whether to join this Union or not. These states were likely to aspire for separate existence, which would be ruinous alike to the states' people and to the national interests. One would also have wished that the States Negotiating Committee should be a representative of the states' people. But this was not to be.

It was good that a representative Interim Government was provided for, but for how long would it work, it was not defined.

FAILURE OF THE MISSION

The history of the Cabinet Mission in India was nicely detailed by Sir Stafford Cripps in the British Parliament on 18 July 1946.[7] According to him the negotiations with the parties could be divided into 4 periods: (1) From the arrival of the Mission in India to the end of April. (2) From the end of April to the 16th of May when the Mission issued its first statement as detailed above. (3) From 16 May to 16 June when the Mission issued its second statement. And (4) From 16 June to 29 June when the Mission left for England.

The First Period

During the first period, Congress insisted that the question of Interim Government be settled first, after which the question of the Constituent Assembly could be taken up. The League on the other hand was equally firm that they could not discuss the question of Interim Government until the long-term question of Constitution-making body was discussed. The League in fact, was committed upto the hilt to a fully sovereign Pakistan, while the Congress was equally strongly pledged to a unitary India though they would not compel people of any territorial unit to remain in the Indian Union against their declared will. The Mission concluded that they should better take up the long-term question first, thereafter immediately tackle the question of the Interim Government.

Second Period

During this period a meeting was called at Shimla where discussions were held regarding the long-term plan. Certain proposals were given and the two parties moved considerably from their initial standpoints. But after a fortnight of discussions, when it was not possible to bring them closer, the meetings were terminated and in the light of the discussions, the Mission finalized its own plan and on its return to Delhi this plan was issued on 16 May.

Third Period

The statement of 16 May having been issued, the League gave a definite acceptance to it on 6 June, though it still criticised the statement particularly on the issue of Pakistan. The Congress, however, was still anxious that the long-term and the short-term questions should be dealt with together, and it had certain misgivings on some of the points of the 16th May statement. On 25 May the Mission issued an explanatory document to remove the Congress apprehension.

The main points of the Congress stressed were: First, as to whether the provinces would be compelled to come into the three sections of the Constituent Assembly (i.e. Sections A, B, and C) in the first instance or they could stay out if they wished. The Mission made it quite clear that it was an essential feature of the Scheme that the provinces should go into Sections, though if groups were subsequently formed they could afterwards opt out of those groups. Fear was expressed that the provincial Constitution might be so manoeuvred as to make it impossible for the provinces to opt out afterwards. Sir Cripps personally, however, did not feel this fear correct. The second apprehension was as to the European vote. The Congress said that the Constitution was to be framed by the Indians. The Europeans had no locus in the matter at all. The European Party in the Bengal Legislature and the Europeans in Assam, however, themselves offered without asking, that they would take no part in the elections at all.

With regard to the short-term arrangement or the Interim Government, the Viceroy started his discussions at Shimla on the proposal that the Interim Cabinet should consist of 5 representatives of the Congress, 5 of the League and 2 of the Minorities. The Congress took strong exception to this parity between the two main parties. The Mission sought to overcome the difficulty by adding a Congress representative of the Depressed Classes to their five representatives, thus making six Congress to the five members of the League, and retaining the two other Minority representatives, one of course a Sikh—thus making a Cabinet of 13 in place of 12. Mr Jinnah was prepared to put this proposal to his Committee, but the Congress still was not satisfied. A meeting between Mr Jinnah and Mr Nehru was proposed which, however, did not materialize and a deadlock was reached.

Now, when the two main parties could not agree on any plan regarding the Interim Government, here again the Mission had to issue its own Plan most likely to be accepted by the parties. This resulted in the second statement of 16 June, which made out the following points (1) An Interim Cabinet consisting of 14 members would be constituted. Of these, six would be the Congress representatives including one representative of the Depressed Classes, 5 would represent the League, and one would come from the Sikhs, one Parsi and one Indian Christian. (2) The Viceroy would arrange the distribution of portfolios in consultation with the leaders of the two major parties. (3) The above composition of the Interim government would in no way be taken as a precedent for the solution of any other communal question. (4) Should this proposal be accepted the Viceroy would aim at inaugurating the new Government on about the 26th June (5) In the event of the two major parties or either of them unwilling to accept this scheme, it was the intention of the Viceroy to proceed with the formation of an Interim Government which would be as representative as possible of those willing to accept the scheme. (6) The Viceroy was also directing the Governors of the Provinces to summon the Provincial Legislative Assemblies forthwith to proceed with the elections necessary for the setting up of the Constitution-making body as put forward in the statement of 16 May.[8]

The Second statement obviously, still sought to retain an unreasonable parity, between the Congress and the League. Still, it was the best in the worst circumstances. The representative of the Depressed Classes added to the Congress and the Sikh and the Parsi most likely to join them, the Congress would not have too uncomfortable position in the Cabinet. Moreover, it was declared that this could not be taken as a precedent for the future. The last point of the statement, by ordering elections in the provinces, set the ball towards the long range plan rolling without waiting that the short range plan be accepted.

Fourth Period

This time Mr Jinnah took up the position that he would await the Congress decision before giving the decision of the League. The Congress on the other hand, still disliked the parity between the Muslims and the Hindus other than the Scheduled Castes. Despite this, Sir Cripps observed, the Congress might have consented but for the unfortunate and widely publicized disclosure of certain letters written by Mr Jinnah at this precise moment, the most important being that which said 'the Muslims League would never accept the nomination of any Muslim by the Congress.' This now at once became an issue. The Congress were, in fact, considering the possibility of asking for the substitution of one of their Hindus by a Muslim in order, in that way to get over the parity difficulty, and they might perhaps, in the opinion of Cripps, have waived the suggestion of nominating a Muslim, had it not been that this public challenge was made as to their right to do so. Sir Cripps observed: "It was made perfectly clear to Mr Jinnah on more than one occasion that neither the Viceroy nor the Mission could accept his claim to a monopoly of Muslim appointments though the Muslim League was certainly to be regarded as the major representative of Muslim interests."

The Congress ultimately accepted the statement of May 16 while rejecting the Interim Government. The Sikhs, however, rejected the statement of May 16, as it, according to them, did not provide similar safeguards for them as for the Muslims. But the Congress ultimately succeeded in inducing the Sikhs also to accept this statement, promising them certain safeguards. This, Cripps observed, was an act of statesmanship on the part of the Congress, as it enabled the progress to be made towards the new Constitution.

Upto that moment the League had arrived at no decision on the proposal of 16 June as they awaited the Congress decision. But now Mr Jinnah went straight and the League Working Committee accepted the scheme of 16 June. Mr Jinnah perhaps thought that the British would proceed forthwith to the formation of an Interim Government with the Muslim League alone, as the statement of 16 June itself had said that in such circumstances the Vicerory would "proceed with the formation of an Interim Government which would be as representative as possible of those willing to accept" the scheme. But Mr Jinnah was disappointed, as this could not be done, the major party having rejected the Plan. In the meanwhile, the Mission left for England on 29 June.

The States

The reaction of the States towards the proposals of 16 May was healthy. They showed their willingness and anxiousness to enter the Federal Union. But close negotiations were necessary between the Negotiating Committee which they set up and the major British Indian parties both as to the representation of the states in the Constituent Assembly and as to their ultimate position in the Union.

Further Developments

The elections to the Constituent Assembly had been ordered and on the day the Cabinet Mission left India, Caretaker Government of officials was set up to carry on the administration of the country and to supervise the elections. In the meanwhile the Viceroy Lord Wavell continued his efforts with regard to the formation of the Interim Government. On 22 July, he sent fresh proposals regarding this to the Presidents of the Congress and the League in which he repeated the proposals of 16 June except that according to the new proposals (1) it would be open neither to the Congress nor the League to object to the names submitted by the other party. (2) The Viceroy said he would "welcome a convention, if freely offered by the Congress, that major communal issues can only be decided by the consent of both the major parties."

The League rejected these proposals, as it could not tolerate Congress nominating a Muslim to the Cabinet. But the Congress accepted them, and the major party having accepted the proposals, the Viceroy invited Mr Jawaharlal Nehru to propose the names for his Ministry. A 14-member Cabinet was proposed which would include 5 Muslims.

League's Direct Action

This was a severe blow to the League, which had not been permitted to form Government when it accepted the June 16 proposals. The League retaliated, withdrew its acceptance both of the short and the long-term proposals of the Cabinet Mission and announced its intention to resort to a direct action in order to achieve Pakistan. The League as the Direct Action day fixed 16 August 1946, and what happened on that day opened the eyes of the nationalist leaders as to the extent to which the horrors of communalism could go. The Direct Action day opened at Calcutta with an unprecedented mob violence, which "plunged the great city into an orgy of bloodshed, murder and terror. Hundreds of lives were lost. Thousands were injured and property worth crores of rupees destroyed," writes Maulana Azad. But the wonder was that despite this, a large military contingent waiting in trucks stood only as spectators. When Mr Azad who happened to be in Calcutta, asked 'why they were not helping to restore order, they replied that their orders were to stand ready but not to take any action."[9] Perhaps the League Ministry of H.S. Suhrawardy, was anxious to demonstrate as to what could happen if League demands were not accepted. It was the innocent Hindus who suffered at the Muslim hands at Calcutta. But the Hindus of other places did not want to remain behind the Muslims of Calcutta, and in October the same year they wreaked an equally inhuman vengeance over the innocent Muslims of Noakhali. And this latter was followed by a terrible bloodshed in the Punjab.

League Enters Governments

Despite all this, however, the efforts to bring the League into the Central Government continued and ultimately Mr Jinnah did agree to nominate five Leaguers, to the Cabinet. But this action was not actuated by any change of heart, for Mr Jinnah wrote to Lord Wavell on 13 October 1946 that the Viceroy having decided to go without the League, "it will be fatal to leave the entire field of administration of the Central Government in the hands of the Congress. Besides, you may be forced to have in your Interim Government Muslims who would not command the respect and confidence of Muslim India, which would lead to serious consequences, and lastly for other weighty grounds and reasons, which are obvious and not to be mentioned, we have decided to nominate five members on behalf of the Muslim League." The words "other weighty grounds and reasons" clearly show that Mr Jinnah had something more nefarious up his sleeves. The League in fact entered the Government only to fight the Congress from within. The League nominee Mr Liaqat Ali was given the charge of Finance which being the mainstay of the whole Governmental machinery, the Finance Ministry was determined to demonstrate as to how without its cooperation the whole Government could be paralysed.

Constituent Assembly

In the meanwhile, to worsen the situation, the League played yet another trick. The elections to the Constituent Assembly as proposed in the Cabinet Mission's Statement of 16 May had taken place in July 1946. The Congress secured an impressive victory in the General electorate where out of 210 it captured 199 seats. The success of the Muslim League in the Muslim electorate, however, was no less spectacular, for it won 73 of the 78 Muslim seats. The date for the first meeting of the Constitutent Assembly was fixed by the Viceroy as 9 December. But long before the Assembly met, the League announced its intention to boycott its meetings. The reason for this was supposed to be a difference of interpretation of the 16 May statement of the Cabinet Mission between the League and the Congress. According to the Congress the true meaning of the statement read as a whole was that the provinces had the right to decide both as to grouping and as to their own Constitution. But according to the League, the decisions in a Section were to be taken by a simple majority vote of all the representatives in a Section, which meant that in Section 'C' Assam could be forced to continue even against its wishes if the representatives of the other provinces in the Section combined to vote for this. Assam, a Hindu majority province, would also accept a Constitution for itself as determined by a simple majority of the Section even if it did not satisfy its requirements.

A Conference of the representatives of the two parties was called in London where Wavell himself accompanied. It could however reach no agreement. The British Government secured an expert legal opinion on the disputed clause, which went in favour of the League and this added fourfold to this party's relentlessness and stubbornness in its demands. The Congress insisted that if the League did not attend the meetings of the Constituent Assembly, it had no right to remain in the Government; the League on the other hand retorted that the Congress, too, had no right to remain in the Government for it also had not accepted the Statement of May 16 as correctly it was.

Despite all this the Constituent Assembly met on its stipulated date of 9 December but the League members were conspicuous by their absence. Dr. Rajendra Prasad being elected as Speaker, the Assembly started its business the whole of which, however, was shrouded in vagueness and uncertainty. Obviously, the working of the Interim Government having already been clogged, the failure of the Constituent Assembly to proceed effectively with its work in the absence of the representatives of a major community of India, proved the whole work of the Cabinet Mission to have failed. If anybody gained from this whole drama, it was the League and its idea of Pakistan; for as a result of the self-centred and strongly irritating behaviour of the League, some of the Congress leaders like Sardar Patel were driven to complete helplessness and they came out openly with the idea that the League should be given its Pakistan so that the peaceful development of the rest of India could be taken in hand. In the meanwhile Wavell retired from India.

After Wavell left India in 1947, he was given an Earldom and later appointed Constable of the Tower of London. Viscount Mersey wrote in 1949: "He maintains his sporting and literary interests. He has had more than a dozen bones broken at different times, and is the author of several books on military subjects and an anthology of light verse.

"Lord Cornwallis, Hastings, Hardinge and Wavell are the only regular soldiers of high rank who have also been Governor-General of India." Lord Wavell "is a listener rather than a talker. One of his favourite remark is supposed to be, 'I see'."[10]

NOTES

1. Azad, *op. cit.*, pp. 112-15.
2. Philips. C.H., *The Evolution of India and Pakistan, 1858 to 1947.* (Select Documents), pp. 355-56; Sitaramayya. *op. cit.*, II, pp. 631-33.
3. Gwyer, Appadorai, *op. cit.*, II, 556-57.
4. Azad, A.K.,*op. cit.*, pp. 131-32.
5. Philips, C.H., *op. cit.*, pp. 378-82.
6. Banerjee, A.C. & D.R. Bose (compiled by), *The Cabinet Mission in India.*
7. *Parliamentary Debates: Commons,* Fifth series, Vol. 425, pp. 1394-1416.
8. Philips.C.H., *op. cit.*, pp. 185-86.
9. Azad, A.K., *op. cit.*, pp. 159.
10. Mersey, Viscount, *The Viceroy,* pp. 151-52.

9

Lord Louis Mountbatten
1947

ON TO INDEPENDENCE

"The Earl Mountbatten of Burma, Knight of the Garter, Knight Grand Cross of the Bath, Knight Grand Cross of the Star of India, Distinguished Service Order, etc., etc., (some thirty-five et ceteras) considers himself forty-first generation in descent from Duke Ydulf, a Frankish Nobleman, who flourished in 600 A.D."[1] Alice Maud Mary, one of the daughters of Queen Victoria and Edward, Prince Consort, married in 1862 Prince Louis of Hesse, who later on became Grand Duke Louis IV of Hesse and the Rhine. They had five children, the eldest being named Victoria, the mother of our hero. Princes Victoria, the grand daughter of Queen Victoria, married Prince Louis of Battenberg, afterwards first Marquess of Milford Haven and Admiral of the Fleet. Louis Mountbatten was born on 25 June 1900. His father was an extremely able sailor and at the beginning of the First World War he was made the First Sea Lord. Louis inherited his qualities and developed a keen interest in naval service. He was educated at Osborne, Dartmouth and Christ's College. He entered the Naval service in 1919. In 1922 he married Hon. Edwina Ashley, grand daughter of a well-known financier and the daughter of Wilfred, Lord Mount Temple. In 1921 he accompanied the Prince of Wales to India, where they were greeted by riots and violence. Gandhi had declared boycott of the Prince's tour. During this visit Mountbatten had an opportunity of developing acquaintance with several princes of India. He also wanted to see Mr Gandhi but the Government of India did not give him the permission. It is during this visit that Mountbatten met Edwina in Delhi and they became engaged. This happened in Room 13 of the building now occupied by the Delhi University. Later on when Louis mentioned this fact to Nehru, the latter told him: "At that moment I was occupying cell 13 in the nearby jail."

Louis had a steady rise in his career. In 1942 he was appointed Chief of Combined Operations, and given the rank of Acting Vice-Admiral and Honorary Lieutenant-General and Air-Vice-Marshal. In 1943 he further rose and became Supreme Allied Commander of the South-East Asia Command, having his Headquarters first at New Delhi, then at Kandy in Ceylon and later on in Singapore. In this capacity he commanded British and American Sea, Land and Air Forces, in Burma, the Malaya Archipelago and the Indian Ocean. He also had to work with Generals Mac Arthur and Stilwell. General Eisenhower spoke very highly of him. When the Surrender ceremonies ended in Singapore and Louis was no more a fighting Commander some political and humanitarian duties were assigned to him. The supplies of food and medicine and the repair of drainage system etc. Based at the Government House at Singapore, he now ruled over enormous areas extending over Burma, Malaya, Singapore, Siam, Sumatra, Dutch East Indies, French Indo-China, etc., about one million square miles of land inhabited by 128 million people. His wife Edwina was the Superintendent-in-Chief of the St. John Ambulance Brigade "and Chairman of its Joint War Organisations with the Red Cross. She had already had a large hand in the recovery of Allied prisoners of war from Germany, so it would be fair to call her an expert on the problem."[2] It is here that Louis had his first acquaintance with Pandit Jawaharlal Nehru, a distinguished figure in the Indian Interim Government, when he came to Singapore to meet the Indian forces and study the condition of the large number of Indians who settled there. The local authorities "wanted to cold-shoulder Nehru, to hamper his movements, and to restrict his contacts with the Indian community. I thought this would be disastrous. This man was clearly going to be the Prime Minister of India. How fatal for future Anglo-Indian relations to treat him like that!...The local authorities had not even arranged to let Nehru have a car, so I lent him mine," thus writes Louis.[3] Mountbatten received him at the Government House and drove with him through the streets where he received a fantastic welcome. This was the beginning of a deep friendship between Louis, Edwina and Nehru, which proved to be quite useful when later on Mountbatten came to India as Viceroy.

The Indian problem had been going quite out of hand. Lord Wavell had lost the confidence both of Gandhi and Nehru and was disliked by the British Prime Minister, Attlee. When Wavell was to be replaced, said Attlee: "Suddenly I had...an inspiration. I thought of Mountbatten." Further he says: "Now Mountbatten was an extremely lively, exciting personality. He had an extraordinary faculty of getting on with all kinds of people as he'd shown when he was Supremo in South-East Asia. He was also blessed with a very unusual life. So I put it to him. Bit of a shock for Dickie (As Louis was known), you know."[4] Mountbatten was not anxious to accept this post. His ambitions lay in the Navy where in 1914 his father had to resign from his post as First Sea Lord. The Mountbattens belonged to the German stock. During the first weeks of the war there was a lot of anti-German feeling in England. Many German shops and churches had been looted, and German individuals in the Government service were suspected of disloyalty. The Mountbatten family was also attacked and it is in these circumstances that his father resigned his post, and they changed their name from 'Battenberg' to 'Mountbatten'. Louis had felt humiliated and since then he had been harbouring an ambition to occupy the post, the pleasures of which had been denied to his father. When the high post in India therefore was offered, Louis naturally had his reservations. He had to be persuaded by Attlee. Louis forwarded several conditions before he accepted the post. He said he would accept the post only if he was invited to do so by the Indian leaders. He was, however, told that it was impracticable. But his condition for a permission to visit the Indian leaders in their homes was accepted. His second condition was that he should be allowed to take his own staff with him. That was also conceded. Then he wanted an authority to act independently of the India House in London. This was asking for plenipotentiary powers, which no Viceroy had so far enjoyed before him. When this condition was forwarded, Mr Attlee was visibly taken aback. Ultimately, however, Mountbatten won this point as well. Mountbatten was also anxious not to prejudice his career in the Navy. Here again Attlee agreed to his request and the order of appointment issued to him read: "Rear Admiral The Viscount Mountbatten of Burma, Second Temporary Duty-Viceroy of India."

As soon as Louis was appointed the Viceroy of India, he occupied himself in the study of the Indian problems. Before actually accepting the offer he had met the king and pointed out to him that there was every possibility that he might fail in his mission to India, which would be bad for a member of his family. The King, however, replied: "But think how good it will be for the monarchy if you succeed." Mountbatten knew that the political situation in India was intricate. Several efforts had earlier been made, i.e., by Simon, Cripps, and the Cabinet Mission, to bring about a solution, but the communal differences and the suspicions that the British were not actually anxious to leave India stood in the way. Mountbatten therefore insisted on Attlee that a time limit when the British would pull out, no matter whether the Indians reached an agreement or not, should be set at June 1948. Attlee supported him here as well. It was generally understood that the existing state of uncertainty in the Interim Government as well as in the Constituent Assembly was fraught with danger and could not indefinitely be prolonged. It was to remove suspicions from the minds of the Indian leaders and to force the pace of events that Attlee willingly agreeing with Louis, issued his historic statement in February 1947.

ATTLEE'S STATEMENT OF FEBRUARY 1947

The statement said: "His Majesty's Government wish to make it clear that it is their definite intention to...effect the transfer of power into responsible Indian hands by a date not later than June 1948." (2) If a Constitution cannot be drafted by a fully representative Assembly as envisaged in the Cabinet Mission proposals by that date, His Majesty's Government will "have to consider to whom the power of the Central Government in British India should be handed over, on the due date, whether as a whole to some form of Central Government for British India or in some areas to the existing Provincial Governments, or in such other way as may seem most reasonable and in the best interests of the Indian people." (3) Although the final transfer of Authority may not take place until June 1948, preparatory measures must be put in hand in advance. (4) With regard to the Indian States, the paramountcy powers would not be transferred to any Government of British India, nor would paramountcy, as a system, be brought to a conclusion earlier than the date of the final transfer of power, but it is contemplated that for the intervening period the relations of the Crown with individual States may be adjusted by agreement.

The statement was indeed a turning point in the history of India. It brought all suspicions with regard to the British intentions to rest. Pandit Nehru reacting to it remarked that it "not only removed all misconceptions and suspicions but also brings reality and a certain dynamic quality to the present situation of India." Mr Jinnah remarked: "For the moment I refuse to comment except to say that the Muslim League will not yield an inch in its demand for Pakistan." He, however, was encouraged by the implied recognition of the demand for Pakistan, for it would force the Congress to come to terms with him before the due date so as to avoid the possible disastrous consequences. The reaction in England was varied. Winston Churchill thus remarked: "In handing over the Government of India to these so-called political classes, we are handing over to men of straw, of whom in a few years no trace will remain."[5] Be that as it may, before Mountbatten left for India, he was sufficiently armed to dispose of the destiny of India as he thought fit.

Mountbatten had been authorized to take own staff to India. Among the men he chose, one was Field Marshall Lord Ismay. Ismay was a Conservative, had started his career, as a soldier in England, was a wartime aide to Churchill and enjoyed enormout influence in England. Mountbatten chose him because he was not sure of his ability to carry the Tory Opposition with him. For this he could rely on this man whom he appointed his Chief of Staff. The Second in Command to Ismay was to be Sir Eric Mieville, who had a sufficient experience of Indian Administration. He had been Private Secretary to the Governor-

General Willingdon, and later on he worked in the capacity of Assistant Private Secretary to King George VI. The four other persons chosen by him had been his aides in Burma. They were Captain Ronald Brockman, Commander George Nicholls, Lieutenant Colonel Vernon Erskine Crum and Alan Campbell-Johnson. The last man was a publicity expert and was chosen with a view to propagating Mountbatten's ideas in the Indian public and press. Besides, his charming wife, Edwina, who soon won the confidence and friendship of Nehru, accompanied him and the important Indian ladies like Patel's daughter and Jinnah's daughter who had a considerable influence over the Indian leaders. His daughter Pamela was one of the regular visitors at Gandhi's prayer meetings. She also freely moved about to "breathe friendship and good-will on every one."

When Lord Mountbatten arrived, the situation in this country was precarious. Interim Government and the Constituent Assembly, thanks to the attitude of the League, were both in a trough of confusion. The recent communal disturbances had left a deep scar in the hearts both of the Hindus and the Muslims and further trouble was brewing up all around. Nor had the February announcement of Mr Attlee resulted in any easing of the situation. "If any hope was entertained that the announcement would have the effect of a shock therapy to bringing the Congress and the League nearer to an understanding, it was unfulfilled. The struggle for power became more intense particularly in the areas in dispute."[6]

Arriving in India Mountbatten took charge of his office on 24 May 1947, and immediately started a round of meetings with the important Indian leaders. He met Mr Nehru whom he frankly told: "I want you to regard me not as the last Viceroy winding up the affairs of the British Raj, but as the first to lead the way to new India." Nehru was impressed and moved and replied: "Now I know what they mean when they speak of your charm being so dangerous." Next Mountbatten met Jinnah. After the interview was over he remarked to Campbell-Johnson: "My God, he was cold! It took most of the interview to unfreeze him." He met Mr Gandhi and in the first meeting just chatted with him. Mountbatten knew that Gandhi's personal influence was enormous. He may not always be able to take Gandhi along with him but he knew he could reach nowhere if he was against him. Mountbatten thought that Mr Gandhi's ideas were often impractical. Thus for instance in the very second meeting with the Mahatma the latter told him that he was willing to agree to Jinnah alone forming the Government at the Centre. Mountbatten knew that it was a mere idle talk and when this idea was referred to the Congress Party they absolutely refused to consider it. Yet the Viceroy was able to win a close friendship with the Mahatma, who called both him and Lady Mountbatten as his dear friends.

THE 'DICKIE BIRD PLAN'

It was Mountbatten's practice that every day after breakfast he would confer with his entourage where the current problems were batted back and forth across the table in a verbal ping-pong, the Viceroy himself acting as an Umpire. Besides the staff that he had brought from England and the English officers, he chose an Indian to help him; there was senior Indian ICS officer, Mr V.P. Menon, who rendered him considerable help.

Within a few days of his arrival in India, Mountbatten was able to prepare his scheme, which was called the 'Dickie Bird Plan' for Indian Independence. This Plan was in fact an adaptation of the Cabinet Mission proposals in which the power was to be transferred unilaterally under the theory that the provinces should first become independent successor states. This plan rejected the idea of the Indian Union or the Two Dominions of India and Pakistan being the successors to power. All the provinces including Madras, Bombay, United Provinces, Central Provinces, Bihar, Orissa, Assam and the Muslim majority provinces of Bengal , Punjab, the North-West Frontier Province, etc. were to be declared independent and they would each separately decide whether to remain in the Indian Constituent Assembly or not. Before giving final touches to this Plan Mountbatten had consulted different Indian leaders informally without placing the details before them. He somehow got himself convinced that they all would agree to it and sent Lord Ismay and George Abell to London with the Plan to get the Cabinet approval. After sending the Plan to England Mountbatten moved to Shimla where Mr Nehru joined him as a guest. One day after dinner on an impulse he decided to take Nehru into confidence and placed the draft plan before him. Mountbatten had thought that Nehru would read it and would be happy, but he was distressed to find that Indian leader's face going red with anger. Mr Nehru tossed the Plan on the desk and remarked, "It won't do, I will never accept a Plan like this!" The next day Mountbatten received a letter from Nehru which said: "The picture presented by the proposals in the Plan is an ominous one. Not only do they menace India but they endanger the future relations between Britain and India...The inevitable consequences of the proposals would be to invite the Balcanization of India; to provoke certain civil conflict and add to violence and disorder."

Mountbatten was aghast. It seemed his whole mission was going to founder before it actually had a start. He cabled to England that the Plan approved by the Cabinet was hereby cancelled, and received a reply: "What in Hell is going on?"

Mountbatten had drawn up his 'Dickie Bird Plan', as it was, fearing that though Jinnah might accept Dominion Status for Pakistan, the Congress would never do so. But he was soon enlightened on this point as well, when Menon told him that he had already had a talk with Sardar Patel and there was every likelihood that the Congress would also accept the Dominion Status. In fact Menon had a lengthy discussion with Patel and convinced him that the dominion status would ensure a peaceful transfer, keep the goodwill and friendship of the British and encourage the British civil servants to stay on to help the Indian Government. The Indian Army also stood stay on to gain that way and the princely states would be willing to federate with India. Moreover he convinced Patel that even after accepting the Dominion Status it would be open to India to opt out of the Commonwealth whenever she like. Sardar Patel had been fully convinced of the arguments and assured Menon that he would use influence with the Congress and have the proposal accepted. When Mountbatten was informed of this he was still hesitant and was not sure whether Mr Nehru would agree to this proposal. Mr Nehru was forthwith called to a meeting where Menon expounded his theory once again. Nehru was actually not very much enthusiastic, because, as he said, although "I myself have always been most anxious for sentimental reasons to have the closest possible relationship with the British Commonwealth" he was afraid that the words "Dominion Status" would irritate the people and they would feel that complete freedom had not yet been acquired. It was not, however, long before Nehru was ultimately persuaded to remain a member of the British Commonwealth and accept the Dominion Status for India. Menon indeed had come to the rescue of Mountbatten at this most difficult hour. The broad lines of the Plan having thus been finalized, Menon himself was called upon to prepare a draft. Menon retired to his hotel and within four hours he came out with the plan, which ultimately was to dispose of the destinies of the 250 million Hindus, 90 million Muslims, 10 million Christians and five million Sikhs who inhabited this land.

To Mountbatten personally, the whole thing was extremely embarrassing. The Home Authorities were already perplexed when they were told that the 'Dicke Bird Plan' on which so much stock had been laid, was now sought to be cancelled. They therefore cabled to Mountbatten desiring his presence in London. Mountbatten, however, did not have the courage to face Attlee and told Menon that he was going to cable back that either they accept the new Plan or his resignation would follow. It shows in what a desperate mood Mountbatten actually was. But before such an unwholesome situation could precipitate Menon was able to persuade him to go back to London and place before the Cabinet the whole truth keeping back absolutely nothing. Lady Mountbatten also advised him to present a bold front and Mountbatten eventually did go with the new plan personally to discuss it in London. As he arrived there the whole matter was reopened. There were lengthy discussions but when it was placed before Mr Attlee in the Cabinet they did not take more than five minutes to accept it.[7] It is in this way that ultimately the scheme for India's Independence and partition matured.

THE MOUNTBATTEN PLAN

This plan, which has come down in history as the Mountbatten Plan consisted of more essential proposals,: (1) Partition of India was inevitable. (2) The representatives of the Muslim majority districts and those (excluding the European Members) representing the rest of a province, in the Legislative Assemblies of both Bengal and Punjab, would meet separately and decide by a simple majority vote whether their respective province was to be divide or not. If either part decided in favour of partition, this would be done. In the event of the partition being decided upon, each part would then decide whether to join the existing Constituent Assembly in Delhi or the new Constituent Assembly to be set up. (3) The Legislative Assembly of Sind as a whole, would decide at a special meeting whether to join the Constituent Assembly of Delhi or the new Constituent Assembly of those not joining Delhi. (4) A referendum would be held in Sylhet, a predominantly Muslim district of Assam, to decide in the event of Bengal being partitioned whether to join East Bengal or to remain with Assam. (5) In the ease of the North-West Frontier Province, a referendum was to be made to the electors of the existing Provincial Legislative Assembly, whether the Province would join Delhi or Pakistan. (6) An appropriate method of giving a similar choice to British Baluchistan was under consideration. (7) The agreement of the major parties of India to the solution of India's political problem made it easy for the power to be transferred much earlier than the date fixed by the Statement of February 20. Therefore, "His Majesty's Government proposes to introduce legislation during the current session for the transfer of power this year on a Dominion Status basis to one or two successor authorities."

According to the procedure laid down in the Mountbatten Plan, the Hindu members of both Bengal and the Punjab Assemblies voted in favour of partition and for joining Delhi. Sind and N.W.F. Province decided to joining Pakistan and Sylhet voted in favour of joining East Bengal.[8]

One may ask how the Congress leaders who had so persistently opposed ultimately agreed to partition India. "My own feeling," said Lord Mountbatten, "was that a United India was, of course, the right answer but...the riots and bloodshed throughout the country made the prospects of its acceptance obviously pretty remote.....All the Muslims League leaders to whom I spoke made it absolutely clear that they desire Partition."[9] Lord Mountbatten therefore was soon converted to the idea of partition. Sardar Patel had already started wavering as a result of the extremely irritating behaviour of the League members in the Central Government. It was not, therefore, difficult for the persuasive manners of Lord Mountbatten and the charming arguments of Lady Mountbatten eventually to win over Pandit Nehru in favour of Pakistan as well. Maulana Abul Kalam Azad, however, persistently opposed the scheme. He told Lord Mountbatten that if the country were divided there would be rivers of blood flowing in different parts of the land. All his forebodings, however, fell on deaf ears and the Viceroy vainly sought to assure him: "I shall see to it that there is no bloodshed and riot. I am a soldier not a civilian."[10] Mr Gandhi, who had earlier told Maulana Azad that Pakistan could be formed only over his dead body, also half acquiesced. When the Congress leaders accepted the partition plan, Gandhi did remark: "Everybody today is impatient for independence. Congress has practically decided to accept partition. They have been handed a wooden loaf, in this new plan. If they eat it, they die of colic. If they leave it, they starve."[11] But he never firmly opposed it.

The arguments of Lord Mountbatten in favour of Pakistan as summed up by Maulana Azad were that "Congress had agreed to a weak Centre only in order to meet the objection of the League. Provinces were therefore given full provincial autonomy, but in a country so divided by language, community and culture, a weak Centre was bound to encourage fissparous tendencies. If the Muslim League were not there, he could plan for a strong Central Government and frame a Constitution desirable from the point of view of Indian unity. Lord Mountbatten advised that it would be better to give up a few small pieces in the north-west and the north-east and then build up a strong and consolidated India."[12] Mr Jinnah agreed against his wishes to the division of Punjab and Bengal and thus accepted a mutilated Pakistan. It is in these circumstances that on 14 June 1947, despite the opposition of Maulana Azad and some others A.I.I.C. passed a resolution accepting partition.

Before the Draft Bill was finally drawn up there were some hurdles to cross. Mr Jinnah thus insisted that he must have a thousand-mile long corridor through India to link Eastern and the Western Pakistan. This proposal of the League leader startled the Congress leaders. Mountbatten however, talked him out of that. There were objections from the Congress leaders as well. They wanted that if India eventually withdrew from the British Commonwealth they should have an assurance that Pakistan also would be expelled. Here again, V.P. Menon came to the rescue of the Viceroy and convinced the Indian leaders that the demand was unreasonable. Another demand that the Congress leaders made was with regard to the N.W.F.P. where Khan Sahib the pro-Congress Muslim leader had started propagating an idea for a separate Pakhtoonistan.

The Congress leaders wanted that the North-West Frontier Province should not only be given a choice to join India or Pakistan but it should be asked if it would like to remain independent. An independent existence of the NWFP however was problematical and with the help of Menon, Mountbatten was able to persuade the Congress leaders to withdraw this demand as well. Another hurdle was the proposal of Mr Suhrawardy that the whole of Bengal should be declared an independent state. Mr Jinnah, however, was never likely to agree to it, and this proposal was also, somehow brushed aside.

The agreed scheme was cabled to England where a Draft Bill was drawn up in record time and cabled back to India on 22 June. Mountbatten wanted that 15 August should be fixed as the date of India's independence. Attlee wanted him to allow some more time but ultimately gave way. Everything having been made ready, the leaders marched to the All India Radio to announce their acceptance, of partition. Mountbatten spoke first expressing his regrets that "It has been impossible to obtain agreement….on any plan that would preserve the unity of India." Nehru followed with the words: "It is with no joy in my heart that I commend these proposals, though I have no doubt in my mind that it is the best course." Jinnah came next arguing that the plan had been accepted only as a compromise. The word 'compromise' probably related to mutilated Pakistan', as he called it. He concluded his speech with the words: "Pakistan Zindabad'!" which some people understood as 'Pakistan is in the bag'.

THE INDIAN INDEPENDENCE ACT

The Indian Independence Bill was brought in the House of Commons on 4 July in order to complete the necessary constitutional formalities. In a fortnight both the Houses passed the Bill. This Act though of such great importance, was simple and short and consisted only of twenty clauses. The more important provisions were: (1) Two separate Dominions of India and Pakistan would be brought into existence on 15 August 1947 and to them would be transferred all the powers previously exercised by the Parliament. (2) Territories of the two dominions were to be defined, but they were empowered to include or exclude a territory themselves. (3) Each dominion would have its own Governor-General though one person could act for both in dual capacity. (4) The Constituent Assemblies of the two Dominions were to work both as Constitution-making bodies and as Legislative bodies in their respective Dominions. (5) All laws in force in the two Dominions on 15 August, would remain so until amended by the respective Legislative bodies. (6) The Members of the Services would continue enjoying their existing rights and privileges and would have a continuity of service. (7) The Government of India Act 1935 and the orders in

Council accompanying it would remain in force as they were, until amended or replaced by the new constitution in a Dominion. The reserved and the special powers of the Governor-General under the Act were, however, abolished. (8) The British paramountcy on the Indian States would lapse and the States would be free to join either of the Dominions or to remain independent. (9) The assent was given for the omission of the words 'Indiae Imperator' and the words 'Emperor of India' from the Royal Style and Titles. (10) The Agreements with the N.W.F. tribes would be negotiated by the successor Dominion. And (11) the office of the Secretary of State of India was abolished: his work being taken over by the Secretary for Commonwealth Affairs.

NOTES

1. Hatch, Alden, *The Mountbattens,* London, 1966, p.6.
2. Terraine, John, *Life and Times of Lord Mountbatten,* London, 1968, p. 133.
3. *Ibid.*, pp. 139-40.
4. Hatch, Alden, *op. cit.*, p.333.
5. Mosley, Leonard, *The Last Days of British Raj*, London 1964, p. 53.
6. Gwyer and Appadorai, *Constitutional Democracy,* p. lxiii.
7. Mosley, Leonard, pp. 125-127.
8. For further details see Campbell-Johnson, Alan, *Mission with Mountbatten*: Terraine, John. *The Life and Times of Lord Mountbatten.*
9. *See* Terraine, John, *op. cit.*, pp. 142-153.
10. Mosley, Leonard, *op. cit.*, p. 129.
11. Mosley, Leonard, p. 128.
12. Azad, A.K., *India Wins Freedom,* Calcutta 1959, pp. 179-81.

10

The Great Divide

THE INDIAN STATES

The actual process of partitioning India, however, was not an easy job. Under the Indian Independence Act the British paramountcy on the Indian states was to lapse, and they were free to join either of the Dominions or to remain independent. The provision was against the wishes of the Indian leaders and had been made on the insistence only of the Viceroy's Political Adviser Sir Conrad Corfield who had personally gone to London to persuade the Labour Government to this effect. The Viceroy Lord Mountbatten had absolutely no soft corner for the princes who numbered 565 and who with the freedom allowed to them were bound to create chaotic conditions in India. Mountbatten called them "a bunch of nitwits", and was sure that they had absolutely no future in India as independent states. The story of the accession of these states to the Dominions of India and Pakistan was therefore painful as well as interesting.

The Political Adviser insisting on the principle of paramountcy, argued that each one of these states had its own treaty relationship with the British crown, and therefore when the British withdrew they were completely within their right to declare their independence if they so wished. In such an eventuality it was natural that they could stop the Indian Railways and the Telegraph lines running through their territories. They were also within their rights to expel the British Contingent Troops and close up the Indian post offices operated within the state. The Congress leaders on the other hand argued that since their foreign policy was completely in the control of the Government of India, these states could not be considered as independent units. Sir Corfield however was in power and wanted to make his authority felt. He wanted the British Contingent Troops to be withdrawn from the Dominions of the Nizam of Hyderabad, though the Defence Minister, Baldev Singh stood in his way. He gave every encouragement to the princes to come together and create a third power in India. When he returned from England after winning his battle with the Labour Government at home, he immediately busied his subordinate staff in the Political Department to check up the files and destroy all important records and communication with the princes, which dealt with their personal character. About four tons of the records were thus consigned to the flames. Large number of records was also dispatched to the Imperial Archives in England. The Indian leaders were naturally incensed and in one of the meetings Mr Nehru said: "I charge the Political Department and Sir Conrad Corfield particularly with misfeasance. I consider that a judicial inquiry on the highest level into their actions is necessary." The Viceroy himself was secretly sympathetic to the Indian view. In that very meeting it was decided that both Mr Jinnah and Nehru would setup their respective State Department to deal with the princes. The Indian States Department was placed under Sardar Patel who invited V.P. Menon to become his Secretary.

The V.P. Menon was a diplomatic genius. The first thing he did was to convince Sardar Patel that the lapse of paramountcy would rather be a blessing in disguise, because in that case India would not inherit all the different types of treaties and conflicting engagements which the British had entered into with the states. The rights and privileges enjoyed by the princes would come to an end and we would start once again with a clean slate. Some princes who showed a refractory attitude were no match to the combined genius of Patel and Menon. The movements were closely watched. Thus when the Maharaja of Jodhpur, having his territories contiguous to both India and Pakistan, contacted Jinnah for the possibilities of some sort of association with Pakistan, Menon reported the matter to the Viceroy and immediate steps were taken to make the Maharaja sign his Instrument of Accession to India. Some trouble arose in the state of Travancore as well. Here Patel had another weapon at his disposal. He encouraged the underground Congress Working Committee of the State to organize demonstrations and within a short time the things were made so difficult for the Maharaja that the Viceroy was telegraphically informed of his wish to sign the instrument.

It was essential in the circumstances that princely states should be persuaded to join one Dominion or the other before actually the independence came on 15 August. For if the matter was permitted to prolong beyond that date, the paramountcy would lapse and the states having become free it would become difficult to negotiate with them. Both Patel and Menon were therefore anxious that the matter should be disposed of as soon as possible. Immediately after they assumed charge they came into clash with Sir Conrad. They approached the Viceroy and Sir Conrad was told to pack his bags. The Viceroy's antipathy towards the Indian princes whose existence he himself considered as an anachronism of history was known, and he was persuaded to help in the matter.

Mountbatten called a meeting of seventy-five of the greatest of the princes on 25 July. The performance on the day, as Leonard Mosley writes, "was probably the most spectacular example of Mountbatten's skill, charm and tremendous art of persuation."[1] As the meeting was held the princes bombarded the Viceroy with all sorts of stupid, acute and sometimes insulting questions. Mountbatten, however, never lost his smile and as Campbell-Johnson writes: "Somehow he managed to infect them with his own spontaneous enthusiasm and powers of decision."[2] Mountbatten had an old friend of the Maharaja of Bikaner, of the days of his first visit to India accompanied by the Prince of Wales. After cajoling, threatening and haranguing the princes, and after painting bright pictures of the possibility of the princes receiving honours from the King of England even after joining the Dominions which had promised to remain in the Commonwealth, he asked Bikaner if he would be the first to sign the Instrument. Bikaner, of course agreed and thus the ball was set rolling. Bikaner was followed by Baroda who after signing the Instrument "threw his arms around surprised Menon's neck and burst into tears. Another Raja had a heart attack after signing. But all were not willing. When Mountbatten called on the *dewan* who represented an important prince who was out of the country, the man said, 'I have received no instruction from my ruler and cannot sign.'

"Surely you know His Highness's mind and can take a decision on his behalf' Lord Louis said.

" 'I do not know his mind,' the *dewan* said stubbornly, 'and cannot reach him by cable.'

" 'Mountbatten picked up a round glass paperweight from the rostrum. 'I will look into my crystal and give you the answer' he said.

" 'For long seconds he gazed, while the princes began to grin. Then Mountbatten solemnly said, 'His Highness directs you to sign the Instrument of Accession.'

"A perfect roar of laughter at last shook the champer. The rest was easy."[3]

As a result of the tactful approach of Mountbatten, the diplomacy of Menon and determination of Patel, out of 565 as many as 562 signed their Instruments of Accession before India became independent on 15 August. The three states that remained behind were Junagarh, Hyderabad and Kashmir and they had a different tale to tell.

Junagarh

Junagarh was a small state in Kathiawar. Its population was about 85 per cent Hindu, but was ruled by a Muslim prince. On all sides it was surrounded by Hindu principalities like that of Baroda and Bhavnagar, which had already acceded to India. Nor were its own territories compact, for right in their midst were other petty principalities ruled and inhabited by the Hindus who also acceded to India. The Nawab of Junagarh was a colourful personality, like others of his tribe, having four wives, a large number of concubines, a pack of hounds and extremely degenerate habits. Junagarh had absolutely no territorial link with Pakistan, the nearest contact being the 240 miles route by sea. The Nawab, while humouring the Congress leaders, kept secretly in touch with Pakistan. The Instrument of Accession was sent to him to sign, but while the Government of India awaited his reply, suddenly they found a news item in the press that he acceded to Pakistan. The Pakistan Government knew the weakness of their case, but while doing almost nothing to incorporate the State territories within their Dominion, in reply to telegraphic enquiries of the Government of India, they did nothing to calm the suspicions. In the meanwhile, the Nawab sent his troops and occupied some Mongol territory in the midst of his state, leading to frantic appeals being sent by the Hindu inhabitants to Government of India for help. The Indian troops were dispatched, but before they actually entered the state, the Nawab loaded his four wives, his dogs and other precious belongings in his private plane to flee. One of his wives was sent back to collect her child who had been left behind. The Nawab waited for a while, but then loading two more dogs instead, he took off. No resistance was offered to the Indian troops, but Pakistan felt outraged. Pakistan considered this a test case, and later on when the Kashmir question arose, where majority of the population was Muslim but the ruling prince a Hindu, they quoted the Junagarh analogy and put forward their claims.

Hyderabad

Another case was that of Hyderabad where, again, about 85 per cent of the population were Hindus, while the ruler, the Nizam of Hyderabad was Muslim. The Nizam repeatedly made his request to the Viceroy and other British authorities pleading his case on the basis of treaties and claiming independence for his state. He, however, received no encouragement either from the Labour Government in England or the Viceroy in India, though Corfield's influence in the state was considerable and the Nizam began to organise Muslim Razakars, the terrorists to resist the Indian designs by force. Mountbatten proposed some special concessions to the Nizam if he acceded to the Indian Dominion, to which he agreed. A plan was drawn up and the

Viceroy somehow secured Patel's approval. But when it was taken back to the Nizam, he rejected it, a settlement based on his own conditions.[4] So long as Mountbatten remained in India, negotiations continued with the Nizam. But two days after he left, the Nizam wrote to the Government of India that he was now agreeable to the Mountbatten plan which he had earlier rejected. The reply he received was that the Mountbatten plan had sailed away with him to England. Shortly after the Indian troops marched. There was not much resistance and Hyderabad was occupied. The Nizam, however, remained as figurehead.

Kashmir

Kashmir was a predominantly Muslim state ruled by a Hindu Prince, Hari Singh, who refused to accede either to India or Pakistan right till the end of the British rule. Pandit Nehru, whose ancestors originally belonged to this State, did not enjoy good relations with the Maharaja. There was a possibility that if either Nehru or Gandhi went to talk with the prince they would be arrested. Mountbatten decided personally to go to Srinagar where he met the Maharaja and his Prime Minister Pandit Kak. The Maharaja was asked to make up his mind and was clearly told that his accession to Pakistan would not be regarded as an unfriendly act. He, however, persisted in his intransigence and invited both India and Pakistan to sign with him Stand Still Agreement so as to afford him a little time to think over. Pakistan agreed and signed the Agreement while India refused to do so. Pakistan, however, wanted the Maharaja to take an early decision. When the Maharaja delayed, the frontier tribesmen were incited to invade the State on 22 October 1947. Several important towns in the valley were overrun, Uri and Baramulla were captured and the raiders now remained only a short distance away from Srinagar, spreading fire and destruction all around and putting even Christian missionaries to death. The Maharaja was shaken and he sent frantic appeals to the Government of India for help. Mountbatten told him that the Indian troops could not enter his state unless the Instrument of Accession was signed. Signatures on the Instrument were hastily put on 26 October and even Sheikh Abdullah, the leader of the National Conference, the largest political party in the state, endorsed the Accession. The Government of India airlifted the troops on 27 October and within a short time the towns like Uri were cleared. The *New Statesman* and *Nation* wrote on 20 February 1948. "There is no possible doubt that if India had not intervened last October, Srinagar and the lovely valley of Kashmir would now be a devastated and blackened ruin."[5]

While marching the Indian troops into the Kashmir valley the Government of India had declared that they had absolutely no intention to stay on in the State, and that as soon as possible the accession issue would be referred to the popular vote. But the raiders had not been completely cleared from the valley when as a result of General Sir Claud Auchinleck's intercession and at the instance of the United Nations to which the case had been referred at the suggestion of Mountbatten, ceasfire had been declared. Obviously the plebiscite could be held only if the territories occupied by the raiders backed by the Pakistan Government, as they later admitted, vacated the aggression. Popular vote could be taken in the whole of the State and not only in the parts held by India. Pakistan, however, refused to vacate the territories conquered by it and the whole issue continued hanging for quite some time till ultimately the Government of India declared that the accession now was final and the State had become an integral part of the country. The argument forwarded was that Pakistan's claim on Kashmir was based only on its being Muslim-majority area. Obviously if the plebiscite was held, communal feelings would be aroused and that would affect the inter-communal relations of the people all over Inidia, leading probably once again to large scale riots and bloodshed.

RADCLIFFE AWARD

The Demarcation Line: Another problem to be solved before the date of independence was that connected with the demarcation line which had to be drawn up between the Hindu and Muslim areas of the two provinces of Punjab and Bengal. There was no such problem in connection with the North Western Province, Sindh, Central Provinces, Bihar and Assam where the minorities were not quite sizeable. But here in these two provinces the population of one community was roughly equal to the other and the problem was indeed complicated because the demarcation line had to cut through long settled and thickly populated areas which together formed an integrated economy and system of communication. Obviously no demarcation line could do full justice to the claims of either of the communities and whatever award in this connection was given was bound to be unpopular and a subject of controversy. Moreover the whole business had to be undertaken as a crash programme and completed within six weeks that now remained upto 15 August.

At the suggestion of Mountbatten two groups were set up, consisting of four members, two from each Dominion. One of these groups was to divide Bengal while the other would cut up the Punjab. It was proposed that the two groups together would elect their own chairman. Mr Jinnah and Pandit Nehru agreed that all the members of this Commission should be High Court judges. The members were appointed, but soon they having failed to select their own chairman, the British Government in England were requested to appoint one. With the full agreement of the two parties, Sir Cyral Radcliffe, a well-known lawyer of England, was appointed to the post. Sir Radcliffe had never been to

India before and therefore was not expected to be acquainted with any of the Indian leaders. This would ensure the impartiality of the award. Besides Radcliffe, the other members of the Commission were: S A Rehman and Saleh Mohammad Akram for Pakistan and C C Biswas and B K Mukherji for India. This group was to partition Bengal. The other group, which would partition Punjab, was to consist of Teja Singh and Mehar Chand Mahajan proposed by the Congress and Mohammad Munir and Din Mohammad nominated by the League. The term of reference was, "the Boundary Commission is instructed to demarcate the boundaries of the two parts of the Punjab on the basis of ascertaining the contiguous majority areas of Muslims and non-Muslims. In doing so it will take into account other factors." What were these other factors? Similar instructions were issued with regard to Bengal. Obviously much was left to the good sense of the Commission itself, and all its members Hindu, Muslim and Sikh having their own notions and difference of opinion, all was ultimately left to Radcliffe, the Chairman himself.

The two groups started working, one at Lahore and the other at Calcutta, Radcliff himself establishing the headquarters in the Viceroy's House in Delhi. It was an extremely tough job but the Commission was able to produce its Award for Bengal on 9 August 1947 and for Punjab on 11 August. The boundary awards of the Commission were bound to produce shock and despair. In East thus the Commission awarded Chittagong hilly tracts to the East Pakistan, which Congress was bound bitterly to resent. Similarly in the Punjab the wealthiest lands built and developed by the Sikhs and most of the great canal system of the Punjab together with some of the most important Sikh shrines like that of Nankana were placed on the side of Pakistan. The city of Lahore itself with its Hindu and Sikh majority population went to Pakistan. The Gurdaspur district, a Muslim majority area was handed to India and incidentally it formed India's only road and rail link with Kashmir. The awards were handed to Mountbatten but he decided not to make them public. "Mountbatten said that if he could exercise some discretion in the matter he would prefer to postpone its appearance until after the Independence Day celebrations feeling that the problem of its timing was one of psychology, and that the controversy and grief it was bound to arouse on both sides should not be allowed to mar Independence Day itself."[6] It was only 16 August, therefore, that the two parties were called to a meeting and the awards were placed before them. There were shocks and dismay, but the job had been done and there was no going back on it.

Later on there was some criticism of the delay in the announcement of the awards. Some pro-Pakistan Muslims like Chaudhri Mohammad Ali claimed that Mountbatten purposely delayed the announcement and in the meanwhile got some changes introduced in favour of India. Headquarters of Radcliffe were in the Viceroy's House, where it was not difficult for Mountbatten to influence the judgement. Chaudhri Mohammad Ali thus reports that on 9 and 10 August he saw a pencil line already drawn on a map in Ismay's office. "I said (to Ismay) that it was unnecessary for me to explain further since the line, already drawn on the map, indicated the boundary I had been talking about. Ismay turned pale and asked in confusion who had been fooling with his map."[7] There was another map dated 8 August found in the office of the Punjab Governor, Sir Evan Jenkins, by his successor Sir John Mudie, the West Punjab Governor, in which the towns of Ferozpur and Zira had been shown on the side of Pakistan. But in the final award they were awarded to India. This is quoted as another instance of the possibility of the Viceroy having influenced the awards. C.H. Philips and Mary Doreen Wainwright however refuse to suspect the motives of the Viceroy. According to them George Abell drew up the map of 8 August on the basis merely of his telephone conversations with the Secretary of the Commission. This map Abell had prepared in response to the urgent requests of the Punjab Governor who wanted to have a rough idea with regard to the boundary line so as to take precautionary measures against communal disturbances. They write: "It seems clear from the evidence that neither Mountbatten nor Radcliffe was personally involved. As for the existence of sketch maps and lines drawn on maps, the simplest explanation is that many such lines must have been drawn on maps at that period, not least in Government offices for administrative purposes. It is not surprising, for example, that in this pre-partition period similar information was sought by and conveyed to the Government of Bengal about the probable line of national boundaries."[8]

THE INDIAN ARMY

Another problem was to split up the Indian Army which had been painstakingly rebuild after the 1857 Mutiny into a magnificent instrument of war. Under the new policy of counterpoise adopted in the time of Lords Canning and Lawrence the Indian regiment had been stratified into "Communal battalions—two Hindu and and one Muslim, two Muslim and one Hindu, or one Hindu, one Muslim and one Sikh so that no sudden upsurge of religious or racial rebellioin could get out of hand. There would always be a loyal battalion round the flag."[9] When General Sir Claud Auchinleck, the Commander-in-Chief of the Indian Army was called upon to do the splitting job, made every possible effort to resist, for he considered the Indian Army as the greatest army of the world and took pride in it. All his arguments however were ruthlessly brushed aside when Mountbatten's proposal for a single army in the Indian subcontinent under the British Command in order to ensure impartiality was summarily rejected both by Nehru and Jinnah. The Indian leaders were anxious not to keep any link between the two dominions each of which they insisted must start with its own army on 15 August. Mr Nehru particularly was so stiff about it that later on when Mr Jinnah asked if the British troops could be allowed to remain in Pakistan after the independence and when Mountbatten enquired from the Indian leader whether he would also agree to such a proposal, he received the curt reply: "I would sooner have every village in India put to the flames than keep the British army here after 15 August."[10]

Auchinleck had to set about his job. The army was split up in two stages. In the first stage the Muslim majority units moved to the Pakistan area while the non-Muslim majority units were moved into India. In the next stage the units themselves were combed out and each personnel was called upon to make his choice subject to certain restrictions as to which dominion he would op for. Six heads were immediately selected, three each for the two dominions, to head the respective navy, army and the air force. The Central administration, however remained under the Commander-in-Chief who himself was under the joint Defence Council. After 15 August the C-in-C was entitled the Supreme Commander and he continued in office till his work was completed.

INDEPENDENCE

All the necessary work, which had to be completed before 15 August having thus been done, the Viceroy flew to Karachi on 13 August where Jinnah had preceded him to take charge as Governor-General of the Dominion of Pakistan. A secret intelligence had been received that after the oath taking ceremony when Mr Jinnah would drive through the streets a bomb would be thrown on him. There were huge crowds as Jinnah and Mountbatten drove together. Jinnah was said to be extremely tense and nervous, but no bomb came and when the two reached back in the Government House safely, in a moment of rare emotion Jinnah laid his hand on Mountbatten's knee and said: "Thank God I've brought you back alive."[11] The ceremonies in Pakistan over, Mountbatten flew back to India, and during the midnight of 15 August he completed his work as the last Viceroy of India, locking up the dispatch boxes emblazoned with the Viceroy's Arms: "The British Empire had joined Ninevah and Tyre." In the meanwhile the necessary ceremonies were being undergone in the Constituent Assembly of India, where Mr Nehru delivered his memorable speech: "Long years ago we made a tryst with destiny, and now the time comes when we shall redeem our pledge, not wholly or in full measure, but very substantially. At the stroke of the mid-night hour, when the world sleeps, India will awake to life and freedom..."[12] About 20 minutes after midnight Dr Rajendra Prasad, President of the Constituent Assembly, and Mr Nehru came to the Viceroy and invited him to be the First Governor-General of free India.

Mountbatten's consent to this effect and the consent of the Labour Government and the Opposition in England had already been secured. Mountbatten had made his efforts after accepting the Indian proposal that Pakistan should also agree to his continuing as the joint Governor-General of the two Dominions for some time. Mr Jinnah, however refused to entertain the proposal and Mountbatten was persuaded to accept the office for India alone. As Dr. Prasad formally invited him to accept the office, Mountbatten replied: "I am proud of the honour and will do my best to carry out your advice in a constitutional manner."

There were huge crowds, hundreds of thousands of them, happy, laughing, to celebrate the day when the midnight hour struck and on 15 August India opened her eyes as an independent and sovereign nation, to take her legitimate place among the free countries of the world.

THE HOLOCAUST

India became independent on 15 August. The people were happy but the happiness was marred by such bloodshed and destruction, as the world had not probably seen before. Earlier there had been riots in Calcutta and Noakhali, which lead to thousands of the innocent people being butchered and maimed. This time the people went berserk in the Punjab. Children were lifted and their heads dashed against the ground, women had their breasts slashed, young girls were raped, sold away to the highest bidders, and trains crossed the border each way with thousands of corpses abroad, and painted on both sides with the legend: 'A Present From India', or 'A Present From Pakistan'. Leonard Mosley writes, it was all started by the Sikhs who had lost their most fertile lands, and their best shrines to West Pakistan. The Sikh population was almost equally divided on the two sides of the border, and they feared being massacred by the Muslims in the West Punjab, and smothered by the Hindus in the East Punjab. Master Tara Singh delivered fiery speeches in the Golden Temple where, as Mosley quotes, he addressed a congregation thus: "Oh Sikhs, know ye that our brethren are threatened in the West by those who call us infidels. Our lands are about to be overrun, our women dishonoured, our children forced to take alien vows..." There was evidence of elaborate preparation, and Mr Jinnah and Liaquat Ali demanded an immediate action against the Master and his associates. But Patel stood in the way and Mountbatten hesitated.

Before Jinnah flew to Karachi on 7 August 1947, several efforts were made to calm the communal passions. On 22 July a joint statement signed by Patel and Dr Prasad for the future Government of India, by Jinnah and Liaquat Ali for the future Government of Pakistan, and by Baldev Singh for the Sikhs, was issued, promising equitable treatment for the minorities, equal citizenship rights for all, safeguard of peace, equal protection and non-discrimination against the political opponents of the period before 15 August, etc. This statement was almost a charter of liberties for the different communities. Besides, as rumours of possible disturbances at the time of partition spread, Mountbatten caused a Boundary Force of 50,000 men prepared under the command of Major-General Rees, who was to be assisted by Brigadier Digambhar Singh for India, and Colonel Ayub Khan for Pakistan. This force was to assist in keeping law and order when Radcliffe Awards were made public. Beyond this, however, Mountbatten did not go. Thus when information was received that in the event of the famous Sikh shrine of Nankana Sahib going to Pakistan, the Sikhs were preparing to start trouble on a big scale, V.P. Menon proposed that Mr Jinnah may be asked to accept a sort of Vatican status for that shrine. The Sikh sacrifices were going to be great, as everybody realised. The Hindu majority town of Lahore was almost certain to be placed in Pakistan, and there were suggestions that Nehru and Patel may be asked to renounce their claims on the town before the announcement of the awards so as to win goodwill of the Muslims. But the Viceroy did not seriously apply his mind to any of such suggestions, which should have gone a long way to mollify the Sikhs and others who felt affected.

The things rather went out of control due to some irresponsible utterances of the Indian leaders as well. Thus, it is said, when Jinnah left for West Punjab, he was in a serene mood, and appealed to all the communities to "bury the past". But after his departure, Patel returned the sentiments with the remarks: "The poison has been removed from the body of India." Some remarks of the Congress President Mr Kripalani, further, were misunderstood in the West Punjab, and Mr Liaquat Ali remarked: "Let me tell Mr Kripalani and other Hindu leaders that they are playing with fire. If Hindu leaders like Kripalani succeed in inciting people, it would be foolish to expect that there will be no repercussions." These remarks of the Prime Minister designate of Pakistan were as much based on shortsightedness as those of Patel.

As the date of Independence drew nearer, tension rose. Had the awards been announced earlier, before actual partition tool place after the independence, people would have been sure as to where they belonged, and the Punjab Boundary Force would have been used to help the people to migrate peacefully. But the people stuck to their homes right till 16 August when the Radcliffe awards were made public, and now when all of a sudden they were told that the lands and houses which they possessed no more belonged to the Dominion they would like to live in, they suddenly started moving in panic to cross the border. Refugees, with cattle and household goods, in sixty or seventy-mile long columns, crossing to the opposite sides preyed by human vultures who swore in the names of their Gurus, their Prophet and Allah, and their Ram and Krishna. Over 600,000 lay dead, cut by swords, daggers and other weapons. Over 14,000,000 lost their homes and had to start a life all over again. How many were forcibly converted? How many girls and women were raped and sold on the auction block? Large number of them died, and larger numbers still remained to bewail their dead and their losses, and to spread the venom of hatred. Such were the fruits of Independence. Men became monsters, the worshippers of God turning into butchers to destroy God's creation. This happened both in Punjab and Bengal, though much more on the West than in the East. The only place saved was Calcutta where only a few months earlier the Hindus and the Muslims had cut each other's throats, but where now 5,000 Hindus and Muslims marched in joint processions shoutings the slogan, *Hindu Muslim Bhai Bhai.* Calcutta at this time was under the magic spell of Gandhi, the *faqir* of Sabarmati who went there and stayed in the Beliaghat slums, to spread the message of peace and keep the people calm. What a Boundary Force of 50,000 men could not do in the Punjab, 'One-man Boundary Force' did in Calcutta.

THE ASSASSINATION OF GANDHI

Mr Gandhi did not participate in the Independence Day celebrations. For his heart was not in them. He had failed to keep the Hindus and Muslims united, and had left Delhi to brood over the feelings of man. He returned to Delhi when India got her Independence and streams of luckless refugees were decending on the capital. Killings and lootings were still going on. Gandhi once again decided to penalize himself for the sins of others. On 13 Januray 1948 he held 'A fast unto death', to be broken only "if and when I am satisfied that there is a reunion of hearts of all communities brought about without any outside pressure, but from an awakened sense of duty…" Within five days Nehru paid up 55 crore rupees which India owed to Pakistan, but which had been withheld as a bargaining point. Intercommunal Committees of Peace came up to bring the different communities once again together. The atmosphere was relaxed, and Gandhi broke his fast. But only 12 days thereafter, on 30 January, an assassin's bullet struck his frail body and he lay dead. Mountbatten rushed to the spot. Somebody shouted out "it was a Muslim who did it." Mountbatten knew that if it were so all was over, and India would witness such orgy of bloodshed as, would turn all the waters, from the river Indus to the Brahmaputra red. He shouted back: "You fool, don't you know it was a Hindu?" Luckily, he was proved correct, though he did not actually know it then. It was Nathuram Vinayak Godse, a young Hindu belonging to Poona who had done it. He had wanted to save Hinduism by taking the life of the Mahatma.

Mountbatten's work in India was now over. He bid goodbye to the country on 21 June 1948 in the midst of tumultuous roars crying and begging him not to leave. When he got into an open landau to move away from the Government House, it was a sea of emotions all around, and even one of his horses went crazy. It reared "and plunged, bucked and almost rolled over. There was nothing for it but to unhitch" the horse.[13] It was obvious perhaps that even the horses did not want Mountbatten to leave. It was indeed now that England really conquered India.

Back home, "the ex-Supremo, ex-Viceoroy, ex-Governor-General, stepped down to the rank of Rear-Admiral, commanding the 1st Cruiser Squadron in Malta."[14] Admiral Sir Arthur Power who had worked under him in SEAC was now his boss. The boss addressed Lord Louis as 'Sir', and Louis addressed him as 'Sir'. Both 'sir-red' each other and observed the rules of the game. In 1951 Churchill came to power again, and raised him to the designation of Commander-in-Chief Mediterranean in 1952. In 1955 he was further raised and appointed First Sea Lord. This was the fulfilment of Mountbatten's life-long ambition. He now stood from where his father had been compelled to resign. Later at his suggestions the British defence forces were reorganized after the American methods, and Mountbatten was appointed Chief of the Defence Staff. His life after retirement has been full of contentment and peace.

WHY DID THE BRITISH LEAVE INDIA?

It now remains only to account briefly for the circumstances, which so dramatically and suddenly brought Mr Attlee to fix the date for the British to quit India and withdraw rather much earlier than the stipulated date.

Michael Brecher writes, "The independence of India was the natural and inevitable outcome of the process of creating natural consciousness and common purpose, accomplished by the Raj, unconsciously and by the Congress consciously, over an extended period of time. In this sense the British Raj contained within itself the seeds of its own destruction."[15] The British rule in India, if it was an evil as an imperialism, it was also a blessing in disguise. It was as a result of the British rule that India was so thoroughly united for the first time in her history, from the extreme North to the extreme South and from her extreme East to the extreme West. One political system, one *lingua franca,* common means of communication, common postal and telegraph systems and a uniform economic exploitation in all parts of the country carried through two centuries of the British rule, created common problems all over India and laid the foundations of nationalism. Urge for independence of the country as a whole developed in intensity till it became a mighty force which the British could not stand. From the great Mutiny of 1857 to the Non-cooperation

Movement organized by Mr Gandhi, to the Quit India Movement and to the part played by the I.N.A., a great change had taken place. The nationalist spirit in the forties of the twentieth century was not as weak as in 1857. The public enthusiasm shown at the time of the I.N.A. trials; the demonstrations of the Calcutta students on 19 November 1945, who despite the police firings and *lathi* charges, could not be prevented from marching to the Dalhousie Square; the violent Mutiny of about 3,000 naval ratings on 19 February, the spread of this trouble to Karachi, Madras, Calcutta and Delhi and sympathetic *hartals* in the cities; all this showed that the fire of dis-affection had spread from students to labourers, peasants, shopkeepers and now even to the common soldier without whose help the British could not stay on even for a day. It was a clear writing on the wall that British would quit, and quit in time, lest they should be consumed in this fire and reduced to ashed.

Then, Locke, Spencer, Mill, Macaulay and Burke of England had not praised democracy as an institution suited only to England. The message of Wordsworth who upheld the dignity of mankind and that of Byron, who glorified in liberty, could not be confined between the coastlines of England. They had travelled to India where the English educational system established by the East India Company made it easy to comprehend and grasp them. A new class of intelligentsia inspired and intoxicated in these new ideas had started developing right from the time of Raja Rammohun Roy, till by the time of Gandhi, Jawahar Lal, Subhas, Azad and Patel it became a force to reckon with. The Churchills and Simons of England were no better arguers and more intelligent than the Motilals and Saprus of India. Their justification to rule this country had, therefore, long since gone. The middle class of India, the class of intelligentsia created by the British themselves in the modern times, was now strong enough to shoulder its responsibilities and the British had no choice but to leave.

For full one century, the British had ruled India only by dividing the Indians among themselves. Right since its inception, the Congress had fought against communalism and therefore its power to fight against the British imperialism had been dissipated. India had tolerated the British rule because she had desired to get her freedom and save her limbs too. But now when the agreement for the severing of a limb had been reached and the Congress accepted the idea of Pakistan, the British imperialism was left with no cause. Thanks to the sincerity and persuasiveness of Lord and Lady Mountbatten, who brought the Congress and the League to an agreement, the British had now no option but to quit.

Then, there were other factors too which led to India's independence. Both Congress and the League had been dead-set in their respective philosophies, with the result that now frustration and helplessness had started creeping into their ranks, which was likely to throw both into the mouth of Communism or some other totalitarian system, unless they were brought to some agreement in time. And if India went Communist, it should have been a shame to Great Britain in the eyes of her own people as well as in the eyes of others of the non-Communist world. It was lucky that Mr Attlee sensed the danger and told Lord Mountbatten: "If we were not very careful, we might well find ourselves handing India over not simply to Civil War, but to political movements of definitely totalitarian character. Urgent action was needed to break the deadlock."

Nor could now the mounting world pressure be resisted for long. The United States of America and the Soviet Union had long since been insisting on the British to make India free. The personal visit of Chiang Kai-Shek to India during the War, though irritating to the British, had convinced them that India's freedom could be delayed only at the risk of England losing her prestige in the world.

The hold on India also was not as much a paying proposition as it used to be. An enormous development of the Indian industries had reduced the markets for the produce of the British industries to the minimum. A free and friendly India could perhaps have some economic ties profitable to the British, but an India seething with discontent and hatred was bound only to be a liability. Particularly so when the British economy had been crippled as a result of the War, the Indian soldiers were refusing to work under the British obedience, and therefore India could now only be retained with the help of the British troops whose number had already depleted to a dangerous level.

Nor was it possible to violate for long, the promises given to India and her soldiers during the War. The blood of the Indian *Jawans* had been shed in torrents and war contributions of the toiling hungry masses of India had been spent in basket-fulls. India had borne all this for the promises that she would get after the War what she was fighting to save for the British and their allies. The fulfilment of these promises could be postponed for long at the risk of dire consequences.

When all this is said, let us also not fail to appreciate the moral compunction that the British masses had started feeling for the illogical and ruthless British regime in India. They were determined to correct the situation and brought the Labour Party to power—the Party, which fought the general elections in 1945 with a pledge to grant India her independence. Nor should we in our hour of freedom, forget to pay homage to the sincerity and tenacity of purpose of Mr Attlee and his colleagues in the Labour Government.

Mr. Chia Luen-lo the Chinese Ambassador to India wrote to salute the free India:

'India be free
Won't that be
A Himalayan dream?
How fantastic
How absurd an idea
That never occurred to me…
Suddenly and incredibly triumphant wisdom
Where the East and West met on common ground.
What a miracle
That Independence can be
Without a war! History will tell you
It has never happened before.
Be brave, forward
Riders on the chariot of time!
While approaching the mountain peak
Redouble your efforts to climb!
Unfailingly you will arrive at your idea.
Lofty and beautiful
Noble and Sublime.'[16]

NOTES

1. Mosley, Leonard, *op. cit.*, p.171.
2. Campbell-Johnson, *Mission with Mountbatten.*
3. Hatch Alden, *op. cit.,* p. 346: Mosley, Leonard *op. cit.,* p.173.
4. See Terraine, John, *op. cit.*, p.164.
5. Kulkarni, V.R., *British Statesman in India*, p.499.
6. Campbell Johnson, *op. cit.*
7. Philips, C.H. and Mary Doreen Eainwright (edited), *The Partition of India*, pp. 22-23.
8. *Ibid.,* Introduction, p.23.
9. Mosley, Leonard, p. 137.
10. *Ibid.*, p. 149.
11. Terraine, John, p.157.
12. *Jawaharlal Nehru's Speeches,* Vol. I, Delhi 1949, p. 25.

13. Hatch, Alden, *The Mountbattens,* p. 361.
14. Terraine, John, *The Life and Times of Lord Mountbatten*, p. 166.
15. Michael Brecher, *Nehru: A Political Biography,* p. 373.
16. Mosley, Leonard, *op. cit.*, pp. 241-42.

11

Some Indian Personalities of the Time

SWAMY DAYANAND SARASWATI

Swami Dayanand was born in 1824 a short distance from North-Western coast of the Indian peninsula in the prosperous town of Marvi, in Kathiawar. His father, a Brahmin of the highest order, held a respectable post in the Government of the State and was "a rigid, austere Brahmin, thoroughly orthodox and uncompromising in his religious beliefs and practices…his mother on the other hand, was the personification of sweetness, gentleness and goodness."[1]

The education of Dayanand whose original name was Mul Shankar, commenced when he was five years of age; his father himself assuming the role of a teacher. He was 14 when his father's piously-intended insistence upon his son's observing the fast of Shivratri, turned the son 'into the most virulent and successful opponent of image-worship of his time." The successive death of his beloved sister and uncle distracted him when he was 19, and when his father made arrangements for his marriage, he fled from home, assumed the ochre-coloured garments and for full 15 years, 1845 to 1860, wandered North, South, East and West, almost all over India in pursuit of knowledge and truth.[2] Ultimately he acquired finishing touches to his education when he waited for two years and a half on Swami Virja Nanda. And then he entered public life, founded the well known Arya Samaj at Bombay in 1875, which coming to Lahore in 1877 developed as a mighty movement in the Punjab. He died in 1883.

In contrast to Raja Rammohun Roy who advocated taking the best from the West, the Swami stood for everything Indian. This was good to a certain extent when India was losing all faith in her old values and in her glorious past, but the Swami, a progressive thinker as he was, fell down from the pinnacle of enlightened philosophy, turned reactionary and to the bad luck of India, left behind a militant and aggressive Hindu Arya Samaj, against the enlightened and progressive Brahmo Samaj of Raja Rammohun Roy.

The Swami was interested in the political sphere even less than Raja Rammohun Roy was, although the British suspected the Samaj of being a political organization. This suspicion of the British arose from the fact that the Arya Samajists believed in Arya for the Aryans and raised the slogans such as 'Go back to the Vedas.' Such slogans were bound to raise hatred against the British rule in this country. and against every race, which came into this country subsequently to the Aryans.

The Swami was basically a social and religious reformer. In the social sphere he condemned early marriage, enforced widowhood and other such evils. The Samaj of the Swami opened Hindu orphanages and organized famine relief. His activities also resulted in the D.A.V. movement, which has established scores of educational institutions all over the country. He was against untouchability and stood for every thing Swadeshi.

In the religious sphere, the Swami was aggressively and fanatically a Hindu. He wrote *Satyarath Prakash*, the religious book of the Arya Samajists, in 1874, and in this book he preached an open hatred against other faiths in order to establish the superiority of the Hindu faith over them all. He was against idol-worhip and considered the Vedas as a storehouse of all knowledge which we have so far gained and which we are ever to gain in future. He professed himself to be the best follower of the Vedas, but in practice, it is doubtful if he rearly understood this highest philosophy of the world. He is survived today by the Arya Samaj which is following the great and enlightened policy of spreading education in this country. But unfortunately, it is mixed with communalistic venom which if allowed to grow will slowly sap all the nationalistic and secular vitality of this great nation throwing it once again, the God of the great Vedas forbid, into a dungeon of medieval depravity.

DADABHAI NAOROJI

Dadabhai, "one of the most perfect examples of the highest types of patriotism" was born on 4 September 1825 at Bombay to a priestly Parsee family. He was only 4 years old when his father died. "His gifted mother," writes R.P. Masani,[1] "however, supplied to a large extent the want of a father's care and protection." Dadabhai was married to Gulbai, a daughter of Sarobji Shroff at eleven. He was educated at the Elphinstone Institution, popularly known as the Siroti School in the Bombay Presidency, where he was the brightest boy of his class. The well-to-do parents of a student colleague helped Dadabhai with books. At that young age he read *Shahnama*, which occupied a pride place among the books he read. Another book, which was his constant companion, was *The Duties of Zoroastrians*, the "burden of which was pure thought, pure speech, pure deed."

In 1840 he received Clare Scholarship, and two years later he was admitted to the newly opened class of Normal Scholars. In "his mastery of natural philosophy and political economy Dadabhai stood unrivalled," and Sir Erskine Perry, the Chief Justice of the Supreme Court of Bombay, was so much impressed with his intelligence that he offered to meet half of his expenses for higher studies in England, if the other half was contributed by Dadabhai's community. But the orthodox in the community having scented a disaster in the generous offer, the scheme fell through.

After completing his education Dadabhai was appointed as the *Head Native Assistant Master* in the Elphinstone School, which two years later proved to be a stepping-stone for his appointment as Assistant Professor of Mathematics and Natural Philosophy. Referring to this appointment the Board of Education in its Report for 1850-51 remarked about him as "one of the most experienced as well as able men ever educated within the walls of the institution." The Government also congratulated the Board for having made this appointment, and Dada himself later said: "Several honours came to me during my lifetime, but no other title created in me that sense of pride which I felt in being known as a Professor."

On 4 August 1849 Behramji Kharshedji Gandhi read a paper on female education, which led some enthusiastic social workers to organize seven schools, 3 Hindi and 4 Parsee, for female education. Teachers worked in these schools on honorary basis, and Dadabhai was in charge of one of these schools–the Baharkote School. This was about the first of his affiliations to social work after which his interest in these activities sharpened.

On 3 August 1851 along with others he founded a society named *Rahnumae Mazdayasnan Sabha,* or the 'Guides on the Mazdayasnan Path', of which Naoroji Furdoonji was President, and Dadabhai the Secretary. "The avowed object of the society was to expound the true tenets of the Zoroastrian creed, to take off the wrappings, to discover the vital and essential elements, and to restore ancient religion to its pristine purity."[4] The Sabha went on working, and Dadabhai lived to see its diamond jubilee.

The first of his political associations was with the *Bombay Association* founded on 26 August 1852, in the first meeting of which Dadabhai delivered his maiden speech. The Association petitioned the Crown for certain political reforms, some of which were actually secured in the Charter Act of 1853, which encouraged Dadabhai, and he now became a more active politician.

On 15, November 1851 securing the financial help of a public spirited friend, Kharshedji Nasarwanji Cama, Dadabhai started a fortnightly journal *Rast Goftar,* or the 'Truth Teller', which soon became popular, and on the demand of its readers it had to be turned into a weekly. Through this paper Dadabhai espoused the cause of the Parsees in India and abroad, and supported England and France against Russia in the Crimean War.

The life of a Professor, however, could not contain the ambitions of Dadabhai for long, and developing a partnership with the Camas, be established the first Indian mercantile firm in England to deal in opium, wine and spirits. The earnings from the business in spirits, etc. however pricked his conscience, and resigning his partnership after about three years he came back to Bombay. He left for England again in 1858, there organized an independent firm—Dadabhai Naoroji & Co—went on working for the political interests of India and organized a *Zoroastrian* association for the Parsee students in that country.

Dadabhai's domestic life was not happy with an illiterate wife, but his business was a grand success as is obvious from certain of his financial contributions to social works, including an offer of Rs. 50,000 to the Bombay University for the endowment of a Fellowship to perpetuate the memory of Lord Canning. Soon, however, his firm failed as a result of the commercial crisis, which supervened on the termination of the American Civil war. Dadabhai took the misfortunate philosophically, and now turned wholly to his struggle for India's political rights.

In collaboration with W.C. Bonnerjee, he started *London Indian Society,* but failing to keep with it, founded on 1 December 1866 the *East Indian Association,* with the object not only of ventilating the grieveances of the Indians, but also of promoting mutual understanding and friendship between the Indians and the Englishmen. Coming to India he established the branches of this Association at Calcutta, Madras and other cities, preached about and wrote papers on the economic grievances of the Indians. The public of Bombay responded to his services, held a function and presented Dadabhai with a purse of Rs. 25,000 for his ill-looked-after personal interests, which however he donated for the activities of his Association.

The Gaekwad of Baroda appointed Dadaji as his Dewan in 1870, where the latter did a lot of work for the administrative reforms, but could not pull on and resigned after 13 months of service. Shortly after he was elected a member of the Town Council of Bombay, which was the Executive Committee of the Bombay Corporation, but refused to accept the usual daily allowances of Rs.

32 and carried on constructive activities gratis.

In 1876, he wrote a remarkable paper on "Poverty in India", followed by a bulky volume named *Poverty and Un-British Rule in India.* The Education Commission of 1882 invited Dadabhai to give his views on certain educational problems of the country. In January 1883, he was appointed Justice of Peace, the same year he started *The Voice of India,* actively supported Ripon's Ilbert Bill, and on Ripon's retirement, collected funds to raise him a memorial. In August 1885, the Governor of Bombay invited Dadabhai to join the Bombay Legislative Council as an additional member. By this time, Dada's reputation as an expert on Indian problems spread far and wide, and many Englishmen came to him for an advice.

In 1886, Dada stood from Holborn, a Conservative constituency, to the English Parliament, but was defeated for his liberal views. Towards the close of 1886, he was invited to attend the second session of the Indian National Congress, which he did, and was elected President of this body. After this he continued his association with the Congress till his death. In 1891 he tried again, and this time was elected to the Parliament from the Central Finsbury constituency with the support of the Liberals. "Dadabhai had now reached the pinnacle of his fame." "For weeks together the first Indian M.P. was deluged with torrents of congratulations from friends as well as strangers from the four quarters of the globe. He was adopted by the Liberals from the same constituency in the next elections, but was defeated. But before being unseated, he had been appointed a member of the Royal Commission to enquire into the financial administration of India, a job in which he acquitted himself admirably well."[5]

When India rose against the ruthless regime of Lord Curzon, Dadabhai declared before a gathering of the *London Indian Society* in 1904: "I earnestly press upon the Indian people to claim unceasingly their birth-right and pledged right of British citizenship, of self-government." He took up the matter of racial persecution of the Indians in South Africa, and helped Gandhiji in this connection.

In 1906, he stood again for membership to the British Parliament, but was defeated, and shortly after when he fell seriously ill, he decided to leave that country and spend the rest of his life in his motherland. Back in India, there being a split in the Congress he supported the Moderates, but generally lived only a retired life. In 1915 Mrs Annie Besant proposed to organize the Home Rule League in India, of which Dadabhai agreed to become President. But before the League was duly constituted, he left this world on 30 June 1917.

Such was the man, the hero of India, about whom Sir N. Chandavarkar wrote: "If we take stock of his life and his example…he was the Prophet Zoroaster's religion personified." "I have always been a hero-worshipper," wrote Gandhiji about him. "And so Dadabhai became real Dada to me." And again: "I never received a typed letter from him…The story of a life so noble and yet so simple…"[6]

Before closing this account, we may quote C.Y. Chintamani[7]: "For 61 long years in England and in India, by day and by night in circumstances favourable and adverse, in the face of discouragement which would have broken the heart of a smaller man, Dadabhai Naoroji served the Motherland with undeviating purpose, with complete selflessness and with vitality of faith to put to shame most young men. Withal, he was the greatest of souls and the most charitable in judgement and never made a personal enemy. In respect equally of the highest personal character and the great public services, Dadabhai Naoroji was the loftiest ideal his countrymen could set before themselves respectively to follow at a distance."

SURENDRA NATH BANERJEE

S.N. Banerjee, the famous writer of the volume entitled *A Nation in the Making,* about whom P. Sitaramayya writes: "For command of language, for elegance of diction, for a rich imagery, for emotional heights, for a spirit of manly challenge, his orations are hard to beat. They remain unapproachable,"[8] was born in 1848, of a Kulin Brahmin family, and of a father who was a very successful medical practitioner of his time. After doing his B.A. he became a member of the Indian Civil Service through an open competition in 1868, but due to his progressive nationalistic ideas, he was dismissed from the Service shortly after joining, and had to content himself with a Professorship in English in the Metropolitan Institute at Calcutta. But by his hard work in politics and journalism he soon distinguished himself, and became one of the popular leaders of public opinion of the day. He founded the Ripon College, which was later on renamed after him, took over the *Bengalee* a weekly jounal, and developed it into a daily. He founded the Indian Association in 1876 as we have already discussed,[9] through which he carried on agitation against the lowering of age of admission in the I.C.S. from 21 to 19, and undertook whirlwind tours of the country, to organize the public opinion. The Indian National Congress was founded in 1885, through the joint efforts of Mr Banerjee and Hume over the sessions of which he presided in 1898 and 1902.

The later life of Mr Banerjea, however, witnessed a steady decline in his career as a popular leader. He had been elected to the Imperial Legislative Council in 1892. He propagated for the acceptance of the Montagu-Chelmsford

Reforms of 1919, left the Congress in 1918, founded the National Liberal Federation, and accepted a Ministry of Bengal under Dyarchy.

In his early career, he was a great and very popular leader. He led deputations to England several times, suffered under *lathi-charges* during the partition of Bengal, and "He was the first Indian leader to popularize public meetings as a means of political propaganda." He was a lover of the path of constitutionalism and his object, "was not the suppression of British Rule in India but the broadening of its basis, the liberalizing of its spirit, the ennobling of its character and placing it on the unchangeable foundations of a Nations's affections, and he hoped for the day when India would find its place in the great confederacy of free states, English in the origin, English in their character, English in their institutions." To him, as he declared: "England is our political guide and our moral preceptor in the exalted sphere of political duty," and the greatest of his political ambitions was to implant the English political institutions in the depths of India's heart,[10] so that they grew and fructified and India gloried in the sunshine of democratic and representative institutions. He died in 1925.

LOKMANYA BAL GANGADHAR TILAK

The "Father of Indian Unrest", as Chirol wrote of him,[11] Tilak was born on 23 July 1856, in a Brahmin family of Maharashtra. After graduating with honours, he started his career as a Professor in the Ferguson College, Poona. His opposition to the Age of Consent Bill converted him into a politician, and his forceful writings in his two weeklies, *Kesari* in Marathi and the *Maharatha* in English, established his reputation in the minds of the authorities, as the Governor of Bombay wrote, "one of the chief conspirators, perhaps the chief conspirator, against the existence of British Government in India, all the weak points of which he has made a careful study."

Tilak joined the Congress in 1889, but being of an extremist view, he could not pull well with the Moderates, who believed in the slow moving process of constitutional struggle for political rights, and broke away with this body in 1907. He organized Lathi Clubs, Anti-Cow-Killing societies and *Akharas*. In 1893, he inaugurated the Ganpati festival, and in 1895, the Shivaji festival. His object was to inspire the Indian youths with memories of the Indian heroes. He said: "With benevolent intentions Shivaji murdered Afzal Khan for the good of others. If thieves enter our house and we have not sufficient strength in our wrists to drive them out, we should without hesitation, shut them up and burn them alive."

He was imprisoned for 4 months in 1882, sentenced to 18 month's rigorous imprisonment in 1897, and to six years' imprisonment in 1908. His second imprisonment in 1897 was important, as it is said to have opened up a new era in India's history of freedom movement. Tilak was charged of sedition and tried by a jury of 6 Europeans and 3 Indians, of whom the Indians found him not guilty, while the Europeans found him guilty. Tilak refused to apologise, and set the first example of being prosecuted for sedition.

This second imprisonment of Tilak changed the Indian atmosphere against the British rule, and *The Madras Times* commented: "The news of Mr Tilak's conviction is received as a national calamity." And according to *The Hindu*: "In the conviction of Mr Tilak the country upholds the beginning of a most mischievous and most deplorable struggle between the Indian people and their enemies in their own country." A petition of mercy was later sent signed by Sir William Hunter, Professor Max Mueller, William Claive, Sir Richard Garth, Romesh Chandra Dutt and Dadabhai Naoroji, and he was released 6 months before the expiry of his term.

In 1908 he was arrested again as a result of his agitation against the partition of Bengal, was tried by a jury of 7 Europeans and 2 Indians, and the story was repeated; Europeans finding him guilty, while the Indians, not guilty. He was sentenced to six years' imprisonment and transported to Malaya, after which there were serious riots, which according to V. Chirol, "assumed at times a very threatening character."[12] In Malaya, Tilak produced his famous works *The Arctic Home of the Vedas* and *the Gita Rahasya.* About the former, Dr Bloomfield said that it was unquestionably "the literary sensation of the year. History, the chronic readjustor, will have our hands uncommonly full to assimilate the result of Tilak's discovery and arrange her paraphernalia in the new perspective."

He was released in 1914 when the First World War commenced, and he asked the people to support the Government. But later finding the Government careless of Indian aspirations, he started, in cooperation with Annie Besant, the Home Rule Movement. He died in 1920.

Tilak, writes Ram Gopal, "had forestalled Gandhi in all the movements that the Mahatma launched after Tilak's dealth; no-rent campaign, boycott of government services, prohibition, Swadeshi were all preached by him. He talked of complete independence as far back as 1897."[13]

Addressing a meeting, Tilak said in 1906: "So many of you need not like...boycott as a political weapon. We shall not give them assistance to collect revenue and keep the peace. We shall not assist them in fighting beyond the frontiers or outside India with Indian blood and money. We shall not assist them in carrying on the administration of justice. We shall have our own course and when the time comes we shall not be taxed. If you can do that by united efforts, you are free from tomorrow." Such was the belief of Tilak. He did not like the Moderates in the Congress, and asserted that India would not get freedom merely by passing resolutions and asking for concessions. India to achieve her goal would have to adopt different means. And so long as the end was noble, one need not bother for the quality of the means, which may be anything, good or bad.

Chintamani writes about Tilak: 'but the historian will not fail to recognize that he was one of the men who by indoubtable qualities and life-long service, laid the foundation of the future India and Swaraj."[14]

BIPIN CHANDRA PAL

A powerful orator of the extremist school to which Tilak belonged, the proverbial Pal was born on 7 September 1858. After completing his education he joined the profession of a teacher. He started his public career by joining the Brahmo-Samaj, proved to be a brilliant writer and became the editor of the *New India.* He took a prominent part in the anti-partition of Bengal, distinguished himself as a powerful supporter of the extremists in the Calcutta session of the Congress in 1906, and put up a strong fight for the candidature of Tilak for Presidentship of the Congress of Surat in 1907. Like the other extremists, immediately after the Surat split he was forced to leave the Madras Presidency. Once he wrote an article 'Anthology of the Bomb' for which he was tried, but he apologised. He died in 1932.

Bipin Chandra Pal was a powerful personality and a forceful speaker who aimed at an immediate and complete independence of the country. Naturally under these circumstances he could have no permanent friendship with the Congress dominated by the Moderates and he had to leave it. National Education and Boycott were among his other favourite subjects, and he played a great part in the development of the extremist movement in this country.

LALA LAJPAT RAI

Lala Lajpat Rai, the 'Lion of the Pubjab', as he was known, was born at Jagraon in distric Ludhiana in 1865 in the house of Shri Radha Krishan who was a teacher in a Government school. Lajpat Rai was lucky in having a mother and a father both of whom were of high character and intellectual habits, and they seem to have left a very good impression of themselves upon their son as he admitted once that all "that I am I owe to my father and mother."

After completing his studies and qualifying for the bar, he started his practice at Hissar, later on shifting to Lahore, and at the latter place he was soon able to establish a high reputation. His father was an admirer of Swami Dayanand, and when Lajpat Rai came of age, he also started taking a close interest in the Arya Samaj activities, more so when he got himself fixed up at Lahore. He spoke from the Arya Samaj platforms, established branches of this Samaj at several places and took a leading part in the establishment of D.A.V. College at Lahore. He also wrote the biography of Swami Dayanand.

The Arya Samaj activities, however, could not satisfy his aspirations completely and therefore he turned to politics in 1888. The All India Congress was then slowly spreading its nationalistic activities, it attracted Lala's attention, and he attended its Allahabad session, thereafter becoming its ardent worker. A hard working and enterprising social worker as he was, he soon rose to the pinnacle of politics, and his name and fame spread far and wide. He established his reputation as a fiery orator, so that in1905 feeling the need of enlightening the public opinion in England regarding the Indian problems, the Congress sent Lajpat Rai together with Gokhale to that country where he undertook a whirlwind tour and impressed the English people of India's capabilities and desires.

Here in Punjab too Lajpat Rai took a daring interest in the public welfare activities. He belonged to the extremist school, and when the Congress was split up into Moderates and the Extremists, the Government following the policy of the suppression of the latter, deported Lajpat Rai in 1907 to Mandalay, where he wrote his famous book, *The Story of My Deportation.*

Due to his extremist activities the British Government becoming very harsh upon him, during the war he left this country and stayed in America from 1914 to 1920; there writing and preaching and living an ideal life from the income of his books. His famous books: *Young India, The Arya Samaj England's Debt to India* were written during his sojourn in the United States.

On his return to this country in 1920 he was elected President of the special session of the Congress at Calcutta. But later as Gandhi rose, disliking the latter's non-cooperation movement he began to follow his independent activities. He got himself elected to the Central Assembly through the Swarajist Party, and there made his mark as a courageous advocate of India's independence. He was specially interested in the Hindu welfare, for which he, together with Malaviya, organized the *Hindu Sangathan Movement.* Chintamani writes: "He never surrendered Hindu interests. He was as keen upon Hindu-Muslim unity as anyone else, but he never believed in the purchase of it by the payment of too heavy a price at the expense of the Hindu Community."[15]

On 20 October 1928 he led a procession in protest against the arrival of the Simon Commission at Lahore. He was violently assaulted, and of this he died a martyr on 17 November the same year.

Lala Lajpat Rai was indeed a commanding personality among the Indian political leaders, and Chintamani compared him to Lloyd George as a public speaker. His hold and reputation in the public can be judged from the fact that he collected as much as nine lakh rupees in only ten days to contribute to the Tilak School Fund. He is said to have played a leading role in the foundation of the *Lakshmi Insurance Company* and any *Punjab National Bank*. His daily Urdu paper *Bande Matram,* and his English journal, *The People,* enjoyed a high reputation among the people.

We may conclude this short sketch of Lajpat Rai's career with a quotation om J C Wedgwood, M.P. who wrote: "I suppose Lajpat Rai would describe himself as one of those we group under Advocates of Constructive Nationalism but he is not a Nationalist as we know the species, he is a hater of injustice and opposition, a living flame of which liberalism of all ages will justly be proud." "Men like Lalaji cannot die so long as the moon shines in the Indian sky," wrote Gandhiji.[16]

ALLEN OCTAVIAN HUME

Among the European friends of India, we must not forget the name of A O Hume who is supposed to be the father of the Indian National Congress. Mr Hume was an Englishman who joined the Bengal Civil Service in 1849, worked with distinction in several capacities and rose ultimately to the office of the Secretary to the Government of India. "As a District Officer," writes Dr P Sitaramayya, "he laboured for the cause of popular education, police reform, the liquor traffic, the vernacular press, the juvenile reformatories, and other domestic requirements. His one interest was the village and its agriculture, his one care and concern was for the people."[17]

Hume was not in favour of the police officers also enjoying the judicial powers. He would prefer to promote popular education through the native agencies. He criticized *Abkari* as follows: "While we debauch our subjects, we do not even pecuniarily derive any profit from their ruin. All this revenue is the wage of sin…And for every rupee additional that the *Abkari* yields, two at least are lost to the public by crime and spent by the Government in suppressing them."

During the Mutiny, Hume found himself in the Etawah district fighting to save the British Empire in India. After the Mutiny was over, he was in favour of following the policy of graceful forbearance, which was not liked by the Government. He received a warning against his over-benevolence. But this made no difference and he continued as he would. *The People's Friend* a vernacular paper was brought out with his help in 1859. Four years after, he was busy establishing a Juvenile Reformatory where the children of the criminals could be reformed and reclaimed. In 1879 he gave birth to an abortive agricultural reform scheme wherein he considered the "civil courts in rural districts directly responsible for the bondage of cultivators to the money lender." He suggested that the "rural debt cases should be disposed of summarily and finally on the spot by selected Indians of known probity and intelligence." For he held "when you get him into court, no witness seems to be able to tell the truth, on his own village platform surrounded by his neighbours, no villager in personal questions like these seems able to tell an untruth. Everybody knows everybody else's affairs."

Hume also worked for some time as the Commissioner of Customs, and in this capacity guided by certain senior officers he introduced a very important reform with regard to the salt tax which had hitherto been levied in different provinces at widely varied rates, thus encouraging the smuggling of salt from one province or from one Indian State to the other. For the prevention of the crime, an impenetrable inland customs line about 2,500 miles in length, running from Attock on the Indus to the Mahanadi in the Deccan, and made at some places of a wall, while at other places of cactus hedge or ditch, had to be established. Such long customs line required as many as 12,000 men to be patrolled by. The whole customs line could be swept away if salt tax in the different provinces was made uniform, and if salt manufacture in the Indian States was controlled. Hume got the required reforms introduced and the whole customs barrier was abolished.

Hume worked as the Secretary to the Government of India from 1870 to 1879. But his ideas being too progressive and independent, he could not be tolerated in this office for long, and was removed. He was offered the Lieutenant-Governorship of the Punjab, which however, he declined and retiring in 1882 he settled at Shimla.

But Hume in retirement was a greater force than Hume in office. After retirement he, according to William Wedderburn, realised with "increasing anxiety that the existing government, administered by foreign officials on autocratic lines, was dangerously out of touch with the people."[18] He met Lord Dufferin whom he convinced that there was a need at the time of some political organization in the country, which could work as Her Majesty's opposition in England. It was desired, as the Viceroy agreed with Hume, that the Indian politicians "meet yearly and point out to the Government in what respects the administration was defective and how it could be improved." Or in other words, the need for an organization, which could act as a safety valve for the rising political ambitions of the Indians, was felt, and Hume decided to organize for the purpose, what was later known as the Indian National Congress. Surendra Nath Banerjee helped him in this. The two jointly issued a circular and convened a conference in 1885, which proved to be the first session of the Indian National Congress. Hume was appointed as the first General Secretary of this organization. This office he held till 1907.

Certain writers like Dr Raghuvanshi[19] assert that the main purpose of Hume in organizing the Congress was to "save the British Empire." But this does not seem correct. In a pamphlet named *An Old Man's Hope* Hume addressed the Englishmen thus: "All men! Well fed and happy! Do you all realise that full misery of these countless myriads?...toil, toil; hunger, hunger, hunger, sickness, suffering, sorrow, these alas, alas, are the keynotes of their short and sad existence." Again, on 1 March 1883 he addressed the graduates of the Calcutta University in a circular letter thus: "Constituting as you do, a large body of the most highly educated Indians, you should, in the natural order of things constitute also the most important source of mental, social, moral and political progress in India...In vain many aliens like myself love India and her children...but they lack the essential of nationality, and the real work must ever be done by the people of the country themselves." And then his vigorous speech in April 1888 at Allahabad advocating a propaganda among the Indian Masses, on the lines of that of the Anti-Corn Law League in England: all these activities were certainly different from those which believers of the 'Save British Empire' theory could safely follow. It was not in vain that the British authorities in India threatened to deport Hume from this country, and in October 1888 Sir A Colvin, the Lieutenant-Governor of the North-West Provinces addressed him a letter running into 20 pages, warning Hume of the consequences of his activities; to which, however, Hume replied in 60 pages.

Still, it would be too much to say that at that early period Hume should have aimed at the complete overthrow of the British Government. His immediate aim was to secure a Government, which should work for India and not for England, with the ultimate end to train the Indians to handle their own affairs.

MAHADEV GOVIND RANADE

Mighty "in intellect, a man of prodigious industry and of vast and varied learning; a profound thinker and ardent patriot," as C.Y. Chintamani[20] called him, Ranade, the political Guru of Gokhale, was born in 1842. A Maharashtrian scholar after a brilliant career, he became a Judge of the Bombay High Court. The Government service was handicap to him, yet he found opportunities to think and plan social reforms, if not political agitation. He started the Deccan

Education Soceity which later established a school at Poona. It was this school which grew into the Ferguson College, the Principalship of which was held for 20 long years by Gokhale, a loyal disciple of Ranade, at a monthly pittance of Rs. 70.

Justice Ranade did not participate in political agitations, yet he was a strong source of strength for the Indian National Congress. A great social reformer, he wrote a book *Social Reforms and Rise of the Maratha Power* in which he criticized the social evils in the Maratha society and explained the necessity of reforming them. The proof of his intimate knowledge of the Indian economic problems is available in his book *Essay on Indian Economics*. He organized what was known as Social Reform Conference and through this body gave practical shape to his social reform ideas. He died in 1901 at the age of 59.

SIR PHEROZESHAH MEHTA

A staunch Moderate who believed in the good sense of the Englishmen and considered the constitutional methods as the most efficacious means towards the political independence of this country, Sir Pherozeshah was one of the important patriarchs of India who played their part in the early years of our fight for independence. Sir Pherozeshah played an important role in the early Congress organization and presided at its 6th Session in Calcutta in 1890. He worked in the different committees of the Congress and made his contributions in them. He was thus one of the members of the committee, which the Congress appointed in 1892 for drafting a petition to the British Parliament with regard to the Public Service Commission. In 1894 he was one of the members of the Congress deputation, who met the Governor-General to acquaint him with the Congress views on some of the existing problems. He was an uncompromising opponent of the Extremists in the Surat Session of the Congress held in 1907. The Extremists being expelled from the organization, they could not re-enter it so long as he lived. His selfless activities received yet another recognition in 1909 when he was elected President of the Lahore Session of the Congress, but he resigned this office before the Session was actually held.

Sir Pherozeshah was indeed one of the illustrious sons of the late 19th century India when the foundation of our freedom struggle was laid. He, together with the others of his age, did the spadework for the political freedom we today possess.

SWAMI SHRADDHANAND

A Hindu reformer who at times showed benevolent attitude towards communal harmony, Swami Shraddhanand earlier known as Munshi Ram, was born as Talwan in the Jullundur district in 1856. In his childhood and boyhood he did not give any promise for his future disciplined and well ordered life. He then had the usual weaknesses of sex till in 1882 he came into contact with Swami Dayanand, was converted to his views and later on became one of the ardent Arya Samajists. In his early years he worked as a Naib-Tehsildar and from 1885 to 1902 he practised as a lawyer. In 1892, the Arya Samaj was divided into two sections, which differed with regard to the lines on which the D.A.V. College of Lahore was to be run. The difference of opinion was whether English, science, or the Vedas should be given the first place in the courses of studies in the institution. Those who held the latter opinion were termed as fanatics and debarred from the management of the College. Swami Shraddhanand was the leader of this party which in 1902 started the well-known Gurukul at Hardwar in order to put their idea into practice.

"The Gurukul," observed Sir James Meston the Lieutenant-Governor of U.P. on 16 March 1913, "is one of the most original and interesting experiments carried on in these provinces, in fact in the whole of India." In the Gurukul, remarked V. Chirol in 1910, "pupils or *chelas* are admitted between the ages of six and ten. From that moment they are practically cut off from the outer world during the whole course of the studies, which cover a period of 16 years altogether—i.e., ten years in the lower school and six years in the upper, to which they pass as *Brahmcharis*. During the whole of that period no student is allowed to visit his family, except in cases of grave emergency, and his parents can only see him with the permission of the head of the Gurukul and not more than once a month."[21]

Such thus was the institution started by the Swami, which reveals his philosophy and way of thinking. From 1902 to 1917 he worked for the Gurukul, but it was in the later year that he adopted *Sanyasa* and began to be known as Swami Shraddhanand. Prior to that he was Mahatma Munshi Ram.

After adopting *Sanyasa,* however, the Swami did not go over to the forests. He participated in the anti-Rowlatt Act agitation in Delhi and led a procession of the agitators, which was stopped by a posse of Gurkha soldiers near the Clock Tower, Chandni Chowk. The Swami bared his breast before them asking them to pierce him with their bayonets before they opened fire at the mob. He won and was permitted to proceed.

The Swami expressed his heart-felt sympathy to the bereaved families of the Muslims who had fallen victims to the police excesses during the Rowlatt Act agitation, and the Muslims of Delhi in the Jama Masjid honoured him. In 1919 he invited the Congress to hold its session at Amritsar and made the necessary arrangements for it. In the following year he sympathized with the

Gurdwara Sudhar agitation of the Sikhs, which landed him in the Montgomery Jail. He joined non-cooperation of Gandhiji, but later resigned from the Satyagraha committee when Gandhiji suspended the movement due to violence having been committed by some mischief-mongers for which according to the Swami, the genuine satyagrahis should not have been held responsible. The communal riots which followed and under which the Hindus generally suffered at the hands of the Muslims, turned him into a reactionary. He started *Hindu Sangathan* movement to meet the situation, organized *Delhi Sudhar Sabha* for the up-lift of the untouchables and also started the *Bharat Shuddhi Sabha.* These activities earned him the enmity of the Muslims and ultimately he fell in 1926 by a shot at the hands of a Muslim assassin.

MRS ANNIE BESANT

Born in 1847, Miss Wood, which her early name was, Mrs Annie Besant lost her father when she was only five. Her early childhood and maidenhood were strewn with all sorts of difficulties. And when she married a clergyman in 1867, her fortune did not improve, it rather worsened. Her husband was a religious man with all that involved only blind faith and absolutely no spirit and desire to understand reality. She had her own ways which were more religious but which, to the sort of society she lived in, seemed atheistic. A daughter was born from this marriage, but still life headed on towards extreme desperation and anguish, till Besant decided to take her life and end the whole game once for all. She prepared herself for the job and was on the verge of committing suicide when second thoughts appeared in her mind and she decided to leave her husband and devote the rest of her life to the welfare of humanity. A penniless and helpless young woman of 25, she, an atheist, plunged into the so-called theistic world, which despised her for her beliefs. A regular employment was a thing utterly difficult to secure. But she was lucky that an article contributed to a journal brought her a small amount of money and opened up a new vista before her. Later on she developed her contacts with Bradlaugh, a gentleman of noble thinking, with whom, through her journalistic and social activities, she launched onto the career of a social reformer. Her fight for the rights of the English girls working in the match factories revealed a great organizer and preacher in her.

Shortly after she joined the Theosophical Society started by Mme. Blavatsky and Colonel Oloott, and came under the intimate influence of the former who trained her into a mystic. As such she came to India in 1893 and for twenty long years kept herself intensely devoted to religious and social uplift of this country. Mrs Besant made a deep study of India's past glory and her glorious literature, discovered how great India was and how great she yet would be. But she was pained due to the existing ignorance and mutual quarrels that existed, and addressed the Indians in her forceful language as; "Children of the Mother, worshippers of one God, the one without a second, why are you shaming both before the world by your quarrels, religious and political? Is not the country greater than your parties? Is not Religion greater than your religions."[22] C.Y. Chintamani writes about her: "in her, greater intellect and learning were united to an indomitable will, concentrated purposefulness, undaunted courage, indefatigable zeal and a determination never to rest until her work was done. And added to these was her matchless oratory."[23] She preached about in India telling the prople of their marvelous fore-fathers, and of the great part they had yet to play. When she spoke, she put the greatest of the Indian Pandits to shame so deep was her knowledge and understanding of the ancient Hindu literature. She translated the *Bhagwad Gita* into English, and started the Central Hindu School and College at Banaras, which later on grew into the Hindu University. India was losing herself into the glare of Western materialistic thought. Mrs Besant preached that India had her own personality and individuality from which the West could much yet learns. She killed the Indian diffidence, breathed courage and will-power wherever she went and prepared India in her own way for the great part which she had in the world politics to play.

Later she became President of the Theosophical Society, and in this capacity she went several times to England between 1908 and 1913. She studied the Irish Home Rule Movement of Redmond, was impressed and back in India decided to start a similar movement in this country. It was in 1914 that she entered Indian politics. "She did not allow the grass to grow under her feet...By temperament she could not be content with merely ordinary. She soon left many of the old political workers behind in the race and even sneeringly referred to them as "men of yesterday." She started a Home Rule League, and under its auspices established organisations throughout the country, distributed vast quantities of propagandist literature and was to be found here, there and everywhere with speeches which always kindled and never restrained."[24] The Home Rule League was started in 1916. In the same year she effected a compromise between the Moderates and the Extremists in the Congress. Prior to that she had started a weekly journal named *Commonweal* and later on brought a daily paper which she named *New India*. Through them she spread her liberal thoughts in this country. All these activities landed her in a jail in 1917, together with Wadia and Arundale. This made a heroin of her, and when she was released after three months, she was honoured by India by electing her the President of the Indian National Congress of 1917.

Mrs Besant did not like the Non-cooperation and Civil Disobedience Movements started by Mr Gandhi. These, according to her, taught lawlessness to the Indians and gave great opportunities to the mischief-makers and criminals.

Her greatest reason for condemning them was that they encouraged violence in the name of nonviolence. Regarding Mr Gandhi, she wrote: "He is not a politician; he is a vague, dreamy mystic, out of touch with ordinary human nature," This is why Perhaps the results of Mr Gandhi's activities were always different from what he aimed at. "Mr Gandhi's influence on politics since he came to India," wrote Mrs Besant, "has always been destructive. I remember how, when I expressed to Mr Gokhale, before Mr Gandhi's arrival in India, my pleasure about his coming, and my hope that he would be of great help in winning Freedom for India, that wise and far-seeing statesman replied: 'No, you are mistaken: Gandhi will cause a great setback to our political movement.' His words have proved to be sadly true. The wild-cat movements of Non-cooperation and Civil Disobedience devastated the political field, blighting the promising harvest that was showing its green shoots above the soil...Gokhale was happy in passing from this world before he saw the ruin of his life's work."[25]

Mrs Besant also criticized the Swarajists who entered the Assembly under the reforms of 1919: "Before they were elected, they roared like lions; now they are even gentler than cooing doves. On the platform they proclaimed the wonders, which would be wrought by them if only the electors would return them. But after entering the Assembly, they forgot all their promises."[26]

Mrs Besant desired complete freedom for India, but she did not want her to break all contact with England. Her aim was rather to establish a British Commonwealth of Nations in which she was sure, India together with England would play a great role in the world politics in times to come. The Commonwealth of Nations has actually been established, and we do hope that Mrs Besant's prophecy will prove correct and India and England together will play this expected role in the future which is in the making.[27]

GOPAL KRISHNA GOKHALE

Born in 1866 at Kolhapur, Gokhale graduated at 18, started his career as a school teacher, but soon rose to the office of the Principal, Ferguson College, Poona. The 'diamond of India, the jewel of Maharashtra and the Prince of workers." As Tilak called him,[28] Gokhale was only 22 when he became a member of the Bombay Legislative Council. A "great master of the possible, a constructive statesman of the first rank, a bringer together of East and West in the common service of the needy, above all an idealist, a foreseer, a prophet of new era of inter-racial goodwill and cooperation," as Hoyland considered Gokhale,[29] his rise in the political field was meteoric. At 39 he became President of the Banaras Congress. His knowledge of the political economy of the country and his knowledge of the general problems of this land was so vast that as early as at the age of only 31, he was invited to England to give evidence on Indian expenditure before Welby Commission.

In his political philosophy, Gokhale was a realist. He understood that the British were in India to perform a Divine mission, and that they would have to continue in the country so long as that mission was not fulfilled. Thus, while he often criticized the Government for its acts of omission and commission, he disliked the people of India thinking of a violent overthrow of this Government to bring about independence to this country. He always advised caution, to the Government and to the people; to the Government to see that they do not bring the interests of the people to suffer, and to the people against trying to force the pace of events. In other words. He was a moderate who disliked both the extremes. Mr Gandhi observed regarding him: "Sir Pherozeshah had seemed to me like the Himalayas unscalable; the Lokamanya like the ocean one could not easily launch forth on the sea. But Gokhale was as the Ganges—it invited one to its bosom."[30]

Gokhale attacked salt-tax, which he considered a tax on poor man's bread; he condemned the Government for not giving the Indians a proper share in the civil services and the higher Government jobs. Nominated to the Imperial Legislative Council in 1902, he criticized Lord Curzon for his reactionary policy and condemned the partition of Bengal made by him; yet Curzon who had the heart of an imperialist, and who despised the Indians for their poor intellect, was forced to observe regarding Gokhale: "God has endowed you with extraordinary abilities and you have placed them unreserved at the disposal of your country."

Gokhale went to England once again in 1905 to place the popular aspirations of India before the thinking minds of England. In the same year he founded the Servants of India Society to train "public workers pledged to work for the Motherland on a pittance and subject to rules of rigid discipline as well as loyalty to the Empire." He played a considerable part in bringing about the Minto-Morley Reforms of 1909 which he considered a solid and definite step forward on India's march towards independence. He struck Pt. Madan Mohan Malaviya and others who criticized the Act of 1909 for its communal electorates and excessive weightage to the Muslims dumb with astonishment, when he declared in unmistakable words: "My Lord, after all we have got to take a large view of this matter. What does it really matter how many Hindus and how many Mohammedans sit in this Council? The more important question is how many of us work and in what spirit we work here?" Gokhale visited South Africa in 1912, and helped Gandhiji in his fight against apartheid. When the reforms of 1919 were in the making, he was one of the experts who were invited to express their opinion with regard to the matter. Gokhale submitted his plan for reforms in the shape of what is known as the "Political Testament of Gokhale." The plan submitted in 1915, demanded complete provincial autonomy, and in the Imperial Legislature 'increased opportunities of influencing the policy of Government by discussion, questions connected with the Army and Navy being placed on a level with other questions." In the same year Gokhale died.

Gokhale felt a great pain for the "starving shrunken, shrivelled-up ryot," and he himself would enjoy no luxury till the lot of these unfortunate masses was bettered. For 20 long years when he was the Principal of the Ferguson College, he would accept not a pie more than Rs. 70 as his monthly salary. He had a great love for the cause of the people of his country, he desired that they should get political independence so that one day they joined the ranks of the sovereign powers of the world. But he never liked them to be gluttons. He wished that they should eat as much as they could easily digest.[31]

MOTILAL NEHRU

Great father of the great son of India—Mr Jawaharlal Nehru, Motilal Nehru was born in a Kashmiri Brahmin family of middle class. He was not very successful in his studies, fled away from his arduous work of the Degree course in the College, but later secured his Degree in law and settled down in Allahabad as a lawyer. In this profession he proved so great a success that his monthly income ran into lakhs. He became a millionaire leading the life of aristocrats. His only son Jawaharlal was sent to England for studies right from his schooling age. It was only after the return of the son from the studies that under the influence of the latter the father entered politics in 1917.

Motilal's sacrifices for India were great. He was a Moderate in the beginning. But the imprisonment of Mrs Annie Besant in 1916 and the Jallianwala Bagh tragedy of 1919 turned him into an Extremist. He presided over the Amritsar session of the Congress in 1919, courted imprisonment under Mr Gandhi's Non-Coperation Movement, but was diassatisfied and together with C.R. Das organized the Swarajist Party which fought elections under the Act of 1919 and entered the Central Assembly. In the Assembly, although the account given by the Swarajists was not as good as expected, yet they did a lot. The 1926-27 budget was rejected, a resolution for the amendment of the Act of 1919 was passed and Round Table Conference was proposed which was actually later on held. Mr Nehru challenged the Simon Commission, prepared what is known as the Nehru Report Regarding the possible Constitutional set up which India could have. It was indeed a comprehensive document, which was rejected by the Government with the result that the Independence Resolution of the Congress was passed in 1929.

Mr Motilal courted imprisonment again in 1930 in connection with the Civil Disobedience Movement. But he was now too old to stand the stress and strain, was released from jail on grounds of health, and died in 1931, at the age of 70.

SARDAR VALLABHBHAI PATEL

Son of Jhaveribhai who participated in the Mutiny of 1857 against the British, Vallabhbhai Patel was born on 31 December 1875. After completing his education in India, he went to England where he got his degree of the Barrister-at-law in 1913 and returned to India to start his legal practice at Ahmedabad where he soon rose to eminence. In 1916, he heard the call of Mr Gandhi and soon renouncing his lucrative practice jumped into the political arena. In the beginning he had not liked the ways of Mr Gandhi, but later on he became so faithful a follower of the Mahatma that he considered the latter as his Guru in a spiritual sense, placing all his independent thinking at his feet and following him blindly as he directed. In 1918 he led the well-known Ahmedabad Labour Strike, and under the directions of Mr Gandhi in 1928 he led the Bardoli Kisan Movement. He had a great love for the cause of *Kisans* of whom he said at Bardoli: "If anyone is fit to walk with his head erect on this earth, it is the peasant. He is the producer, the others are parasites." It was his great success in organizing the Bardoli Kisans, which won him from Mr Gandhi the title of Sardar.

Sardar Patel was a man of strong will and iron determination. He showed his organizational skill in the Congress party and was elected its President in 1931. This office he held till 1934. John Gunther observed regarding him: "He is the party boss *par excellence.* He is the Jim Farely, the ruthless party fixer and organizer."[32] When in 1935 the Congress accepted office, Mr Patel was appointed chairman of the Congress Parliamentary sub-Committee, which office he held till 1940. During this period he directed the working of the Congress ministries in the provinces and definitely proved how iron-discipline could be enforced upon them, making the Ministers to dance to his tunes.

He offered his individual civil disobedience in 1941 and courted arrest. He was put behind the bars and released in 1941 on grounds of health. He was arrested once again in 1942, and put inside the Ahmednagar Fort from where he was released only in 1946. He was appointed Home Minister in the Interim Government formed by Mr Jawaharlal Nehru in 1946. He was not in favour of partition of this country, but to the astonishment of Maulana Azad, he changed his colours under the influence of Lord Mountbatten and silently gave his acquiescence in the matter.[33] As a Home Minister, he had to face the ruthless communalism of the Muslim League which was determined to destroy all peace and order of the country in order to secure its goal. It was perhaps this, which convinced him that no peaceful reconstruction of the country was possible till the League demands were conceded.

After the independence, the Sardar was appointed in 1947, as Deputy Prime Minister in the Nehru Cabinet. It was he who successfully solved the problem of the accession of the Princely States of India, at a moment when the British paramountcy on them having lapsed, they were developing the most fatal separatist tendencies. The old Political Department was abolished, and at his suggestion a State Ministry was set up, of which he was appointed as head. In this position he used persuasion as well as threats, and to his great credit, without firing a single shot of gun, he was able to rope the princes in for union with India. Hyderabad and Junagarh were the only States in which, due to peculiar situations, a stern action had to be taken to secure the desired effect.

When his mission was completed and India stood united and consolidated, this Bismarck of India was removed in 1950 from this mortal world. With the loss of Sardar Patel, India lost one of her most faithful and loyal servants who considered no sacrifice too great for the welfare and freedom of the toiling millions of this country.

MAULANA ABUL KALAM AZAD

Born in a refugee family at Mecca in 1888, from an Arab lady, Abul Kalam came to Calcutta with his father in 1898. Here he received his education and was sent in 1905, to the Azhar University of Cairo for higher education. Soon he returned to India and plunged into politics in 1908. He was a great scholar of the Arabic language. A selfless worker, an opponent of narrow Muslim communalism throughout his life, he started his *Al Hilal* weekly in 1912 through which he impressed the people with his scholarly attainments and mature political thinking. From the alien Government, however, he earned only a wrath. He was removed to Ranchi in 1915 and kept behind bars till 1920.

Maulana Azad was one of the loyal followers of Mahatma Gandhi, but not a blind follower. He participated in the Non-Coperation Movement in 1920 and courted arrest. Later when this Movement was withdrawn he took a leading part in bringing about a compromise between the two parties in the Congress, one in favour and the other against the Council-entry programme. He criticized the Mahatma for his giving too much importance to Mr Jinnah, which, according to him, was in a way responsible for developing the Muslim communalism. He was repeatedly elected as the President of the All India Congress. He held this office during the Second World War and negotiated as such with the Cripps and the Cabinet Missions. He remained steadfast in opposition to the creation of Pakistan, and was bitterly pained when Mr Gandhi who had declared that Pakistan could be formed only on his dead body, was changed. In his *India Wins Freedom*, he expresses wonder how, even the most responsible leaders of this country were blinded in their independent thinking, the moment they came close to Mr Gandhi. He was appointed Education Minister in the Interim Cabinet. This office he continued to hold till his death in 1958.

SUBHASH CHANDRA BOSE

Born in 1897, Subhash Chandra Bose was selected into the Indian Civil Services after a brilliant academic career. But in the Service, when he was called upon to take an oath of allegiance to the Crown, he refused to do so and left the Services in 1921. Already during his college career, he had shown what he was going to be, when he beat an Englishman black and blue for his having criticized the culture of India. After leaving the services, Subhash joined the Non-Coperation Movement, but was not satisfied with Mr Gandhi's ways and supported Motial and C R Das in their organizing the Swarajist Party. C R developed a great liking for him and when he became Mayor of Calcutta, he appointed Subhash as the Chief Executive Officer under him. But the progressive activities of Subhash soon invited the wrath of the Government, he was deported to Mandalay, but his countrymen showed him their gratitude and elected him to the Bengal Legislative Council in his absence.

Subhash represented the young and the extremist element in the Congress, was elected its President in 1938 and again in 1939. When he could not pull well with Mr Gandhi and others of his way of thinking, resigned his Presidentship and organized the famous Forward Block. Subhash did not believe in the non-violent activities of Mr Gandhi, and criticized him like Annie Besant for his rather having brought about a setback to the political progress of India. He criticized Mr Gandhi's ways in the Second Round Table Conference in 1931, and said Mr Gandhi was a greater force during the First Round Table Conference when he was absent from it than what he was in the Second Conference where he was present. He strongly believed that India could not achieve her independence without foreign aid. During the Second World War, he was put under house-arrest but he escaped and via Afghanistan, Italy and Germany, reached Japan where he organized the Indian prisoners of war and others into the Indian National Army, attacked India on her eastern borders, but was defeated. He died in 1945, in an air crash. Many in India believe that he escaped death in the air crash and still lives somewhere as a Yogi.

M.K. GANDHI

Great "as a politician, as an organiser, as a leader of men, as a moral reformer," but "greater than all these as a man," as Rabindra Nath Tagore writes of him M.K. Gandhi, popularly known as Mahatma Gandhi, was born at Porbander in Kathiawar in a Vaish family in 1869. He was only 12 when he was placed under marital ties. But this did not block his career, and at the age of 19, despite the opposition of his orthodox kinsmen who considered going overseas a sin for a Hindu, he managed to leave for England to qualify as a Barrister-at-Law. He returned to India in 1893 and started his practice at Rajkot later shifting over to Bombay. Shortly after he left for South Africa to conduct a case in which an Indian firm was involved. Here, within a short time he established his reputation as a leading barrister, something which he had not been able to do in India. He was literally amassing wealth when certain events took place which converted him into a non-violent agitator and a fighter for the cause of the oppressed. This happened in 1906 when Asiatic Registration Act was passed, which made it compulsory for all Asiatics settled in South Africa to register their names and give their thumb impressions even if they could give their signatures. Mr Gandhi called upon the Indian in South Africa to refuse to do as required by the humiliating Act, he led a deputation to England to appeal to the better sense of the British authorities there, but failed in his mission and returning to South Africa started what was known as the Civil Disobedience Movement. It was a novel movement under which the Indians were to disobey the Act and rather court arrests. Soon jails began to be filled up with these Indians. Mr Gandhi himself was sentenced to two months imprisonment. But the Government could not carry on their repressive policy for long and had soon to seek a compromise with Gandhi. Gandhi carried similar Movements against some other racial enactments of the South African Government as well, and won a good measure of success in his ventures.

Having thus evolved the novel weapon of disobedience and non-cooperation against a Government persisting in evil practices, Gandhi came back to India in 1914 because, as he observed, "I wanted to acquaint India with the method I have tried in South Africa and I desired to test in India the extent to which its application might be possible."[34] In 1915 he got his first opportunity in this regard, though small, when the people of Virgam threatened under his leadership if the customs cordon newly imposed there was not abolished. The threat paid off and the authorities took the required step. He made second trial of this weapon in 1917 to stop the emigration of indentured labourers from this country; the third trial to secure his right to make enquires into the agrarian grievances of the Champaran people; the fourth trial at Ahmedabad where the mill-owners had to grant the legitimate rights of their workers; and fifth to secure remission of rent from the Kheda peasants in Gujarat where crops had failed. Thus from 1915 to 1920, he had tried this weapon on five different occasions, as we have seen earlier and in all these he secured a success. Thus encouraged, he suddenly, brought his weapon before the whole nation in 1920, to be used as a mass-weapon for wresting political freedom from the Government. It appealed to the majority of the Indians and hence the history of India after 1920 became the history of the failure or success of the non-violence philosophy of Gandhi, as we have already discussed in detail. Gandhi died a martyr in 1948, falling from the pistol-shot of a fanatical Hindu assassin, Nathuram Godse.

Since, for 28 long years, from 1920 to 1948, Gandhi was the virtual dictator of the political movement in this country, because of which he also earned the title of the Father of the Nation, it should be advisable to study in brief, his philosophy which is also known as Gandhism.

Mr. Gandhi's Philosophy

Politically, in the early years of Mr Gandhi's public career, he believed in the good sense of the British and observed: "I discovered that the British Empire had certain ideals with which I have fallen in love and one of those ideals is that every subject of the British Empire has the freest scope for his energies and honour and whatever he thinks is due to his conscience...And I have found that it is possible for me to be governed least under the British Empire" But later on the Rowlatt Act agitation, the Jallianwala episode and the Khilafat Movement exploded his faith in the British; he was convinced that the British could be 'unscrupulous, immoral and unjust" also, and in a letter to the Viceroy he declared: "I can retain neither respect nor affection for such a government."

But this does not means that he developed any hatred towards the British. For he declared that if the British committed certain wrongs in India, they could be converted only through love and through the force of truth. Gandhi believed that "ends must be justified by means," which in other words meant that if India was to attain her independence, which was a noble end, she must also use only noble means to attain that end. The means that Mr Gandhi adopted to attain the noble end, were Satyagraha, civil disobedience and non-cooperation. Non-violence, self-sacrifice and truth were the keynotes of this programme, and if in any agitation these two notes were absent, he would call off the agitation than carry it on however near the ultimate goal he may be. The word *satya* means truth, and *agraha* means an intimate grasp of it. All the agitation carried on through self-suffering, fasts, etc. is Satyagraha, or an action which is based on truth and aims at reconciling the enemy to truth. Disobedience also involves a courageous self-sacrifice, for one who disobeys a law, must be prepared to face its consequences peacefully. "The idea of non-cooperation is that the victim of injustice and tyranny should withdraw his cooperation from the tyrant and therefore from tyranny. If he tolerates wrong and does not non-cooperate with it he is an accessory to wrong." Obviously, the methods he advocated were not the methods of the weak or of the cowards. They involved rather the greatest of courage and deliberate self-sacrifice. The people were to offer satyagraha knowing full well that the satyagrahis preceding them were being subjected to the most inhuman and barbaric atrocities.

Mr Gandhi believed, by disobeying the laws made by the British, and by non-cooperating with the Government which involved the boycott of the English goods, of the educational institutions established by them and of, in fact, every amenity they provided, the whole governmental machinery could be brought to a standstill in one day and the British could immediately be forced to leave this country. From this belief of Mr Gandhi evolved the *Swadeshi* Movement, or the movement, for using everything Indian. Wearing of khadi was made compulsory for his followers, the khadi cap which became famous as Gandhi cap, donned their heads and since this khadi was to be manufactured in the cottages, the *Charkha* or the spinning wheel became a symbol of the whole movement.

Nationalism in the Gandhian era differed from the earlier schools in one respect. It did not share with liberals their unqualified admiration of the West and had no appreciation of the communal fervour of the Nationalists." "The nationalism of Mahatma Gandhi, was not merely a doctrine of national emancipation in the narrow sense. It was a way of life which he considered it a privilege of this ancient land to show to the world, sick of blood-spilling and violence, full of the harsh and grating strife of tyrants and foes."

"Mahatma Gandhi had profound faith in the essential goodness of human nature."[35] The men, according to Mr Gandhi, differed from one another with respect to their natural aptitudes, inclinations and limitations. In free India, therefore, he would give maximum liberty to the individual and no centralization of authority. According to him, that government is the best, which governs the least. The modern state he condemned as violence in concentrated and organized form. It was, according to him, a soulless machine, which "can never be weaned from violence to which it owes its very existence." Mr Gandhi condemned the growing craze for machinery, which debased personality. According to him, although machinery had come to stay, the cottage industry should not be entirely destroyed. The salvation of India particularly lay in her cottage industry and land.

Man being the supreme consideration with Mr Gandhi, he was never impressed with the marvelous progress in science. He would like to use things natural, as far as possible, and would avoid all sorts of aids and luxuries provided by science. "According to him India's salvation consists in unlearning what she has learnt during the past fifty years. The railways, telegraphs, hospitals, lawyers, doctors and such like have all to go, and so-called upper classes have to learn to live consciously, religiously and deliberately the simple peasant life, knowing it to be a life giving true happiness."[36]

Mr Gandhi not only believed in the merits of the Hindu-Muslim unity, but also was sure that it could be established. He not only supported the Khilafat movement of the Muslims, which aimed at pan-Islamism and at securing to Turkey a favourable settlement after the First World War, but led it.

In the social sphere, Mr Gandhi condemned the existing caste system, early-marriages and the depressing condition of the women. But it would be wrong to say that he desired to introduce revolutionary changes in the Hindu social structure. For he believed in the basic value of some of the social practices of the Hindus which had become evil due to excrescences. Regarding caste thus he said: "In my opinion, it is not caste that has made us what we are. It was our greed and disregard of essential virtues, which enslaved us. I believe that caste has saved Hinduism from disintegration. But like other institutions, it has suffered from excrescences. I consider the four divisions alone to be fundamental, natural and essential. The innumerable sub-castes are sometimes a convenience, often a hindrance. The sooner there is fusion the better."

Mr Gandhi wanted to uplift the depressed classes, which he called rather Harijans or God's people. He would like to make the education system more utilitarian, as revealed in his Wardha scheme, which required the pupils to learn through their local crafts right from the beginning. And he favoured prohibition even at the cost of a heavy sacrifice of revenues.

There was a time when the philosophy of Mr Gandhi caught the imagination of the people. But this philosophy, according to his critics, postponed India's complete independence for at least twenty years, and for a short period at least, it "hindered the progress of the spirit of enquiry and critical reason in modern India."[37]

Much of Mr Gandhi's political programme was unrealistic. His philosophy of non-violent Satyagraha could be successful only if those who wielded this weapon were perfect human beings. But since this was not so, twice he used this weapon on a mass-scale, in the 'twenties and in the thirties, and twice he bitterly failed. The people could not carry on a non-violent struggle with violence in their hearts. The irresponsible mob-behaviour in Amritsar, which brought about the alien retribution of Jallianwala, is only one instance of it. Nor could one appreciate Mr Gandhi's philosophy of breaking the law and bringing about lawlessness in the country. It was bound only to encourage the spirit of irresponsibility and lawlessness among the ignorant and the criminal classes. Mrs Annie Besant called him "a vague, dreamy mystic, out of touch with ordinary human nature."[38] The best way to the political independence of India, according to Mrs. Besant, was a swift reform "instead of turning into the supposed non-violent inaction which would inevitably break into violence."[39]

"If Mahatma Gandhi had not come forward with his nostrum of non-cooperation just on the eve of the introduction of the present reform, (of 1919)," wrote Sir C Y Chintamani, "the whole politics during the last fifteen years would very likely have been different. Indian nationalists would have remained a united body of men, and would have in offices, in legislatures and in outside public life brought to bear upon the British Government a pressure the result of which would in my opinion have been very different from what has actually been the consequence of the divisions in public life brought to a head and rendered inevitable by Mr Gandhi's policy. His non-violent non-cooperation is just one of those double negatives, if there be any, which do not make an affirmative."[40]

Mr Gandhi aimed at Hindu-Muslim unity, and that was good. But one really wonders how a brain supposed to be so great could commit the blunder of supporting communalism in the name of unity. For everybody knew that the Khilafat Movement was a purely communal movement based on the principles not of Indian nationalism but on those of pan-Islamism over and above it.

Mr Gandhi enjoyed a great influence during his lifetime. "The question, however," writes Mr K M Pannikar, "is not the influence that Gandhiji exercised in his lifetime, but how far it is a continuing process in independent India."[41] And if we consider the question from this view point, Mr Gandhi does not seem to have been much success. Khadi, which according to Mr Gandhi represented an ideal of civilization, is nowhere used widely in this country. Mahatma Gandhi's policy of non-violence has been replaced by India's efforts to arm herself to the teeth. Satyagraha as a weapon to realise political ideals received a death blow after Master Tara Singh's failure of political fasting. Nowhere in India can one see his ideas of utilitarian education making any progress.

Even during the very lifetime of Mahatma, his philosophy failed in most of its aspects. Everywhere a non-violent movement resulted into the most inhuman violence. And his efforts for a Hindu-Muslim unity exploded into ultimate bifurcation of this country into two parts. Mr Gandhi's ways rather encouraged the Muslim communalism than discouraging it, as Maulana Azad believed. For it was Mr Gandhi who all of a sudden brought Mr Jinnah to the forefront of Muslim politics by giving him the title of Quid-e-Azam.[42]

When all this is said, we fail, however, to understand the violent remarks of Dr. Raghuvanshi that his "utterances suggest a deep longing for the barbaric simplicity of life in the woods…Is the conversion of a system, capitalistic or imperialistic, through non-violence really possible?"[43] Nor would it be just to say that whole of his philosophy has been rejected by free India. For the abolition of untouchability, the development of village Panchayats, etc. which were dear to Mr Gandhi, are still aimed at and being carried into practice. During his lifetime too, it was only Gandhiji who was able to convert the Independence Movement of this country from a middle-class movement into a mass movement. The general awakening he brought about in India was tremendous. Nor was anything wrong with his simplicity, which is so essential if the modern world is to enjoy some peace. Nor could we condemn his non-violence policy as such. For if this policy failed, it was not due to its worthlessness, but due to the immaturity of the masses who could not understand it in essence. Our criticism of Mr Gandhi would be that he recommended a cure for the disease, which though correct, was too difficult to adopt in the circumstances. And it is a tragedy that a man who abhorred violence so much, had still to live in the midst of that violence which resulted from his own activities, and ultimately died of this violence.

"In a large measure," comments Mr Nehru, "he made this country during the last thirty years or more, attain to heights of sacrifice which in that particular domain have never been equalled elsewhere. He succeeded in that. Yet ultimately things happened which no doubt made him suffer tremendously though his tender face never lost its smile and he never spoke a harsh word to anyone. Yet, he must have suffered for the failing of this generation whom he had trained, suffered because we went away from the path that he had shown us."[44]

DR RAJENDRA PRASAD

Born in 1884, Dr Rajendra Prasad had a brilliant academic record, sweeping almost all the records of the Calcutta University before him. He was offered State Scholarship for studies in England, but he declined the offer and preferred to settle down in the law practice where soon he earned a great name and lucrative business. He was among those who sacrificed their all, including the professional practice and future in response to the call of Mahatma Gandhi for India's fight for independence. He participated in the Civil Disobedience and Non-cooperation Movements of Mr Gandhi to whom he was fanatically loyal in his beliefs and practices. A great social worker as he was, he rendered great service during the Bihar earthquake, was later elected President of the Congress and when the Constituent Assembly met in 1946, he found himself unanimously installed in the high office of Speaker to guide the framing of India's Constitution. He also worked for some time as the Food and Agriculture Minister in the Nehru Cabinet, and when in January 1950, the present Constitution of India was put into force, he became the first President of the Indian Republic. A great writer in Hindi, he won many honours as such. As a President, he brought his simplicity to bear upon his office. He voluntarily offered cut down his allowances and other emoluments. He acted as President for two terms, till 1960, when he retired. He died in 1962.

NOTES

1. Lajpat Rai, *The Arya Samaj,* p.4.
2. *Ibid.,* p.18; Census, *op. cit.,* p.534.
3. Masani R.P., *Dadabhai Naoroji,* p.26.
4. *Ibid.,* p.48.
5. *Ibid.,* p.145-47.
6. Gandhi, M.K., *My Experiment with Truth,* p. 233.
7. Chintamani, *op. cit.,* p.283.
8. Sitaramayya, pp. 59-62.
9. See the chapter on the *Nationalistic Movement.*
10. See Raghuvanshi, *op. cit.,* p.72.
11. Chirol, V., *Indian Unrest,* p. 251.
12. *Ibid.*
13. Ram Gopal, *Lokmanya Tilak,* p. 321.
14. See Chintamani, *Indian Politics Since the Mutiny,* p. 118. See also Tehmanker, D.V., *Lokmanya Tilak;* Tilak, B.G., *Writings and Speeches* (Madras); Athalye, *The Life of Lokmanya Tilak.*
15. Chintamani, *op. cit.,* p.231.
16. Gandhi, *op. cit.,* p. 214.
17. Dr. P Sitaramayya, *The History of Indian National Congress,* I, p.77.
18. Wedderburn, *A.O. Hume,* p. 142.
19. Raghuvanshi, V.P.S., *The Indian Nationalist Movement and Thought,* pp. 44-47.

20. Chintamani, C.Y., *Indian Politics Since Mutiny,* p. 37.
21. Chirol, V., *Indian Unrest,* p. 121; see also *Census Report of Punjab,* 1911.
22. Besant Annie, *The India that Shall Be* (1914), p.1.
23. Chintamani, C.Y., *Indian Politics Since Mutiny*, p. 102.
24. *Ibid.,* pp. 101-103.
25. *Ibid.,* p. 102-103.
26. Besant Annie, *op. cit.*, p. 103.
27. See Pal, B.C., *Mrs. Annie Besant.*
28. Tilak, *Writings and Speeches,* see for a detailed study.
29. Hoyland, J.S., *Gopal Krishna Gokhale (His Life and Speeches),* Calcutta, 1930, p. 235.
30. Gandhi, *My Experiments with Truth,* p. 236.
31. See Shahani, T.R., *Gopal Krishna Gokhale*, Bombay, 1929.
32. Gunther, John, *Inside Asia.*
33. Azad, Maulana A.K., *India Wins Freedom,* pp. 179-81.
34. See Gandhi, M.K., *My Experiment with Truth* (his autobiography), for full details.
35. Raguvanshi, Dr V P S, *Indian Nationalist Movement and Thought*, pp. 309-310.
36. *Ibid.*, pp. 315-316.
37. Karunakaran, K.P., *Modern Indian Political Tradition*, p. 26.
38. Besant Annie, *The India that Shall Be,* p. 194.
39. *Ibid.*, p. 221.
40. Chintamani, Sir, C.Y., *Indian Politics Since Mutiny,* p. 187.
41. Pannikar, K.M., *A Survey of Indian History.*
42. Azad, *op. cit.*, pp. 112-15.
43. Raghuvanshi, *op. cit.*, p. 311.
44. *Independence and After,* a collection of Mr Jawaharlal Nehru's speeches, p. 21. See for further details, Tendulkar, *Mahatma,* 8 vols.; Pyarelal, *Mahatma Gandhi,* 2 vols.

Bibliography

Adye, J.M., *Indian Frontier Policy,* 1897.

Aggarwala, R.N., *Nationalist Movement and Constitutional Development of India,* Delhi, 1967.

Ahluwalia, B.K., *Facets of Gandhi,* New Delhi, 1968.

Ahluwalia, M.M., *Freedom Struggle in India,* Delhi, 1965.

Ahmad, Z.A., *Indian Federation.*

Aiyangar, N. Rajagopala, *The Government of India Act,* 1935.

Aiyar, Sir, P.S.S., *Indian Constitutional Problems.*

Alder, G.J., *British India's Northern Frontier,* London, 1967.

Alexandrowicz, C.H., *Constitutional Development of India,* 1957.

Ambedkar, B.R., *Evolution of Provincial Finance in British India.*

Anand, C.L., *History of Government of India.*

Andrews, C.F., *The Rise and Growth of Congress in India,* Calcutta, 1967.

———*India and Her Neighbours.*

Andrews, W.P., *Our Scientific Frontier.*

Appadorai, A., *Dyarchy in Practice.*

Asok, Chanda, *Freedom in India,* London, 1963.

Azad, Maulana, A.K., *India Wins Freedom,* Calcutta, 1959.

Aziz, K.K., *Britain and Muslim India,* London, 1963.

———*The Making of Pakistan,* London, 1967.

Bains, J.S., *India's International Disputes,* Bombay, 1962.

Banerjee, A.C., *Indian Constitutional Documents,* 3 vols. (1946).

Banerjee, A.C., and Bose. D.R., *The Cabinet Mission in India.*

Banerjee, S.N., *Speeches and Writings.*

———*A Nation in Making.*

Barker, A.J., *The March on Delhi,* London, 1963.

———*The Neglected War Mesopotamia 1914-1918,* London, 1969.

Barker, A.T., (ed.) *The Mahatma Letters.*

Barton, Sir William, *The Princes of India.*

Basu, B.D., Major, *Rise of the Christian Power in India.*

Basu, Durga Das, *Constitutional Documents,* Calcutta, 1969.

Batra H.C., *The Relations of Jaipur State with East India Company,* Delhi, 1958.

Bell, Sir Charles, *Tibet, Past and Present,* London, 1968.

———*The People of Tibet,* London, 1968.

Bellow, H.W., *North-West Frontier and Afghanistan.*

Besant, Annie, *Builder of New India,* speeches and writings.

———*India a Nation,* 1930.

———*India and the Empire,* 1914.

———*The Future of Indian Politics.*

———*How India Wrought for Freedom?*

———*India That Shall Be.*

———*India Bound or Free,* 1926.

Bhagat, K.P., *Decade of Indo-British Relations,* Bombay, 1959.

Bhatia, B.M., *Famines in India,* Bombay, 1967.

Bhatia, O.P. Singh, *History of India,* 2 vols., New Delhi, 1965.

Bhutto, Zulfikar Ali, *The Myth of Independence,* London, 1969.

Birdwood, Lt. Colonel C.B., *A Constitutional Experiment.*

Bissoondoyal, S., *A Concise History of Mauritius,* Bombay, 1965.

Bombwall, K.R., *The Foundations of Indian Federalism,* Bombay, 1967.

Bose, N.K., *Culture and Society in India,* Bombay, 1967.

Bose, Nemi Sadhan, *The Indian National Movement,* Calcutta, 1965.

Bose, Subhas Chandra, *The Indian Struggle,* Calcutta, 1964.

———*An Indian Pilgrim,* London, 1965.

Bose, Suresh Chandra, *Dissentient Report*, Calcutta, 1961.

Bose, S.M., *The Working of Constitution in India.*

Brailsford, H.N., *Subject India.*

Breecher, Michael, *Nehru—A Political Biography.*

Brockway A.F., *A Week in India.*

Bruce George, *Retreat From Kabul,* London, 1968.

Buchan, *Lord Minto.*

Budha Prakash, *India and the World*, Hoshiarpur, 1964.

Caswell, W.A., *India Independent,* London, 1968.

Chalapathi Rau, *The Press in India,* London, 1968.

Chaman Lal, *The Vanishing Empire,* New Delhi, 1969.

Chandra Jagpravesh, *Delhi, a Political Study,* Delhi, 1969.

Chatterji, Amiya, *The Constitutional Development of India,* 1937-1947, Calcutta, 1958.

Chatterji, Atul Chandra, *The New India,* London, 1968.

Chatterji, A.C., *India Struggle for Freedom,* 1947.

Chatterji, B.C., *The Heart of Aryavarta.*

Chakraverti, Arulanand, *Hindus and Muslims of India.*

Chailley, J., *Administrative Problems of British India.*

Chaudhuri, Ramnarayan, *Nehru—in his own words,* Ahmedabad, 1959.

Chintamani, C.Y., *Indian Politics Since Mutiny.*

Chesney, G.M., *India Under Experiment,* 1918.

Chesney, Sir George, *The Indian Polity.*

Chirol, Valentine, *Indian Unrest.*

———*India, Old and New,* London, 1921.

Choudhary, V.S.P., *Imperial Policy of British in India,* Calcutta, 1968.

Choudhary, Radha Krishna, *History of Bihar,* Patna, 1958.

Coatman, J., *Indian Riddle,* 1932.

———*The Road to Self-Government.*

Comming, Sir John, *Political India,* Delhi, 1968.

Connell, John, *Wavell Scholar and Soldier,* India, 1964.

Cotton, Sir Henry, *India Old and New.*

———*Indian and Home Memories.*

———*New India: India in Transition.*

Coupland, R., *India, A Restatement.*

———*The Indian Problem 1833-1935,* 1945.

Cowell, Herbert, *History and Constitution of the Courts and Legislative Authorities in India,* 1936.

Craddock, Reginald, *Dilemma in India.*

Curtis, L., *Dyarchy.*

Curzon, George Nathaniel, *British Government of Modern India*, Calcutta, 1959.

———*Russia in Central Asia.*

———*His Speeches.*

Cust, Rober, *Linguistic and Oriental Essays.*

Das, C.R., *India for Indians,* 1918.

Das, M.N., *The Economic and Social Development of Modern India,* Calcutta, 1959.

———*India Under Morley and Minto,* London, 1969.

———*The Political Philosophy of Jawaharlal Nehru,* London, 1959.

Datta, V.N., *Jallianwala Bagh,* Ludhiana, 1969.

Davies, *The Problem of North-West Frontiers,* 1932.

Desai, A.R., *Social background of Indian Nationalism,* 1948.

Dharum Kumar, *Land and Caste in South India,* London, 1966.

Dhebar, U.N., *Gandhiji: A Practical Idealist,* Bombay, 1964.

Digby, *Prosperous British India.*

Diwakar, R.R., *Mahayogi Sri Aurobindo,* Bombay, 1967.

Dodwell, H.H. (ed.), *The Cambridge History of India,* vols. V & VI, Delhi, 1964.

Doke, Joseph J., *M.K. Gandhi,* 1959.

Dongerkery, S.R., *Memories of two Universities,* Bombay, 1966.

Durga Das, *India from Curzon to Nehru and After,* 1969.

Durrani, F.K. Khan, *The Meaning of Pakistan.*

Dutt, R. Palme, *India To-day,* Delhi, 1955.

Dwarka Das Kanji, *India's Fight for Freedom,* Bombay, 1966.

Edwards, Michael, *British India,* London, 1967.

———*Last Years of British India,* Bombay, 1963.

———*A History of India,* Bombay, 1961.

Farquhar, J.N., *Modern Religious Movements in India,* Delhi, 1967.

Fischer, Louis, *The Life of Mahatma Gandhi.*

Fisher, *History of Europe.*

Gandhi, M.K., *Socialism of My Conception,* Bombay, 1966.

———*Man v. Machine,* Bombay, 1966.

– – – –*The Village Reconstruction,* Bombay, 1966.

———*Message of Jesus Christ,* Bombay, 1966.

———*All Men are Brothers,* Ahmedabad, 1960.

———*The Science of Satyagraha,* Bombay, 1962

———*Gospel of Swadeshi,* Bombay, 1967.

———*Self-Restraint v. Self-Indulgence,* Ahmedabad, 1956.

———*True Education,* Ahmedabad, 1962.

———*The Collected Works of Mahatma Gandhi,* Ahmedabad, 1968, different vols.

———*India of My Dreams,* Ahmedabad, 1962.

———*Bapu's Letters to Mira,* Ahmedabad, 1959.

———*My God,* Ahmedabad, 1962.

———*To the Students,* (Ahmedabad, 1965).

———*My Experiments with Truth.*

———*Freedom's Battle*, 1921.

———*India's Struggle for Swaraj.*

Gaekwad, V.R., *The Anglo Indians,* London, 1967.

Garratt, G.T., *Legacy of India.*

Ghose, Dilip Kumar, *England and Afghanistan,* Calcutta, 1960.

Ghose, Shankar, *The Western Impact on Indian Politics,* Bombay, 1967.

———*The Renaissance to Militant Nationalism in India,* Bombay, 1969.

Ghose, K.K., *The Indian National Army,* Meerut, 1969.

Ghose, P.C., *The Development of Indian National Congress,* Calcutta, 1960.

Ghose, *Press and Press Laws in India.*

Ghoshal, U.N., *A History of Indian Public Life*, London, 1966.

Gibb, H.A.R., Mohammedanism, *An Historical Survey*, London, 1949.

Gledhill, Alan, *The Republic of India.*

Gopal, S., *The Viceroyalty of Lord Irwin*, London, 1967.

———*British Policy in India*, Cambridge, 1965.

Gour, Hari Singh, *Government of India Act, 1935.*

Graham, Pole, Major D. and Shiva Rai, B., *The Problem of India.*

Griffiths, Percival, *The British Impact on India,* London, 1952.

Gupta, Subhash Chandra, *Agrarian Relations and Early British Rule in India*, Calcutta, 1963.

Gwyer, Maurice and Appadorai, A., *Speeches and Documents on the Indian Constitution,* 2 vols.

Haqqi, S.A.H. (ed.), *Union-State Relations in India,* Meerut, 1967.

Hall, D.G.E., *Burma*, London, 1950.

Handa, R.L., *History of Freedom Struggle in Princely States,* New Delhi, 1968.

Hardinge, Lord, *My Indian Years, 1910-1916.*

Hardinge, Charles Viscount, *Viscount Hardinge.*

Hassanain, S.E., *Indian Muslims: Challenge and Opportunity,* Bombay, 1968.

Holland, W.E.S., *The Indian Outlook,* 1927.

Hunter, W.W., *A History of British India,* vol. II.

———*The Indian Mussalmans.*

Hussain, Zakir, *The Dynamic University,* 1965.

Hutheesing, Krishna Nehru, *We Nehrus,* Bombay, 1963.

Hyde, H.M., *Lord Reading,* London, 1967.

Ilbert, C.P., *The Government of India.*

———*Historical Introduction.*

Ishwari Prasad and K.S. K. Subedar, *A History of Modern India.*

Jagdisan, J.N., *Letters of Sriniwas Sastri,* Bombay, 1963.

Jarmani Das, Diwan, *Maharaja,* Bombay, 1969.

Jayakar, M.R., *The Study of My Life.*

Jha, Jagdish Chandra, *Bhumij Revolt,* Delhi, 1967.

Johnson, Alan Campbell, *Mission with Mountbatten,* Bombay, 1951.

Kabir, Humayun, *The Indian Heritage,* Bombay, 1964.

———*Muslim Politics and other Essays,* Calcutta, 1969.

Karandikar, M.A., *Islam in India's Transition to Modernity,* Bombay, 1968.

Karan Singh, Dr., *Prophet of Indian Nationalism, Study of Sri Aurobindo Ghosh,* London, 1963.

Karunakaran, K.P., *Religion and Political Awakening in India,* Calcutta, 1965.

———*Modern Indian Political Tradition.*

Kaushik, P.D., *The Congress Ideology and Programme,* Bombay, 1964.

Keer, Dhananjay, *Veer Savarkar,* Bombay, 1966.

Keith, A.B., *A Constitutional History of India,* Allahabad, 1961.

———*Speeches and Documents on Indian Policy,* vols, I and II.

Kerala Putra, *Working of Dyarchi in India,* 1919-1929.

Khan, Aga, H.H., *India in Transition,* 1918.

Khera, S.S., *India's Defence Problem,* Bombay, 1968.

Khushwant Singh, *History of the Sikhs,* vol.II.

Kochanek, Stanely A., *The Congress Party of India,* 1968.

Krishna, K.B., *The Problem of Minorities.*

Kulkarni, V.B., *British Dominion in India and After,* Bombay, 1964.

———*British Statesmen in India,* Bombay, 1961.

Kumar, Krishna, *Democracy and Non-Violence,* New Delhi.

Kunzru, *Public Services in India.*

Lajpat Rai, *Young India,* 1917.

———*Unhappy India.*

———*The Political Future of India,* 1930.

Latif, Abdul, *The Muslim Problem in India.*

Linlithgow, *Marquess of Speeches and Statements.*

Lovett, Verney (Sir), *A History of the Indian Nationalist Movement 1600-1919.*

Loveday, *A History and Economics of Indian Famines.*

Ludlow, *British India,* 2 vols.

Lyall. Alfred, *The British Dominion in India.*

Macdonald, J R, *Government of India.*

Macdonald, Ramsay, *The Awakening of India.*

Macdonell, *India's Part, 1927.*

Macnicol, N., *The Making of Modern India.*

Madhok, Balraj, *Portrait of a Martyr,* Bombay, 1969.

Maheshwari, H., *The Philosophy of Swami Rama Tirtha,* Agra, 1969.

Majumdar, A.K., *Advent of Independence,* Bombay, 1963.

Majumdar, B.B., *Indian Political Associations and Reform of Legislature,* Calcutta, 1965.

Mujumdar, B., *Political Thought from Ram Mohan Roy to Dayanand.*

Majumdar, B.C., and others, *An Advanced History of India,* 1963.

Majumdar, R.C., *History of the Freedom Movement in India,* 3 vols. Calcutta, 1963.

———*Three Phases of India's Struggle for Freedom,* Bombay, 1967.

MaMun, Lieut-General Sir George, *The Indian States and Princes,* 1936.

Mary, Countess of Minto, *India, Minto and Morley, 1905-1919,* 1934.

Masaldan, P.N., *Evolution of Provincial Autonomy in India.*

Masani, M.R., *The Communist Party of India, A Short History,* Bombay, 1967.

Masani, R.P., *Britain in India.*

Mason, Philip, *The Men Who Ruled India.*

Mathur, J.S., *Indian Working Class Movement,* Allahabad, 1964.

Mathur, L.P., *History of the Andaman and Nicobar Islands,* Delhi, 1968.

Marx, *On India.*

Menon, V.L., *Ruskin and Gandhi,* Varanasi, 1965.

Menon, V.P., *Montagu Chelmsford Reforms,* Bombay, 1965.

———*The Transfer of Power in India.*

———*The Story of the Integration of Indian States.*

Mersey, Viscount, *The Viceroys and Governor-Generals of India,* Ahmedabad, 1949.

Mira Behn, *The Spirit's Pilgrimage,* London, 1960.

Misra, K.P., *India's Policy of Recognition of States and Government,* Bombay, 1966.

Mitra, Sisir Kumar, *Resurgent India,* Bombay, 1963.

Mody, Sir H., *Pherozeshah Mehta.*

Molesworth, G.N., *Afghanistan 1919,* London, 1962.

Montagu, Edwin, S., *An Indian Diary.*

Moon, Penderel, *Divide and Quit.*

Moreland, W.H., *A Short History of India.*

Morley, J., *Recollections,* 2 vols.

———*Speeches on India.*

Mosley, Leonard, *The Last Days of the British Raj,* London, 1961.

Mukerjee, Hirendranath, *India's Struggle for Swaraj,* Calcutta, 1958.

Mukerjee, Hari Das, *Sri Aurobindo and the New Thought in Indian Politics,* Calcutta, 1969.

———*Bipin Chandra Pal and India's Struggle for Swaraj,* Calcutta, 1958.

Mukerjee, Nilmaṇi, *The Ryotwari System in Madras*, Calcutta, 1962.

Mukerjee, P., *Indian Constitutional Documents.*

Mukerjee, Radhakamal, *Land Problems in India.*

Mujeeb, M., *The Indian Muslims,* 1967.

Munshi, K.M., *Gandhi's View of Life,* Bombay, 1968.

———*Gandhi's Philosophy in Life and Action,* Bombay, 1965.

———*Indian Constitutional Documents,* 2 vols., Bombay, 1967.

———*Pilgrimage to Freedom.*

Narayan, Jayprakash, *My Life and Struggle,* Delhi, 1969.

Natrajan, S., *A Century of Social Reforms in India,* 1959.

———*A History of the Press in India,* London, 1962.

Nehru, Jawaharlal, *Discovery of India.*

———*An Autobiography,* Bombay, 1962.

———*India and the World.*

———*Independence and After, a collection of speeches.*

Newton, A.P., *A Hundred Years of the British Empire,* London, 1967.

Norman, Mohammad, *The Muslim India.*

Novinson, *The New Spirit in India.*

Palande , M.R., *An Introduction to Indian Administration.*

Pandey, B.N., *The Introduction of English Law into India,* Bombay, 1967.

———*Rise of the Modern India,* 1967.

Panikar, K.M., *Foundation of New India.*

———*Ideas of Sovereignty and State in Indian Political Thought,* Bombay, 1963.

———*The Native States of India.*

———*Relations of Indian States.*

———*Studies in Indian History,* 1963.

———*Introduction to Study of Relations of Indian States to Government of India.*

———*Evolution of British Policy Towards Indian States, 1774-1858,*

Panjabi, K.L., *The Indomitable Sardar,* Bombay, 1962.

———*Civil Servants in India,* Bombay, 1965.

Parvate, T.V., *Makers of Modern India,* Delhi, 1964.

Patel, M.S., *The Educational Philosophy of Mahatma Gandhi,* Ahmedabad, 1958.

Pawar, A.G., *Studies in Indian History,* Kolhapur, 1968.

Percival Spear, *India: A Modern History.*

Percival, Griffith, *Modern India.*

———*The British Impact on India.*

Phadnis, Urmila, *Towards Integration of Indian States,* Bombay, 1968.

Philips, C.H., *Select Documents on the History of India and Pakistan.*

———*The Evolution of India and Pakistan*—Select Documents, 1962.

Poles, D. Graham, *India in Transition*, London, 1932.

Power, Paul F., *Gandhi on World Affairs.*

Powell-Price, J.C., *A History of India.*

Pradhan, R.S., *India's Struggle for Swaraj.*

Prasad, Amba, *The Indian Revolt of 1942,* Delhi, 1958.

Prasad, Basheshar, *Origins of Provincial Autonomy.*

Prasad, Beni, *Hindu-Muslim Question,* Allahabad, 1947.

Prasad, Bishwanath, *The Indian Administrative Service,* Delhi, 1968.

Punniah, K.V., *The Constitutional History of India*, Delhi, 1964.

Purani, A.B., *Sri Aurobindo: Some Aspects of his Vision,* Bombay 1966.

Pyare Lal, *Mahatma Gandhi: The Last Phase,* 2 vols., Ahemdabad, 1956.

Pylee, M.V., *Constitutional Governments in India,* Bombay, 1965.

Raheja, P.C., *Land Transformation,* Bombay, 1962.

Raghuvanshi, V.P.S., *Indian Nationalist Movemment and Thought.*

Rai, Satya, M., *Partition of the Punjab,* Bombay, 1965.

Raj Gopal Acharya, *Gandhiji's Teachings and Philosophy,* Bombay, 1967.

Ram Gopal, *British Rule in India,* Delhi, 1963.

———*Indian Muslims,* Bombay, 1964.

Radcliffe, S.K., *Sir William Wedderburn*, London, 1923.

Rau, Sir Benegal, *India's Constitution in the Making,* Bombay, 1960.

Rawlinson, H.G., *The British Achievement in India,* 1948.

Ray, P.C., *Life and Times of C.R. Dass*, Oxford University Press, 1927.

Reed, Sir Stanely, *The India I Knew.*

Rees, *Russia, India and Persian Gulf,* 1903.

Reynolds, Reginald, *The White Sahibs in India.*

Risley, Herbert H., *The People of India,* Delhi, 1959.

Roberts, P.E., *History of British India,* 1958.

Roy, B.N. Dutta, *Sir N.N. Sircar's Speeches and Pamphlets,* Calcutta, 1934.

Roy, Naresh Chandra, *The Civil Service in India,* Calcutta, 1960.

Roy, Smith William, *Nationalism and Reforms in India.*

Rudra, A.B., *The Viceroys and Governors-Generals.*

Rushbrook William, L.F., *What About India?*

Russell, Sir W., *My Diary in India.*

Ruthnaswamy, *Some Influences that Made British Administrative System.*

Sahai, Govind, *'42 Rebellion.*

Sadiq Ali, *The Congress Ideology and Programme.*

Sanwal, B.D., *Nepal and East India Company,* Bombay, 1965.

Sapre, B.G., *The Growth of the Indian Constitution and Administration.*

Sarma, D.S., *Renascent Hinduism,* Bombay, 1966.

Savarkar, V.D., *The Indian War of Independence 1857,* New Delhi, 1963.

Scrafton, *Reflections on the Government of Indostan.*

Seal, Anil, *The Emergence of Indian Nationalism,* Cambridge, 1968.

Sharma, B.M., *Federal Polity,* Bombay, 1966.

———*The Republic of India,* Bombay, 1966.

Sharma, Beni Shankar, *Swami Vivekananda,* Calcutta, 1963.

Sharma, Jagdish Saran, *India's Struggle for Freedom,* 3 vols. (Documents), Delhi, 1962.

Sharma, M.P., *Local Self-Government in India.*

Sharma, S.R., *The Founding of Maratha Freedom,* Bombay, 1964.

———*Swami Rama Tirtha,* Bombay, 1965.

———*Evolution of Administration in India,* Allahabad, 1965.

Shridharani, Krishnalal, *War Without Violence,* Bombay, 1962.

Singh, Brigadier Rajinder, *Soldier and Soldiering in India,* Ambala, 1959.

Singh, Gurmukh N., *Land Marks in Indian Constitutional and National Development 1600-1919,* Benaras, 1930.

———*Indian States and British India.*

Singh, Hira Lal, *Problems and Politics of the British in India,* Bombay, 1963.

Singh, S.N., *The Secretary of State for India and His Council 1858-1919,* Delhi 1962.

Singh, V.B., *Economic History of India,* Bombay, 1965.

Singhal, Damodar, P., *Nationalism in India and other Historical Essays,* Delhi,

1961.

Sinha, N.K., and Banerjee, A.C., *History of India,* Calcutta, 1963.

Sitaramayya, P., *History of the Intlian National Congress,* 2 vols. Delhi, 1969.

Smith, Vincent A., *The Oxford History of India,* London, 1961.

Smith, W.R., *Nationalism and Reform in India,* 1938.

Spear Percival, *Indian Modern History,* 1961.

———*The Oxford History of Modern India,* London, 1965.

Srinivasan, N., *Democratic Government in India,* 1954.

Sri Prakasa, *Pakistan Birth and Early Days,* Calcutta, 1965.

Subramanyam, M., *Why Cripps Failed?*

Suda, J.P., *Indian Constitutional Development and National Movement.*

Swinson, Arthur, *North West Frontier,* Delhi, 1967.

———*Six Minutes to Sunset,* London, 1964.

Tagore, Sir Rabindranath, *Nationalism,* 1921.

Tara Chand, *History of the Freedom Movement in India,* vols. I & II.

Tendulkar, D.G., *Abdul Ghaffar Khan,* Bombay, 1967.

———*Mahatma,* 4 vols., Bombay, 1960.

Terraine, John, *The Life and Times of Lord Mountbatten,* London, 1968.

Thakore, B.K., *Indian Administration to the Dawn of Responsible Government.*

Thomas, F.W., *British Education in India.*

Thompson, E., *The Other Side of the Medal,* 1925.

Thompson, E.C.M., *India of To-day,* 1913.

Tinkar, Hugh, *Reorientations,* 1965.

———*The Foundations of the Local Self-Government in India, Pakistan and Burma,* Bombay, 1967.

Titus, *Indian Islam,* 1930.

Topa, I. N., *The Growth and Development of Nationalist Thought of India,* 1930.

Toynbee, Arnold, *One World and India.*

Vajpeyi, J.N., *The Political Movement in India.*

Waley, S.D., *Edwin Montagu,* Bombay, 1964.

Walter,, H.A., *The Ahmadiya Movement,* 1918.

Wasti, S.R., *Lord Minto and the Indian Nationalist Movement,* 1964.

Watson, Francis, *Talking of Gandhi,* Bombay, 1965.

Wellock, Wilfred, *Gandhi as a Social Revolutionary.*

Woodruff, Philips, *The Men Who Ruled India, The Guardians,* London, 1963.

Zacharias, H., *Renascent India,* 1933.

Zetland, Lord, *Steps towards Indian Home Rule.*

INDEX

A

Abdul Ghaffar Khan, Khan, 51, 54, 55, 62, 193
Abdullah, Sheikh, 200
Abell, George, 190, 203
Abkari, 223
Afghan War, third, 53
Africa, 26
Afridis, 54-55
Afzal Khan, 219
Agha Khan, 155
: Agha Khan's Palace, Poona, 149
Agrarian Bill, 2
Agrarian grievances of Champaran, 236
Agricultural problems, 160-161
Ahmedabad, 1, 16, 50
: labour strike, 233
Ahmednagar, 149
: Ahmednagar Fort, 233
Aishevpur, 166,
Ajmer-Marwara, 82
Akram, Saleh Mohammad, 202
Ali brothers, 14, 15
All-India Federation, 73-74
All-India Services, 40
All-Parties Conference, 41-42, 44
All-Parties Convention, 44
All-White Commission, 37
Allah Baksh, 123
Allies, 21, 130, 138, 143, 148-149, 160, 161, 167, 169
Alwar, 82, 83
Ambedkar, 52, 63, 133, 138
Amery, L.S, 130, 135, 156, 169
: Amery-Wavell plan, 169
Amritsar, 3, 4, 8, 10, 11, 21, 150
: Congress session at, 2, 227, 232
: Jallianwala Bagh, tragedy at, 2, 9-11, 21, 34, 50, 59, 232, 240
: Golden temple, 21
Andaman and Nicobar Islands, 73
Aney, M.S, 154
Anglo-Indians, 61, 82, 83, 108, 186
Anglo-Japanese Commercial Convention (1905), 116
Ansari, M.A, 12, 42, 47, 60, 64
Anti-Corn Law League, 225
Arab provinces, 12
Army, Indianization of, 40
Arundale, 229
Arya Samaj, 213, 214, 222, 227
: Arya Samajists, 214, 227
Asia Minor, 12
Asiatic Registration Act, 236
Assam, 61, 63, 69, 73, 82, 106, 107, 108, 120, 124, 125, 150, 168, 175, 177, 179, 190, 192, 201
Atlantic Charter, 130, 131
Attlee, Clement, 128, 136, 173, 186, 187, 192, 194, 210
: Statement of (1947), 188-189
Auchinleck Claud, 201, 203, 204
August Offer (August Declaration), 127-132, 133, 140, 141
: Cripps Mission and, 127-132 (see *also* Cripps Mission)
Australia, 125
Ayub Khan, 206
Azad, Maulana Abul Kalam, 15, 27, 35, 125, 138, 143, 144, 147, 148, 149, 153, 154, 167, 182, 193, 209, 233, 234-235, 241

B

Bajaj, Jumnalal, 13
Bajaur, 116
Baldev Singh, 196, 204
Baldwin, 24
Ballasore, 150
Baluchistan, 39, 73, 82, 168, 175
Banaras
: Congress session at, 230
Banerjee, Surendra Nath, 2, 218, 219, 225
Baramulla, 200
Bardoli, 48, 134
: Bardoli Kisan Movement, 233
Baroda, 198, 199, 216
Belgaum, 27
Bengal, 28, 30, 42, 61, 62, 63, 69, 70, 73, 82,

83, 101, 106, 107, 108, 119, 120, 123, 126, 135, 150, 161, 168, 169, 173, 175, 179, 190, 192, 194, 202, 207, 219
: East, 192
: Famine, 161; Bengal Famine Enquiry Commission, 161
: Bengal National University, 13
: partition of, 231
Benn, Wedgwood, 46, 60
Berar, 71, 82, 108
Besant, Annie, 2, 11, 12, 16, 17, 18, 30, 37-38, 47, 65, 217, 220, 228-230, 232, 235, 240
Bhagalpore, 150
Bhagat Singh, Sardar, 52, 53
Bhave, Vinoba, 132
Bhavnagar, 199
Bihar, 1, 2, 63, 73, 82, 106, 107, 108, 119, 121, 123, 150, 175, 190, 201
: earthquake in, 242
Bikaner, 23, 56, 82, 83, 198
Birkenhead, Lord, 24, 32, 36, 37, 41
Biswas, C.C, 202
Blavatsky, 228
Bloonfield, 220
Bolshevik, 4
Bombay, 8, 14, 16, 38, 42, 60, 61, 73, 82, 101, 106, 108, 119, 126, 150, 151, 154, 175, 190, 217
: Bombay Presidency, 114
Bonnerjee, W.C, 216
Bose, Rash Bihari, 171
Bose, Sarat Chandra, 135
Bose, Subhash Chandra, 45, 46, 52, 53, 61, 65, 135, 166, 171-172, 209, 235
Boundary Commission, 202
Brahmo-Samaj, 214, 221
Brailsford, 50
Brecher, Michael, 208
British (Britain; England; Great Britain U.K.)
: British-Baluchistan, 82, 175
: British Commonwealth of Nations, 130, 131, 139, 140, 174, 191, 193, 230
: British East India Company, 209
: British Parliament, supremacy of, 67
: British Raj, 208
: Why did leave India?, 208-211
Brockman, Ronald, 189
Broomsfield, 2, 16
Bull, John, 72
Bulsar, 50
Burke, 209
Burma, 70, 76, 115, 136, 185, 189
Butler, Harcourt, 56
: Butler Committee, 56
Byron, 209

C

Cabinet Mission Plan under Wavell, 171-184, 187, 190, 235
: Circumstances, 171
: Constituent Assembly, 175-176, 183-184
: Failure of, 178-184
: Indian National Army (INA) trials, 171-172
: interim arrangement, 176
: Labour in power, 173-174
: Muslim League enters government, 182-183
: Muslim League's direct action, 182
: naval mufiny, 172
: states, 176-178, 181
: treaty, 176
: Union of India, 174
Calcutta, 14, 22, 44, 50, 202, 207, 209, 216
: Congress session at, 45, 64, 226
Cama, Harshed ji Hasarwan ji, 216
Campbell-Johnson, Alan, 10, 189
Canada, 59, 125, 137
Canning, Lord, 203
Cattle
: All-India Cattle Show, 160
Central Legislature, 39
Central Provinces (CP), 8, 28, 30, 31, 50, 71, 73, 119, 121, 175, 190, 201
Centre and States, relations between, 92-94
Chamberlain, 130
Champaran, 1
: agrarian grievances of, 236
Chanda, 150
Chandavarkar, N, 218
Charter Act of (1853), 216
Chauri Chaura, violence at, 15
Chelmsford, Viscount, 1-18, 21, 107
Chia Luen-lo, 211
Chiang Kai-Shek, 137, 210
China, 52, 115, 116, 136, 137, 148
Chintamani, C.Y, 16, 56, 218, 221, 222, 223, 225, 229, 240
Chirol, V, 219, 220, 227
Chittagong, 202

Christians, 51, 63, 82, 83, 108, 180, 200
Churchill, Winston, 47, 81, 130, 131, 133, 135, 137, 138, 147, 160, 169, 173, 188
Civil Disobedience Movement, 27, 48, 49, 52, 58, 64, 126, 132, 229, 230, 233, 236, 237-238, 241-242
Civil services, 26, 40, 68, 101, 121, 125
Claive, William, 220
Colvin, A, 225
Communalism, 209, 234, 241
: Communal Award, 62-63
: Intercommunal Committees, 207
Communism, 210
: Communist Party, 35
: Communists, 149
Congress (Indian National Congress), 2, 12-15, 18, 21, 23, 25-26, 35, 37, 38, 41, 47, 49, 51, 52, 54, 60, 61, 62, 64, 96, 119, 120, 122, 123, 125-126, 127-128, 131-133, 135, 137, 141, 143, 148, 150-151, 153, 154, 158, 163, 167, 170-172, 177-184, 188, 191, 193-194, 196, 199, 202, 206, 208-209, 217-219, 221, 223, 225-226, 229, 233-235, 242
: All India Youth Congress, 53
: Committees of, 152
: Quit Indian resolution, 148-149
: Sessions of : Ahmedabad, 14-15; Allahabad, 222; Amritsar, 2, 227, 232; Banaras, 230; Calcutta, 12, 221, 222, 226; Delhi, 27; Gaya, 26; Karachi, 53; Lahore, 48-49, 226; Nagpur, 12-13; Patna, 64; Surat, 221, 226;
: Working Committee, 47, 62, 140, 148-149, 153, 167, 197; resolution of 1942, 140
Congress Socialist Party, 152
Constituent Assembly, 175-179, 181, 183-184, 187, 189, 190, 204, 242
Constitutional reforms, 36
: of (1935), 157
Coorg, 8
: Ajmer-Marwara, 73
Corfield, Conard, 196, 197
Cornwallis, Lord, 184
Council of States, 39-40
Coupland, R, 125, 156
Criminal Law Amendment Act (1923), 25
Criminal Law Amendment Repeal Act (1922), 25
Cripps, Stafford, 173, 180, 181, 187
Cripps Mission, 127-144, 147-235
: Contact with Japanese, 135-136
: Council expansion, 133
: enlightened opinion in England, 136-137
: Indian liberals, 135
: release, 133-134
: war and its effects, 134-135
: World opinion, 137-138
Cripps Mission, August Offer and, 127-132
: appraisal, 131-132
: Congress resignation, 127-128
: talks re-opened, 128-131
Cripps Mission : proposals of, 138-144, 147
: Immediate, 139-144
: long-term, 138-139
Crum, Vermon Erskine, 189
Curzon, Lord, 217, 231

D

D.A.V. Movement, 214
Dalai Lama, 116
Dandi March, 49-50
Das, C.R, 12-15, 26, 28, 30, 232, 235
Day of Deliverance, 129
Dayanand Saraswati, Swami, 213-214, 222, 227
Defence of India Act, 6
Defence of India Rules, 90, 135
Defence Rule (26), 151-152
Delhi, 16, 24, 42, 45, 47, 59, 64, 73, 75, 82, 150, 154, 160, 173, 192, 202, 209
Depressed classes, 61, 63, 65, 141, 179, 180, 239
Desai, Bhulabhai, 169, 172
Desai, Mahadev, 129, 151-152
Dhillon, Col., 172
Dickie Bird Plan, 190-192
Digambhar Singh, 206
Din Mohammad, 202
Dominion status, 24, 33, 42, 45, 46, 47, 67, 106, 128, 130-132, 140, 153, 190-192, 194, 196
Doveton, 10
Dual policy of repression, 113-117
Dufferin, Lord, 224
Dunichand, Lala, 4
Durham, Lord, 137
Dutt, Romesh Chandra, 220
Dyarchy, 28-29, 38, 69, 78, 219
Dyer, Gen, 9-11

E

Economy
: economic depression, 58
: economic reforms, 115
: Imperial Economic Conference, Ottawa, 115
Eddi, Sherwood, 153
Education, 239
: basic, 157
: Education Commission (1882), 217
: Wardha scheme, 157-158, 239
Egypt, 24
Electorate, 70
England (see British)
Europe (Europeans), 5, 9, 61-62, 82-83, 108, 110, 179, 192, 220
Extremists, 222, 226, 229

F

Famine, 161 (*wf also* Bengal)
Fazalul Haq, 123
Fazi Hussain, 54
Federal Court, 70
Federal Executive, 75-78
Federal Government, States and, 92-97
: Centre and States, relations between, 92-94
: Federal government, 94-97
: Federal scheme, 94-97
Federal Legislature, 79, 82-92
: Council of States, 82
: Federal Assembly, 82-83, 87, 93
: Federal Court, 88-90, 93, 94, 99
: Federal Railway Authority, 90-91
: Financial adviser and advocate-general, 91-92
: legislative powers, 83-88
: organs, 88-92
: Reserve Bank of India, 91
Federal Structure Committee, 60
Federation and Federal Government, 68-69
Finance Bill, 28
Fischer, Louis, 148
Foreign relations, 115-116
: Foreign relations Act (1932), 113-114
Forest laws, 50
Forest service, 40
Forward Block, 235
France, 5, 12
: French Revolution, 153
Furneaux, Rupert, 9

G

Gandhi, Behramji Kharshedji, 215
Gandhi, Mahatma, 1-4, 8, 11-18, 21-23, 26-27, 31-32, 34-35, 45-55, 59-61, 63-65, 71-72, 121, 128, 132-134, 137-138, 142, 147-154, 163, 166-168, 185-186, 189, 193, 209, 217, 220, 222-223, 228-232, 234-241
: assassination of, 207-208, 237
: at Round Table Conference, second, 61-62
: Dandi march, 49-50
: fast and release, 154-157
: Gandhi-Irwin pact, 51-53, 59, 71
: Harijan work, 64,
: Irwin-Gandhi pact, 52-53, 60
: Movements of 1920-21 and 1930, 65
: Non-Cooperation movement (section-Cooperaction movement)
: passive resistance in South Africa, 1, 4
: philosophy of, 237-241
: Satyagraha against Rowlatt Bill of (1919), 1
: Satyagraha Ashram on Sabarmati river, Ahmedabad, 1
: sentenced to six years imprisonment, 16
: truth and non-violence advocated by, 54
: twenty-one day fast in Yervada jail, 64
Ganga Singh, 23
Garth, Richard, 220
George VI, King, 189
George, Lloyd, 23, 26, 223
Glendevon, John, 162
Godse, Nathuram Vinayak, 207, 237
Gokhale, Gopal Krishna, 1, 18, 225, 226, 230-232
: "Political Testament of Gokhale", 232
Golden Temple, 21
Gorakhpur, 15
Government of India Act (1919), 13, 53, 67, 69, 98, 100, 112, 232
Government of India Act (1935), 41, 66-117, 119, 127, 161, 170-171, 177, 194
: proposed federation, 73-74
: safeguards, 71-73
Governor-General, 75-77, 79-81, 84-85, 87, 89, 92-94, 96, 98, 101-102, 109, 120-122, 195
: extraordinary legislative powers, 77

: financial powers, 77
Gujranwala, 10
Gujrat, 10
: Gujrat Vidaya-Peeth, 13
Gunther, John, 233
Gurdaspur, 10, 202
Gurudwara Sudhar movement, 21
: *Gurudwara Sudhar* agitation of Sikhs, 228
Gwalior, 23

H

Halifax, Lord, 144
Hardinge, Lord, 3, 184
Hari Singh, 200
Harijans, 239
: welfare work for by Gandhi, 64
Harkishan Lal, Lala, 4
Hastings, Lord, 184
Hindu Mahasabha, 45, 138, 142, 149
Hindu-Muslim Accord, 31
Hindu-Muslim front, 15
Hindu-Muslim problem, 59
Hindu-Muslim riots, 31
Hindu-Muslim unity, 31, 239-241
Hindu Press, 144, 154
Hinduism, 239
Hindus, 12, 23, 31, 35-36, 43, 51, 61, 63, 65, 82, 83, 114, 119, 129, 170, 172, 189, 201-203, 205, 207
Hitler, 81
Hoare, Samuel, 60
Holocaust, 205-207
Home Rule League, 217, 229
Home Rule Movement, 58, 220
Hume, Allen Octavian, 218, 223-225
Hunter, William, 11, 220
: Hunter Committee, 10
Hyderabad, 83, 198-200, 234
: Nizam of, 55, 71

I

Imperial Legislative Council, 218
Imperialism, 72-73
India
: dominion status of (see Dominion)
: partition of, 192-193, 196-211, 206
(see *also* Indian Independence)
Indian Army, 203-204
Indian Civil Services (see Civil Services)
Indian Independence movement, 241
: independence declared, 48-49, 204-205
: independence day celebrations, 64, 202
: Indian Independence Act, 193-194, 196
: Mountbatten on, 185-187
Indian National Army (INA), 166, 209, 235
: Trials of, 171-172
Indian National Congress (see Congress)
Indian National Union, 35, 36
Indian Police Service, 40
Indian States Protection Act (1934), 114-117
Individual Civil Disobedience, 132
Instrument of Accession, 73, 92-94, 197-200
Instrument of Instruction, 76, 78-81, 104, 106
: appraisal, 80-81
Interim Government, 176-181, 186-187, 189
: Interim Cabinet, 235
Ireland, 24
: Irish Home Rule Movement of Redmond, 229
Irrigation service, 40
Irwin, Lord, 34-37, 59-60
: broken promises, 46-48
: Irwin-Gandhi pact, 52-53, 60
Ismay, Lord, 188, 190, 203
Italy, 62
Iyengar, S. Srinivas, 38

J

Jallianwala Bagh, tragedy at, 2, 9-11, 21, 34, 50, 59, 232, 240
Jamia Milia, Delhi, 13
Japan, 135-136
: Anglo-Japanese Commercial Convention (1905), 116
Jayakar, 51, 138
Jenkins, Evan, 203
Jinnah, M.A, 8, 12, 29, 38, 44, 48, 51, 52, 96, 122-123, 128-130, 137-138, 141, 167-168, 170, 179-181, 183, 188-190, 193, 197, 201, 203-206, 234
: fourteen points of, 44-46
Jobbery, 61
Jodhpur, 197
Johnson, Frank, 10
Johnson, Louis, 144
Joint Parliamentary Report, 71
Joint Select Committee Report, 67
Joseph, 9
Junagarh, 198, 199, 234
Justice Party, 119

K

Kaira, 64

Kak, Pandit, 200
Karachi, 204, 209
Karur, 3
Kashgar, 115
Kashmir, 23, 198-202
Kasur, 9-10
Kathiawar, 199
Kenya, 26
Khare, N.B, 121
Kheda, 237
Khilafat Movement, 8, 12-18, 26, 31, 237, 240
: All India Khilafat Committee, 12
: Appraisal, 16-18
: Khilafat Agitation, 31
: Khilafat Committee, 17
: Khilafat Conference, Delhi, 12
: Khilafat Republic, 14
: suspension of, 15-16
Khudai-Khidmatgars or Servants of God, 54
Kitchlew, 4, 8
Kohat, 54
Kripalani, Acharya, 149,152, 206

L

Labh Singh, 4
Labour Party, 28, 37, 60
Lahore, 3, 8, 10, 21, 38, 202, 213, 221, 222, 227
: Congress Session at, 48, 49, 226
Lajpat Rai, Lala, 15, 26, 38, 221, 223
Land Revenue, 49
Laski, 142, 143, 144
Lausanne, 23
Land of Sedition, 18
Lawrence Pethics, 173, 203
League of Nations, 62
Lee Commission, 40
Legislatures, Bicameral Enlarged, 69, 70
Liaquat Ali, 183, 205, 206
Liberals, 12, 25, 37, 119, 132, 135, 138, 142
: All India Liberal Federation, 135
: Liberal party, 25, 36
: Liberalism, 37
: National Liberal Federation, 2, 25
Linlithgow, Lord, 66, 118, 144, 147 154, 156, 159, 160, 161, 162, 166
: Estimate, 163, 164
: Provincial Autonomy in Operation, 118-127
: working of, 120-127
Locke, 209
London, 51, 59, 62
Lothan Lord, 109
: Lothian report, 67
Lowell, 81
Lucknow, 44
Lumly, R, 155
Lyalpur, 10

M

Macaulay, 209
MacDonald, Ramsay, 28, 46, 60, 61, 108
Maclagan, Eric, 21
Madras, 38, 58, 59, 61, 73, 82, 83, 101, 106, 107, 108, 112, 119, 126, 150, 175, 190, 209, 216
Magee, Bishop, 17
Mahajan, Mehar Chand, 202
Mahsuds, 54
Malabar, 14, 17, 59
Malaviya Madan Mohan, 11, 12, 21, 47, 60, 63, 222, 231
Mangal Sen, Diwan, 4
Manipur, 166
Martial Law, 55
Martin, Kingsley, 143
Masani, R.P, 214
Mashobra, 75
Max Muller, 220
Mayo, Katherine, 37
: *Mother India* by, 37
Mehta, Pherozeshah, 226
Meerut, 49
Menon, V.P, 190, 191, 193, 194, 197, 198, 206
Mersey, Viscount, 184
Mesopotamia, 13
Meston, James, 227
Mieville, Eric, 188
Mill, 209
Minorities Sub-Committee, 60
Minto Lord, 23, 55
: Minto-Morley reforms of (1909), 231
Mira Ben (Miss Slade) ,149, 151, 152
Moderates, 2, 25, 45, 217, 219, 221, 222, 229
Modi, M.S, 154
Modified Forward Policy, 53
Mohammad Ali Chaudari, 202, 203
Mohammad Ali Maulana, 12
Mohammad Munir, 202
Mohan, Pearay, 3
Mohmands, 54

Monghyr, 150
Montagu, E.S, 2, 22, 23, 107
: Montagu Declaration of (1917),34
: Montagu reforms, 24, 58
: Montagu Chelmsford reforms, 24, 218, 219
Montford Reforms, 27
Moore, R.J, 163
Moplahs, 14, 15
: Uprising (Rebellion), 14, 31, 59
Mosley, Leonard, 198, 205
Mountbatten, Lady (Edwina Ashely), 185, 189, 209
Mountbatten, Lord, 22, 185-194, 196, 198, 200, 201, 203, 204, 205, 206, 207, 208, 209, 210, 233
: Attlee's Statement of (1947), 187-189
: Dickie Bird Plan, 190, 192
: Indian Independence Act, 193, 194
: Mountbatten Plan, 192, 194
: On to Independence, 185, 187
Muddiman, Alexandar, 29, 32
: Muddiman reform enquiry committee, 29, 32
Mudie, John, 203
Muhammad Shafi, 45
Mukherji, B.K, 202
Mukherjee, Hirendranath, 11
Mukherjee Shayama Prasad, 123
Multan, 5
Munshi, K.M, 12, 14
Muslim League, 31, 37, 44, 45, 63, 65, 96, 119, 122, 127, 130, 131, 132, 140, 141, 149, 154, 163, 169, 171, 173, 177, 178, 180, 181, 182, 183, 184, 189, 192, 193, 202, 209, 233, 234
: Direct action of, 182, 183
: enters government 182, 183
Muslims, 12, 21, 23, 31, 35, 43, 51, 53, 60, 61, 63, 82, 83, 84, 108, 112, 114, 119, 142, 172, 175, 176, 181, 182, 199, 201, 202, 203, 207, 227, 228, 231, 239
Mussolini, Siginor, 62, 81
Mutiny of 1857 (Rebellion), 153, 230, 208, 209, 223
Mysore, 23, 82, 83

N

Nabha, 82, 83
Nadia, 150
Nagpur
: Congress Session at, 12, 13
Naidu, Sarojini, 60
Nail, 126
Nair, Shankaran, 11,
Nair, Sushila, 152
Naoroji, Dadabhai, 214, 218, 220
Naoroji, Furdoonji, 215
Narain, J.P, 153,
National College, Lahore, 13
National Conference, 33, 130, 135, 200
National Liberation Federation, 2, 25
National Muslim University Aligarh, 13
National Party, 28
Nationalism, 5, 238, 240
Nationalist Movement, 1, 55
Nationalists, 238
Naval Mutiny, 172
: In Bombay, 172
: In RAF at Dum Dum Airport, Calcutta, 172
Nawonagar, 23
Nehru, Jawaharlal, 15, 38, 45, 46, 47, 49, 51, 52, 54, 61, 62, 65, 73, 96, 120, 122, 126, 129, 132, 134, 137, 138, 147, 149, 153, 154, 171, 179, 182, 185, 186, 188, 190, 193, 194, 197, 200, 201, 203, 204, 206, 207, 209, 232, 233, 241
: Nehru Cabinet, 234, 242
Nehru Motilal, 11, 13, 15, 26, 29, 31, 35, 41-46, 47, 48, 51, 209, 232, 233, 235
Nehru Committee Report, 41, 46, 47, 48, 49, 67, 157, 232
: Estimate, 46, Jinnah's Fourteen Point, 44-46, Recommendations, 42
Nepal, 3
Nicholls, George, 189
Nizam of Hyderabad, 55, 71
Non-Cooperation Movement, 1-6, 12, 13, 15, 16, 22, 31, 49-51, 59, 113, 208, 209, 232, 234, 235, 242; Second, 113
Non-Violence, 26, 237
: non-violent movement, 35
North-West Frontier Provinces (NWFP), 35, 39, 62, 70, 73, 82, 108, 114, 120, 123, 168, 175, 177, 190, 192, 195, 201
: Red Shirts and, 53-57
Northcliffe, 22

O

Oloott, 228
Omoore, 6

Orissa, 63, 73, 82, 108, 121, 124, 126, 150, 169, 175, 190

P

Padanur, 59
Pakhtoonistan, 193
Pakistan, Demand for, 141, 167, 168, 170, 173, 174, 176, 178, 179, 182, 184, 188, 193, 194, 199, 200, 201, 204, 207, 209
: Dominion Status for, 190, 191, 194, 196
: West, 205
Pal, B.C, 12, 221
Palwal, 8
Pamela, 189
Panehayats, 24
Pannikar,K.M, 240
Pant, G.B, 38, 125
Panth-Piploda, 73
Paris, 62
Parsis, 180
Passive Resistance, 4
Patel, Sardar Vallabhbhai, 49, 119, 125, 152, 171, 177, 184, 189, 191, 193, 197, 198, 200, 206, 209, 233, 234
Patel Vithal Bhai, 13
Pathans, 54
Patiala, 23, 82, 83
Patna, 64, 150
: Congress Session at, 64
Pearl Harbour, 134,
Pears, 54
Peasants
: Conditions of, 1-2
: Kheda Peasants, 237
Perry, Erskine, 215
Peshawar, 50, 55
Phillips, C.H, 166, 203
Phippls, D.H, 163
Pirpur Report
: U. P. Crisis and, 122,-124
Police Act, 11
Politico-Economic Reforms, 113, 117
Poona, 149, 166, 207, 226, 230
: Poona Pact, 63, 65, 108
Power Arthur, 208
Press, 62,
: Press Act (1931), 113
Princely States, 4
Princes, 53, 55-57, 94, 137, 138
: Chamber of Princes, 23, 24, 55
: Princes Protection Act, 25
Proposed Federation, 73, 74
Provincial administration, 38, 39
Provincial and Subordinate Services, 40
Provincial Autonomy, 70, 97-113, 118-127
: Appraisal, 105, 106, 112, 113
: Composition and Rights, 107, 108
: Council of Ministers, 104, 105
: Executive Machinery, 100, 101
: Executive Powers, 101-103, 111, 11
: Executive Relations, 98, 99
: External Control, 98, 100
: Financial Powers, 104, 110, 111
: Financial Relations, 99, 100
: Financial Qualifications, 108, 109
: Governor 101, 102, 103, 104, 105, 106
: Instrument of Instruction, 104
: Internal Responsibility, 100-113
: Legislative Council (Second Chamber), 107
: Legislative Powers, 103, 104, 109, 110
: Legislative Relations, 99
: Provincial Legislature, 106
Provincial Councils, 40
Provincial Funds, 40
Provincial Legislatures, 68, 106
Public Service Commission, 226
Punjab, 3, 4, 5, 6, 8, 10, 21, 22, 42, 53, 60, 61, 64, 73, 82, 108, 114, 119, 120, 124, 168, 173, 175, 176, 190, 192, 193, 201, 202, 203, 205, 206, 207, 213, 224
: East, 205
: Horrors, 2
: Punjab Legislative Council, 9
: West, 203
Punjabis, 3
Purna swaraj, 47, 49 (see *also* Swaraj)

Q

Quit India Movement, 147-164, 209
: Agricultural Problems 160-161
: Circumstances, 147, 148
: Congress Resolution, 148, 149, 154, 155, 171
: Crisis Precipitated, 149, 150
: Developments other, 157, 163
: Fakir of IPI, 162, 163
: Famine, 161
: Gandhi's Fast and Release, 154-157

: India's Sterling Balance, 159, 160
: Sargeant Scheme of (1943), 158, 159
: Violence Responsibility, 150 154

: Wardha Scheme of education, 157-158
Quit India Resolution, 148, 149, 154, 155, 171

R

Radcliffe Cyral, 201-203, 206
: Radcliffe Award, 201, 203, 206
Raghuvanshi, 225, 241
Rahnumae Mazdayasnam Sabha, 215
Railway Authority, 90, 91
Raisman, Jeremy, 159
Rajagopalachari, C, 63, 119, 132, 134, 167
: C.R. Formula 167-169
Rajah, M.C, 138,
Rajendra Prasad, 13, 63, 119, 125, 128, 129, 149, 152, 184, 204, 205, 241, 242
Ram Gopal, 220
Ram Mohan Roy, Raja, 209, 213, 214
Ranade, Mahadev Govind, 225, 226
Rangachariar, Diwan Bahadur T, 25
Ras, 64
Razmak, 53
Reading, Lady, 24
Reading, Lord, 14, 18, 20-33, 36
Red Fort, Delhi, 172
Red Shirt movement, 55, 114
: Red Shirts and North-West Frontier, 53, 57
Reed, Stanley, 37
Rees, 206
Reforms of (1919), 2, 114, 230
: Reforms Act of (1919), 21, 25, 34, 36
(see *also* government of India Act 1919
Regulation IIIrd of, (1818), 29
Rehman, S.A, 202
Reserve Bank of India, 70, 72, 74, 91
: Reserve Bank of India Act, 100
Reynolds, Reginald, 49
Romain Rolland, 15, 62
Roosevelt, 137, 144, 155
Round Table Conference, 14, 28, 29, 32, 33, 47, 53, 57, 67, 114, 131, 232
: First, 51, 52, 59, 71, 235
: Second, 59, 60-63, 71, 235
: Third, 65, 66; White Paper, 65, 66, 67
Rowlatt Act, 2, 4, 6-9, 34
: Agitation against, 227, 237
Rowlatt Bill of (1919), 1
Roy, B.C., 64
Royal Commission, 30, 123
Russia, 25
: Czar of, 81
: Russian Revolution, 153

S

Sabarmati Ashram, 64
Saklatwala, 37
Salt Law, 50
:Salt Tax, 26, 27
Sapru, Tej Bahadur, 29, 37, 45, 47, 48, 51, 71, 135, 138, 209
Sarcar, N.R., 154
Sarda Act, 54
Sargeant, John, 158
: Sargeant Committee ,158, 159
: Sargeant Scheme (1943), 158, 159
Satyagraha (Satyagraha Movement), 49, 62, 64, 133, 134, 237, 239, 240
: Satyagraha committee, 228
Satyapal, 4, 8
Savarkar, 138,
Scheduled Castes, 51, 52, 63, 82, 180
Schuster, George, 136
Seal Privy, 57, 137, 138
Secretary of State and his Council, 67, 68
Sedition Law, 50
: Seditions Meetings, 14
Sehgal, Major, 172
Servants of India Society, 1, 231
Serves, Teaty of, 12, 21, 23
Shah, K.T., 80
Shah Nawaz Khan, 172
Shardhanand Swami, 35, 226, 227
Shaukat Ali, 12
Shimla, 21, 24, 60, 75, 178, 179, 190, 227
: Conference , 170, 171, 179
Shivaji, 219
Sikandar Hayat Khan, 123, 124, 132
Sikhs, 21, 45, 51, 63, 82, 83, 108, 172, 173, 175, 177, 180, 181, 202, 203, 205, 206
: *Gurudwara Sudhar* Agitation of, 228
: *Gurudwara Sudhar* Movement, 21
Simon Commission, 24, 32, 36, 38, 45, 71, 187
: At Lahore, 223,
: Indian Opposition, 36-38,
: Report, 38-41, 47, 67,
: Army, 40; Centre, 39; Civil Services, 40; Council of States, 39-40; Execu-

tive, 40; For India Office, 40-41, Indian States, 41; Provinces, 38, 39
: Simon Go Back, 38
Sind, 53, 73, 108, 114, 120, 123, 126, 168, 175, 201
Sinha, Lord, 37
Sitaramayya, P, 128
Skeen Committee, 31
Slade, Medeleine, 50, 149 (see *also* Mira Ben)
Social Reform Conference, 226,
Socialist, 37
Socialist, Party, 149, 150
Solocombe, George, 51
Special Law Repeal Act (1922), 25
Spencer, 209
Srinagar, 200
Staffood, 143, 144
and Still Agreement, 200
States Negotiating Committee, 177, 178, 181
Statutory Commission, 36
Steel Protection Committee, 31
Suhrawardy, H.S., 182, 194
Surat, 221
: Congress session at, 221, 226
Swadeshi, 13, 220, 238
Swaraj Party (Swarajist), 25-33, 35, 64, 222, 230, 232, 235
Swaraj, 13, 17, 22, 38, 48
: Appraisal, 30, 33
: At Polls, 28,
: Muddiman Committee Report, 29, 30,
: Programme of, 27
: Work, 28, 29,
Swinson, Arthur, 163,
Switzerland, 62
Sylhet, 192

T

Tagore, Rabindranath, 11, 182, 236
Talchera, 150
Tambe, S.B., 31
Tamulk, 150,
Tara Singh, Master, 205,240
Teja Singh, 202
Theosophical Society, 228, 229
Thompson, Edward, 136
Thrace, 12
Tibet, 116
Tilak, Bal Gangadhar, 2, 13, 34, 219-221, 230
: Tilak Mahasabha Vidya Peeth, 13
: Tilak School Fund, 223
Tin Tut, 135, 136
Trade
: Indian Trade Union Congress, 49
: Trade Unions, 51
Transvaal,
: Anti-Asiatic legislation of, 1
Trench, Victor, 58
Turkey, 2, 8, 12, 21, 31

U

U.P, (United Provinces), 15, 38, 61, 62, 63, 73, 82, 83, 106, 107, 108, 112, 119, 121, 125, 150, 175, 190, 227
U. Saw, 135, 136
U.S.A., 71
Udaipur, 82
United Kingdom, 76, 79 (see *also* British)
United Nations, 139, 201
Uri, 200

V

Vincent, William, 25
Vinoba Bhave (see Bhave)
Virja Nanda, Swami, 213,

W

Wadia, 229
Wainwright, Doreen, 163, 203
Wales, Prince of, 14, 15, 16, 22, 185, 198
Wana, 53
War Cabinet, 135, 136, 140, 142, 144
Wavell, Lord, 161, 166-184, 186
: Cabinet Mission plan, 169-184 (see *also* Cabinet Mission)
: Amery-Wavell Plan, 169
Wedderburn, William, 224
Wedgwood, J.C., 223
Welby Commission, 231
Wilkie, Wendell, 153
Willingdon, Lord, 58-66,. 113, 144, 117, 189
: Round Table Conference, second, 60-63
: Willingdon Committee of Inquiry, 59
Willoughby, R.W.D., 15
Women
: Depressing condition of, 239
Wood, Kingsley, 159
World War
: First, 1, 166, 220, 239
: Second, 127, 157, 166, 234, 235
Wordsworth, 209

Y

Yakub Hasan, 38
Yervada, 64,
: Yervada jail, 51, 64
Youth
: National Youth Movement, 159

Z

Zacharias, 42, 46
Zetland, Lord , 105, 130, 163
Zoraster, Prophet, 218